What Johnny Shouldn't Read

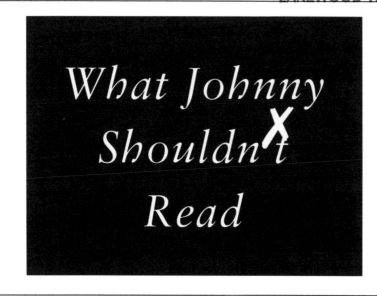

What Johnny Shouldn't Read

Textbook Censorship
in America

Joan DelFattore

YALE UNIVERSITY PRESS ■ NEW HAVEN AND LONDON

Published with assistance from

Designed by Jill Breitbarth and set in Sabon type by Rainsford Type,
Danbury, Connecticut. Printed in the United States of America by Vail–
Ballou Press, Binghamton, New York.

Library of Congress Cataloging-in-Publication Data
DelFattore, Joan
What Johnny shouldn't read : textbook censorship in America / Joan
DelFattore.
p.   cm.
Includes bibliographical references and index.
ISBN 0-300-05709-1 (cloth)
0-300-06050-5 (pbk.)
1. Textbooks—Censorship—United States—Case studies.
2. Censorship—United States—Case studies.   I. Title.
LB3045.7.D45   1992
379.1'56—dc20   92-3585
                                                           CIP

A catalogue record for this book is available from the British Library.

The paper in this book meets the guidelines for permanence and
durability of the Committee on Production Guidelines for Book
Longevity of the Council on Library Resources.

6   8   10   9   7

To my parents
with love and thanks

Contents

Acknowledgments

As this book evolved, colleagues and friends—Deborah Andrews, Jerry Beasley, Heyward Brock, Carl Dawson, Robert Day, and George Miller—read parts of it and offered invaluable advice and encouragement. I am warmly grateful for both. I also appreciate the help of the long-suffering graduate students who worked on the book in its various incarnations: Marguerite Quintelli, Jeffrey Mathers, Kathleen Therrien, Mary Loaec, and Gayle Allen. Finally, I acknowledge with thanks the financial support of the American Association of University Women Educational Foundation, the University of Delaware, the College of Arts and Science, and the English Department.

CHAPTER ONE

Romeo and Juliet
Were Just Good Friends

Is uniformity attainable? Millions of innocent men, women, and children, since the introduction of Christianity, have been burnt, tortured, fined, imprisoned; yet we have not advanced one inch towards uniformity. What has been the effect of coercion? To make one half of the world fools, and the other half hypocrites.
—THOMAS JEFFERSON

A few years ago, I taught a summer course in literary classics for high school English teachers. When the class began talking about *Romeo and Juliet,* two of the teachers had trouble following what the others were saying. Those two teachers were using high school literature anthologies; the rest of the class had read paperback versions of *Romeo and Juliet.* We compared the high school anthologies with the paperbacks and found more than three hundred lines missing from the play in each anthology. Neither textbook mentioned that its presentation of *Romeo and Juliet* was definitely not Shakespeare's.

In the anthologies, lines containing sexual material—even such mild words as *bosom* and *maidenhood*—were missing. Removing most of the love story shortened *Romeo and Juliet* considerably, but the publishers did not stop there; they also took out material that had nothing to do with sex. Both anthologies, for example, omitted Romeo's lines,

> When the devout religion of mine eye
> Maintains such falsehood, then turn tears to fires;
> And these who, often drown'd, could never die,
> Transparent heretics, be burnt for liars! (I, 2)

1

I later found that this speech is routinely removed from high school anthologies because it associates religion with falsehood and violence, thus offending people who demand that religion must always be presented favorably.

The realization that publishers can simply drop three hundred lines from a Shakespeare play was startling, and I set out to discover what other material is being deleted from textbooks, why, and by whom. I found excellent books and articles discussing various aspects of textbook censorship from the 1950s through the early 1980s. The work of Lee Burress, James Davis, Kenneth Donelson, Frances FitzGerald, Edward Jenkinson, Nicholas Karolides, Judith Krug, James Moffett, Robert O'Neil, and Diane Shugert was particularly helpful in clarifying the extent and importance of textbook censorship issues.

Along with books and articles, I was also reading newspapers. Throughout the 1980s, one censorship lawsuit after another made front-page headlines. *Mozert v. Hawkins County Public Schools* was filed by Tennessee parents who maintained that an entire elementary school reading series, including "Cinderella," "Goldilocks," and *The Wizard of Oz*, violated their fundamentalist religious beliefs. More than half a century after the Scopes "monkey trial," *McLean v. Arkansas Board of Education* and *Aguillard v. Edwards* evaluated attempts to promote the teaching of creationism in public schools. In *Smith v. Board of School Commissioners of Mobile County*, a federal district court ordered the removal of forty-four history, social studies, and home economics textbooks from public school classrooms on the grounds that the books violate the First Amendment by promoting the religion of secular humanism. *Farrell v. Hall* and *Virgil v. Columbia County School Board* pitted parents and teachers against school boards that had banned literary classics, such as *Lysistrata, Macbeth*, and *The Autobiography of Benjamin Franklin*.

Behind each court case was a red-hot local controversy fanned by national organizations that eventually funded the lawsuits they had helped to bring about. The dynamics leading up to legal action, the educational agendas of national lobbying groups, and the rulings in the lawsuits all have powerful implications for the future of education in this country. *What Johnny Shouldn't Read*, which is based on court documents, textbook adoption records, and interviews, adds to the ongoing discussion of textbook censorship in twentieth-century America by describing how these lawsuits combined with the textbook adoption process to affect textbooks sold nationwide.

All six of the federal court cases discussed in this book involve attempts by religious fundamentalists to influence the content of public education.

The *American College Dictionary* defines fundamentalism as "a movement in American Protestantism which stresses the inerrancy of the Bible not only in matters of faith and morals but also as literal historical record and prophecy." Trying to decide how to use the word *fundamentalist* in a discussion of textbook censorship is, however, more problematic than the dictionary definition suggests. Over the past five years, I have given more than a hundred talks on this subject at public gatherings as well as at professional conferences. That experience has made it clear that the term *fundamentalist* does not, in practice, describe a monolithic belief system. Time after time, audience members have stood up and said something to this effect: "I am a fundamentalist, but I do not agree with what the textbook protesters are doing. I am embarrassed when extremists use the name *fundamentalist* because it makes people think we are all like that." Conversely, others proclaim that they do not consider themselves fundamentalists but do oppose evolution or nontraditional female roles.

A similar dilemma arises with regard to the word *conservative*. Textbook protesters often describe themselves as conservatives, but when George Will and James Kilpatrick write scathing columns condemning a textbook challenge, it is difficult to believe that that challenge represents mainstream conservative thought. Problems also arise when it comes to identifying the locations in which textbook controversies take place. While visiting southern states where court cases and controversial textbook adoption activities had occurred, I often met people who opposed the textbook activists and were irritated that the names of their states were associated with them. The same thing happened in California with regard to textbook protesters who call themselves liberals but represent viewpoints that mainstream liberals consider extreme and that many Californians do not endorse.

It would be inappropriate and unfair to suggest that extremist views, on either the right or the left, are more widespread than they are. On the other hand, it is necessary to call textbook protesters something that reflects what they call themselves and to acknowledge that they live somewhere. Whenever possible, I have specified particular groups, such as the *Smith* plaintiffs or health food lobbyists, rather than saying *the fundamentalists* or *the Californians*. When a more general term is necessary, my use of that term does not imply that everyone who is a fundamentalist, liberal, Texan, Californian, or whatever agrees with the protesters' views.

The reason for focusing on recent federal textbook lawsuits that involve fundamentalist ideology is simple: there is none that does not. In some cases, parents and teachers who describe themselves as fundamentalists initiate lawsuits against a school district for using books that violate their religious beliefs; in others, a school board bans books because of fundamentalist lobbying, whereupon other parents and teachers file suit.

Apart from lawsuits, there are hundreds of incidents every year in which parents or teachers try to convince school boards to include or exclude certain materials. Such controversies are reflected on a wider scale in the textbook adoption process in large states. Challenges initiated by people who identify themselves as fundamentalists not only outnumber the protests of all other groups combined but also involve far more topics. The National Organization for Women (NOW), for example, advocates the depiction of women in nontraditional roles, and the National Association for the Advancement of Colored People (NAACP) lobbies for more favorable presentations of African Americans. One may agree or disagree with the stands taken by NOW and the NAACP, but neither group is likely to comment on such issues as the age of the earth, the development of language, or the probable domestication of dinosaurs. Fundamentalist textbook activists, on the other hand, lobby for geology and history books that conform to their interpretation of *Genesis* by teaching that the earth is about five thousand years old and that dinosaurs once coexisted with humans Flintstones-style. Their interpretation of the Bible also rejects biological evolution and, by extension, gradual development of any kind, such as the evolution of language over time.

The fundamentalist textbook activists discussed in this book are determined to color the education of all students with their entire world view. Their protests therefore target a wide range of subjects, including personal decision making, imagination, conservation, world unity, tolerance for cultural diversity, religious tolerance, negative portrayals of religion, unflattering depictions of the military or the police, empathy toward animals, anti-pollution laws, pacifism, socialism, gun control, nontraditional roles for women, minority issues, and evolution.

Because the word *fundamentalist* means different things to different people, it is impossible to tell exactly how many fundamentalists there are in the United States. Estimates generally range from 3 percent to 20 percent of the total population, with a few enthusiasts claiming that more than half of all American citizens are fundamentalists. But even if no more than three Americans out of a hundred are fundamentalists, and some of them do not support all of the textbook protesters' views, they are effective out of all proportion to their numbers because of their intense dedication to what they see as the salvation of American children from political, social, economic, and spiritual ruin. In most local elections, a very small proportion of qualified voters shows up at the polls, and few of them have paid close attention to the candidates for school board seats. Under those conditions, how many determined voters does it take to elect a sympathetic candidate to the school board? It is also important to remember the cardinal rule of any political dynamic: the number of people needed to make a difference is inversely proportionate to their level of expertise at working the system. Saying that a relatively small number of intense activists cannot have much effect on textbooks is like looking at the shape of a bumblebee and saying, "That thing can't possibly get off the ground." Maybe it can't, but it does. Far Right national organizations have become very adept at supporting grass-roots legal challenges and at influencing the state-level textbook adoption process, thus affecting the content of textbooks purchased by school districts and private schools throughout the country.

Textbook protests are nothing new to the United States. As Kenneth Donelson explains in "Obscenity and the Chill Factor," activists of one kind or another have influenced the selection of classroom materials since colonial times. Nevertheless, according to the American Library Association, challenges to reading materials, including textbooks, have increased dramatically since 1980—the year in which Ronald Reagan was first elected president of the United States. Far Right perspectives are reflected in the vast majority of these challenges, suggesting that the increase in textbook protests is probably related to the overall upswing in ultraconservative activism surrounding the Reagan victory. Moreover, the changing content of textbooks themselves has motivated protesters to proclaim loudly—and accurately—that education is not what it was in the old days. From presenting traditional family, religious, and patriotic themes, textbooks have moved to endorsing multiculturalism, environmentalism, and globalism while discouraging militarism, stereotyping, and unbridled capitalism. The gradual change in textbooks began in the 1960s, but it was not until the 1970s and early 1980s that nationally organized campaigns were mounted against the new books.

In the Dick and Jane readers some of us remember from our childhoods, a family consisted of a married couple, two or three well-behaved children, and a dog and a cat. Father wore suits and went out to work; mother wore aprons and baked cupcakes. Little girls sat demurely watching little boys climb trees. *Home* meant a single-family house in a middle-class suburban neighborhood. Color the lawn green. Color the people white. Family life in the textbook world was idyllic: parents did not quarrel, children did not disobey, and babies did not throw up on the dog.

With the advent of civil rights and feminism, and with the rise of pollution, overpopulation, drug use, and the threat of nuclear war, the key word in textbooks became *relevance*. People who were not white or middle-class and did not live in traditional nuclear families began to demand representation in textbooks. Textbooks also began to talk about the importance of international understanding and independent thinking in today's complex and troubled world.

The new books are deeply disturbing to people who do not want education to describe a changing social order or promote independent decision making. At its extreme, fundamentalist textbook activism is based on the premise that the act of creative thinking is evil in itself, regardless of content, because it might lead to thoughts that are displeasing to God. Pictures of little girls engaging in activities traditionally associated with boys, such as playing with toy cars or petting worms, threaten American family life because girls might grow up craving male roles. Pollution is a humanist myth promoting international cooperation, which could lead to world unity and thus to the reign of the Antichrist, which will signal the end of the world. Conservation is an act of human pride and an offense against God. Humans have no business worrying about the extinction of whales; if God wants whales to exist, they will exist. If not, then preserving them is an act of rebellion against God.

Textbook activism often begins at the grass-roots level, but successful drives to ban or change books require the support of powerful national groups. The Far Right organizations that are most vocal about textbook content are the American Family Association, based in Mississippi and headed by Donald Wildmon; Citizens for Excellence in Education (California, Robert L. Simonds); Concerned Women for America (Washington, D.C., Beverly LaHaye); the Eagle Forum (Illinois, Phyllis Schlafly); Focus on the Family (California, James Dobson); and the National Legal Foundation (Virginia, Pat Robertson). These well-funded, politically sophisticated national organizations supply legal representation for local textbook protesters and support efforts to lobby school boards and state legislatures.

It would be misleading to suggest that all textbook activism—conservative or liberal—is censorship, since decisions about what to teach and what not to teach are a necessary part of every educational system. Some material may be too advanced, academically or socially, for students of a particular age. Besides, human knowledge is cumulative: as scientific discoveries are made, as poems and novels are written, as historic events occur, information previously taught is pushed aside to make room for newer material. The school day has just so many minutes, and the school year has just so many days. For every fact that is put into a textbook, something else is left out. Given that some degree of selectivity is essential to education, advocacy groups will, naturally, try to influence textbook content in directions they consider appropriate. A certain amount of activism is part of the normal functioning of an educational system in a nontotalitarian state; the challenge is to determine the point at which attempts to influence textbook content shade into attempts to censor education.

The verb *to censor* operates according to its own peculiar grammatical rules. It is used almost exclusively in the second or third person: "You are censoring" or "They are censoring." It is almost never used in the first person: "We are censoring." A much more common self-perception is "We are participating in the common-sense selection of material suitable for children and adolescents." In order to make the point that even by the most rigorous definition censorship is occurring in American schools, neither conservatives nor liberals are called censors in this book unless their goal is to obliterate from the store of human knowledge all trace of ideas with which they disagree. By that stringent definition, relatively little of today's textbook activism is actually censorship, but the incidents that do fall under that heading are very serious indeed. Only two major groups thereby qualify as textbook censors: fundamentalists and politically correct extremists.

The changing image of textbooks has aroused liberal advocates who are as dedicated to intensifying the new trend as their opponents are to reversing it. Some liberal protesters call for an increase in the representation of women, minorities, and non-Western cultures in textbooks without specifically targeting anything for removal. It would be naive to suggest that such inclusion does not involve exclusion; given the constraints of textbook space and classroom time, *something* that used to be covered has to be eliminated to make room for the new material. "Inclusionary" liberal textbook activists also tend to encourage the selection of facts that place previously underrepresented groups in the best possible light. By the definition of censorship given above, however, such lobbyists are not censors. Their efforts certainly contribute to the fragmentation of textbooks, but they do not tend toward the systematic elimination of any particular idea or fact.

Somewhere along the continuum of liberal textbook activists, however, "inclusionary" advocates give way to liberal censors. *Battle of the Books,* Lee Burress's study of literary censorship in the schools, describes organizations whose attempts to eliminate racism and sexism from textbooks have become so extreme that they are themselves censoring part of the truth. Since Burress's book was written before the term *politically correct* came into vogue, it is clear that the movement preceded its current label. Regardless of what liberal censors are called, the exact point at which they take over from "inclusionary" liberal activists is difficult to identify because the difference is in degree, not in kind. The noncensor leans toward additional, and favorable, representation of minorities and women. The politically correct censor is determined to eliminate all depictions of women in traditional roles, or every statement that could possibly be construed as disparaging a particular racial, ethnic, or religious group. The accuracy of a statement and the context in which it occurs are dismissed as irrelevant. Politically correct extremists, like their fundamentalist counterparts, operate on the assumption that education has two functions: to describe what should be rather than what is, and to reverse the injustices of yesterday's society by shaping the attitudes of tomorrow's. Balanced portrayals of reality—some women *are* full-time homemakers, while others *do* have careers—get lost in the shuffle.

Taken to its extreme, the term *political correctness* denotes a form of intellectual terrorism in which people who express ideas that are offensive to any group other than white males of western European heritage may be punished, *regardless of the accuracy or relevance of what they say.* Racism, sexism, and other forms of prejudice are abhorrent and cannot be tolerated by any culture that claims to be civilized. Nevertheless, if we were *trying* to perpetuate mutual hostility and suspicion, we could not find a better way to do it than by suppressing honest questions because somebody might not like the answers, or by selecting and altering facts solely to shape opinion. Politically correct censors, like fundamentalist censors, also ignore the broader implications of their activities. By what logic can people defend their own freedom of expression while denying the rights of others to state facts and express beliefs? Once a culture decides that the truth can be suppressed because it is offensive to some, all that remains is a trial of strength to determine whose sensibilities take precedence. In this regard, the only difference between fundamentalist and politically correct extremists lies in the specific truths they wish to promote or suppress; the principles on which they operate are the same.

What Johnny Shouldn't Read discusses only elementary and secondary school textbooks, not because college texts are immune from outside pressures, but because the same forces do not apply to them. College attendance is voluntary and most college students are legally adults, which makes college instruction less vulnerable to lawsuits than public education is. Moreover, the selection procedure for college textbooks is different from the method of adopting books for public school classes. Students in multisection college courses may use a common textbook selected by a faculty committee, but most college texts are chosen by the individual professor teaching a particular course. College professors in their right mind (admittedly not 100 percent of us) would simply refuse to use a version of *Romeo and Juliet* with three hundred lines missing. The book would not make a profit because it would not sell, and that would be that. At the pre-college level, however, textbook selection is handled in a more centralized way. A small proportion of elementary and secondary school teachers may serve on textbook selection committees, but on the whole, teachers at the pre-college level are assigned textbooks that have been developed and selected by a highly politicized process. Regardless of anyone's opinion about what the teaching profession should look like, the truth is that individual college professors generally have more autonomy and more power than individual elementary or secondary school teachers. As a result, college textbooks tend to be produced to the specifications of professors, whereas elementary and secondary school books are more likely to reflect the wishes of school boards, administrators, and other nonclassroom personnel.

College professors' relative freedom to select and shape course material does not mean that textbook censorship does not affect college education. When students have spent twelve years reading books based more on market forces than on scholarly excellence, they may not come to college prepared to do college-level work. The increasing use of short sentences and simple words—often called "dumbing down"—in elementary and secondary school textbooks has generated a great deal of print since the mid-1970s, but the watering down of ideas is at least equally dangerous. In response to this problem, the American Association of University Professors (AAUP) recently published a report prepared by its Commission on Academic Freedom and Pre-College Education. The report, entitled "Liberty and Learning in the Schools: Higher Education's Concerns," points out that students whose pre-college education was based primarily on "official" textbooks are not likely to understand how to deal with shades of meaning or with controversial topics.

Religious private schools that want to promote a fundamentalist viewpoint can purchase textbooks from small presses specializing in religiously oriented instructional materials. An example is A BEKA Publishers, located in Pensacola, Florida. A BEKA is the largest fundamentalist textbook publishing company in America. Its mathematics books feature problems involving the tribes of Israel; its reading books glorify Christian heroes; its history books attribute world events to God; and its science books teach creationism rather than evolution.

Secular private schools, and religious private schools that do not use specifically religious textbooks, have no choice but to buy their books from the same publishers that supply public school districts. Private schools have far fewer students and operate in a less centralized way than public schools, which means that they do not have the economic clout to tell publishers what to include in textbooks or to induce publishers to produce special editions just for them. As a result, parents who think that they are sidestepping public school politics by sending their children to private schools are only partially correct. The same is true of parents who live in school districts that do not advocate censorship. Their children's textbooks were not developed for their particular schools; they were designed for a national market that includes heavily populated states where textbook activists are very influential. Further, private schools are not necessarily exempt from state authority over curriculum. Robert M. O'Neil, in his 1981 book *Classrooms in the Crossfire*, discusses several lawsuits touching on state regulation of private schools.

Overall, the textbook development process in America has less to do with educating a nation than with selling a product. In the world of publishing, the consumers who matter most are not the students and teachers who use textbooks but the school boards that buy them. Some school boards choose to accept the recommendations of teachers almost automatically, but recent federal court decisions have shown that school boards can, if they wish, simply order teachers to use certain textbooks. Since school boards are either elected themselves or appointed by elected officials, they are vulnerable to lobbying by pressure groups. In American public education, the most important decisions are made not by educators but by politicians. Activists can affect textbook content by persuading politically vulnerable school boards to put pressure on publishers to change what the textbooks say. Given the realities of the free-enterprise system, school boards overseeing the largest markets have the most power over textbook content. What schoolchildren throughout America learn is heavily influenced by states like Texas and California in which large populations are combined with strong state-level textbook activism.

Because negative publicity is likely to reduce textbook sales, a series of nationally publicized federal court cases throughout the 1980s alarmed publishers into becoming more and more careful about what their books include. The real importance of the legal cases discussed in this book is not, however, their immediate effect on textbook content. In larger terms, these cases try to balance the religious rights of individuals with the separation of church and state in public education. Some cases deal with conflicts between the right to a free public education and the right to practice a religion that opposes what is taught in public schools. Other cases respond to the claim that the religion of secular humanism, defined as worshiping humanity in place of God, is being taught in American public schools in violation of the First Amendment. In many situations, different groups of parents in the same district come into conflict over what should be taught in the schools, and the courts do their best to arbitrate. Courts also weigh the rights of parents against the authority of school boards, and as chapter 7 explains, the school boards are well ahead. The courts' support of school board authority is a two-edged sword as far as censorship is concerned: it discourages extremists from going to court to challenge the use of textbooks they do not like, but it also leaves other parents little recourse when activists succeed in persuading a local school board to ban certain books.

In the movie *1776*, a messenger from Valley Forge periodically interrupts the Continental Congress with George Washington's plaintive cry for support. "Is anybody there?" Washington asks. "Does anybody care?" The same questions may well be asked about the fight for freedom of information in the schools. Who, if anyone, is doing what, if anything, to sustain it?

Not surprisingly, national organizations representing educators and librarians play an important role in responding to censorship issues. Describing their anti-censorship activities could easily fill a chapter by itself; in fact, Diane Shugert's "A Body of Well-Instructed Men and Women: Organizations Active for Intellectual Freedom" (1979) is devoted to just this issue. To give a few examples: the American Library Association distributes its *Newsletter on Intellectual Freedom* every two months, documenting the latest challenges to library collections, textbooks, films, plays, and news stories. The Modern Language Association, which sponsors an active Committee on Academic Freedom, is planning to focus on literature and censorship in an upcoming issue of its prestigious journal, PMLA. The National School Boards Association featured textbook censorship at a 1987 convention in Washington, D.C. Some of the most useful books on textbook censorship, such as *Dealing with Censorship* (James E. Davis, 1979), *How Censorship Affects the School and Other Essays* (Lee Burress, 1984), and *Celebrating Censored Books* (Nicholas Karolides and Lee Burress, 1985), are published by the National Council of Teachers of English and its state affiliates.

Professional associations are not the only groups active against censorship. In each of the legal cases discussed in this book, the anti-censorship side was underwritten by the American Civil Liberties Union (ACLU) or People for the American Way (PAW). The ACLU, PAW, and the National Coalition Against Censorship also mount mailing campaigns informing the public of challenges to reading materials and soliciting contributions for the fight against censorship. Dedicated as these national groups are, however, the real power lies with the people—conservatives, moderates, and liberals alike—who oppose the extremes to which the textbook censors go. Until the publicity generated by professional organizations, advocacy groups, and books like *What Johnny Shouldn't Read* provoke a loud and sustained outcry from opponents of the textbook censors, the balance of power described in this book is unlikely to change significantly.

CHAPTER TWO

Power
Struggle

It boils down to who is going to tell who to read what.
—A HAWKINS COUNTY VICE-PRINCIPAL

One hot August afternoon in 1983, just after the Tennessee schools had opened for the fall term, a sixth-grader named Rebecca Frost was having trouble with her homework. She was reading a story called "A Visit to Mars," in which astronauts from Earth meet a tribe of Martians. At first, the Earthlings think that they can understand the Martians' language, but it turns out that the Martians do not use words at all. Instead, they transfer their thoughts directly to the minds of their "listeners," where the ideas are translated into whatever words each individual would use; so a medical doctor might hear *fractured tibia* where someone else would hear *broken leg*.

Rebecca was trying to answer the questions at the end of the story, but she got stuck on one which asked why two of the Earthlings called the Martian tribe the Beautiful People, while the others thought that the tribe's name was the Lovely Ones. According to the teachers' manual, the correct answer was, "The thought behind both expressions is the same." Rebecca asked her mother, Vicki, to explain the question to her. As Vicki Frost later testified, "With this one question, with this one question, this was the very start of the controversy" (Deposition, April 3, 1986, p. 368). Within a few months, the bitter dispute beginning "with this one question" had escalated into a nationally publicized federal court case that lasted for four and a half years.

To Frost, a devout Christian fundamentalist, anything that is beyond present human capacity—such as thought transference—is a form of magic forbidden by the Bible. Besides, the ability to read thoughts belongs to God alone, and attempting to share that power reflects a sinful human desire to take the place of God. The notion of fantasy as entertainment was entirely foreign to her; in her later testimony, she rejected any form of imaginative thinking as a temptation that might lead the born-again Christian away from biblical truths. She was also troubled by the notion of communication without language barriers, regardless of how it is achieved. If everyone could understand everyone else, she reasoned, American Christians might be contaminated with foreign ideas and religions. Even worse, global unity might result. A united world is only one step away from a one-world government, and Frost feared the end of the free enterprise system and a decrease in the American standard of living.

Frost read the rest of Rebecca's textbook, along with the readers used by her other children in the first, second, and seventh grades. She did not like any of them. All four children were using the brand-new Holt, Rinehart and Winston Basic Reading Series, which had just replaced the school district's eleven-year-old Economy readers. The change was not, to their mother's way of thinking, an improvement. She associated the old readers with what she considered good American Christian values, such as patriotism and traditional nuclear families. The new books, to her dismay, were full of minorities, foreigners, environmentalism, women in nontraditional roles, and open-ended value judgments without clear right and wrong answers.

Frost and the other fundamentalists who later joined her protest wanted their children to grow up sharing the values of their parents and grandparents, and they accused the school authorities of trying to use reading instruction as a way to promote social change. Their accusation was perfectly accurate: the Holt books do promote certain ideas, just as earlier generations of textbooks emphasized other ideas. There is not, and never has been, any such thing as a values-free education, but people generally do not object to the schools' inculcating attitudes that resemble their own. The furor in Hawkins County arose, not because textbooks were suddenly teaching values, but because they were suddenly teaching values to which some fundamentalists objected. Where the protesters wanted their children to see themselves as a separate people unto God, regarding all others as inferior and misguided, the Holt books emphasized tolerance for diversity. The protesters wanted their children to obey without question, but the new readers promoted creative thinking and independent decision making.

If Frost's protest had been an isolated incident, it would have represented no more than a ripple in Hawkins County school politics and, perhaps, in Holt public relations. But the stand she took was by no means unique. It reflects the educational agendas of national Far Right organizations, such as Phyllis Schlafly's Eagle Forum, Robert Simonds' National Association of Christian Educators (NACE) and Citizens for Excellence in Education (CEE), Beverly LaHaye's Concerned Women for America (CWA), Pat Robertson's National Legal Foundation (NLF), and Donald Wildmon's American Family Association (AFA). These groups oppose public education for teaching what they define as the religion of secular humanism. As a handbook written by Simonds explains:

> There are only *two* general world views. Though there are many ideas on life's worth and purpose they all boil down to two basic views. One is *God's view*—the other is *man's view*.
>
> These two views produce two different people. The humanist or worldly person is basically EGO, or *self-oriented*. The Christ-ian person or follower of God is "*other person*" oriented.
>
> Humanism says there is *no* God. Christianity says there *is* a living Creator God. Each of these two views, philosophies, or belief patterns comprise their own world-view. All belief systems fit into one of these two diametrically opposite camps, even though there is every shade and color in each of these fundamentally opposite philosophies. (*Communicating a Christian World View in the Classroom: A Manual* [Costa Mesa, Calif.: NACE, 1983], p. 1)

Simonds and others like him use the word *Christianity* to mean their own Protestant fundamentalist beliefs. By their definition, secular humanism is a competing religion encompassing all the ideas that their interpretation of the Bible rejects. Since their religion is not being taught in public schools, and the only other world view is secular humanism, it follows that public schools are violating the First Amendment by promoting one religion at the expense of the other.

Far Right organizations do more than just write handbooks about secular humanism in the schools. They monitor newspapers nationwide in search of grass-roots disputes, like the one in Hawkins County, that give them the opportunity to move from abstract argument to legal action or political lobbying about a specific situation. Although Frost's protest began modestly enough, it was only a matter of time before the involvement of national organizations elevated it from a local debate to a national controversy over secular humanism in the schools.

Frost herself began expressing her objections to the Holt books in terms of secular humanism after talking with a friend, Jennie Wilson, who had recently taken a course on humanism at Graham Bible College in Bristol, Tennessee. Until she spoke with Wilson, Frost had simply been going from neighbor to neighbor, asking people whether they had read the new books and, if so, what they thought of them. Now Frost and Wilson decided to organize a full-fledged campaign to have the Holt readers removed from the Hawkins County schools on the grounds that they promoted the religion of secular humanism. They began by holding an informational meeting attended by about seventy-five parents and school officials. According to a newspaper report, Frost and Wilson accused the readers of promoting idolatry, demon worship, gun control, evolution, and feminism while opposing free enterprise, the military, lawful authority, and Christianity.

A week after the informational meeting, Frost, Wilson, and several of their supporters addressed the Hawkins County School Board. Frost alone spoke for over an hour about the ways in which children were being indoctrinated rather than educated by the Holt books. The protesters were confident that the board members would withdraw the reading series as soon as they heard what was in it. As Wilson later testified, she had expected the board to tell the publisher, " 'Hey, you've sold us a bill of goods, and you take these back and give us some books that do not teach secular humanism, the religion of it' " (Deposition, February 26, 1986, p. 148).

Wilson's expectations were doomed to disappointment. Expressing open contempt for the protesters' arguments, the board refused to take the Holt series out of the schools. The resulting confrontation between the protesters and the school authorities was an eye-opener for both sides. Like many fundamentalists who become involved in textbook controversies, Frost associates mainly with people who think much the way she does. She and her family are not so separated from the secular world as the Amish are, but they read primarily religious newspapers and magazines, avoid movies and television programs, and socialize with others of the same religion. It came as a great surprise when churchgoing local school officials, including some of her former schoolmates, did not agree with what seemed perfectly obvious to her. On the other side, the school officials took it for granted that everyone supports multiculturalism, environmentalism, and the other contemporary "isms" presented in the Holt books. Between the protesters' shocked rejection of the school

board's views and the board's contemptuous impatience with the protesters' demands, communication in Hawkins County was at low tide.

When the school board refused to remove the Holt readers, Frost went
to see James Salley, principal of Church Hill Middle School, where Rebecca and her older brother, Marty, were students. After Frost and the
parents of eight other students had spoken to Salley, their children were
allowed to use alternate readers that were acceptable to them.

The protesters' request put Salley in a precarious position. On the one
hand, parents undoubtedly have primary responsibility for their children's upbringing. Few people would want to see the United States become a totalitarian nation in which children are forced to attend classes
that alienate them from their parents' religious beliefs. On the other hand,
the fact that someone finds certain ideas offensive does not necessarily
mean that they can be avoided in public school instruction. It would be
unreasonable for people who believe in polygamy to put their children
in public schools and then object to stories involving monogamous marriages. The problem, of course, is deciding *what* ideas can be omitted
from the public school curriculum, at least for students receiving individualized instruction. The twenty-five-year-old readers Salley gave the
protesters' children were harmless in themselves, but they represented a
tacit agreement that certain children did not have to learn to think independently, or understand anyone who was different from themselves,
or grapple with contemporary world issues.

Another problem with the Church Hill Middle School alternate reading
arrangement was that the state has a duty at least to try to teach reading
effectively, and the instruction offered to the protesters' children was far
from ideal. The children were not all in the same grade and did not have
reading class at the same time. Rebecca and another child worked in a
small cubby next to their regular classroom; the others stayed in their
classrooms or went to the library or cafeteria. They spent the class period
reading stories on their own and answering assigned questions. As they
testified later, they often finished their work well before the end of the
period. Moreover, the students who worked outside their classrooms
were supervised by any adults who happened to be nearby, including
cafeteria workers whom one student called "the cafeterians." The teachers checked the worksheets handed in at the end of the period, but apart
from that, the children received little if any reading instruction. This
arrangement went on for several weeks. When the parents later testified
about their children's reading instruction during this time, they said either
that they did not know how it had been handled or that they were not
concerned; they were interested only in avoiding the Holt books. One

mother said that she was not worried about her son's reading classes because he was in the sixth grade and already knew how to read. Overall, Salley's compromise was just that: a compromise that served, briefly, to ease a difficult situation but did not offer a permanent solution to the philosophical and educational problems raised by the controversy.

Salley was not the only principal who had to make a decision about alternate readers. The protesters were determined, as a matter of principle, to involve as many schools as possible to make the point that schools have no right to teach children anything that their parents disapprove of. Jennie Wilson could not contribute to this aspect of the dispute at first because she had no children of school age. Then, early in October, she invited her two little granddaughters to come and live with her. Heather, who was in the second grade, and Vicky, a year younger, had started the school year in a district that did not use the Holt readers. When they went to stay with their grandmother, they were transferred to Carter's Valley Elementary School, where the controversial readers were in use.

The principal of Carter's Valley Elementary School, Archie McMillan, was one of the school officials who had attended the informational meeting organized by Wilson and Frost. He thought that their views on mental telepathy, in particular, were just plain silly, and said so in front of a reporter: " 'I remember sitting in church with my friends and cutting up, then I got a look from my mother that was definitely mental telepathy—I knew what she was saying,' he said, as several persons laughed. 'I've read the stories, and I saw no evil in them' " (*Kingsport Times-News,* September 2, 1983).

Unlike Salley, McMillan would not allow students in his school to use alternate readers. He believed that the school's first responsibility was to see that primary grade children learned to read, and for that, he concluded, they needed to be in their regular classes. He refused to provide one-on-one instruction for the protesters' children or to allow first- and second-graders to skip class in favor of reading on their own. He also rejected Heather's mother's choice of an alternate textbook: the Christian version of the McGuffey readers, copyright 1836–38.

One of the biggest obstacles to communication between the protesters and the school officials was the parents' insistence that they had absolute rights over their children's education. To them, school authorities had no control whatsoever over what their children learned or over their own behavior in public school buildings. This aspect of the controversy began to heat up one day in the middle of October, when Wilson went to Carter's Valley Elementary School to visit her granddaughters' class-

rooms without consulting McMillan. When a teacher asked whether she
had the principal's permission to be there, she replied that it was "all
right." She later explained that she "had no notion a public school was
no longer public" (Letter to the Board of Education, October 14, 1983).
McMillan eventually asked her to leave, and she later said that he had
"expelled" her from school. According to Wilson, McMillan told her
that the teachers felt threatened by her presence because she was one of
the textbook protesters. She also quoted him as saying that "the school
children belonged to [the school authorities] because the parents wanted
it that way" (Letter to the Board of Education, October 14, 1983).
McMillan confirmed that he had asked her to leave the school but denied
the rest of her account.

Three days after Wilson's abbreviated classroom visit, her husband
drove to the school and took both of his granddaughters home. The
children, who had been in Carter's Valley for about two weeks, were
transferred to a private Christian school. The Wilsons accused McMillan
of expelling both girls. McMillan asserted that the Wilsons had withdrawn their grandchildren voluntarily in protest against the Holt readers.

The disagreement between McMillan and the Wilsons was the first of
several arguments that occurred because the protesters saw no difference
between removing a child from a school and having a child expelled. In
their view, school officials were required to conform absolutely, without
argument or explanation, to whatever parents wanted for their children.
If a principal refused to meet their demands, they reasoned, then they
had no choice but to remove their children from the school; and what
is expulsion but the forced removal of a child from a school because of
the actions of school officials?

As the controversy progressed, the Hawkins County protesters began
corresponding with national organizations. Their attitudes about parental
control of education had from the beginning coincided with those of Far
Right national groups; now, as they received handbooks and other mailings confirming that they were not alone in their beliefs, their opposition
to the schools became even stronger.

The idea that parents and public school officials are locked in competition for the minds and souls of children was the focus of *Humanism*,
a handbook sent to Hawkins County by Mel and Norma Gabler, whose
textbook activism is discussed in Chapter 9. The handbook includes a
reprint of "Parental Guide to Combat the Religion of Secular Humanism
in the Schools," originally distributed by Parents of Minnesota, Inc. The
flier urges parents not to "fall victim" to the notion of academic freedom
because schools operate *in loco parentis,* which means that "they [public

school officials] MUST honor the objections of the parents" (p. 1). According to "Parental Guide," "As long as the schools continue to teach ABNORMAL ATTITUDES and ALIEN THOUGHTS, we caution parents NOT to urge their children to pursue high grades or class discussion, because the harder students work, the greater their chance of brainwashing" (p. 2).

The view of public education as the enemy of Christian parents has persisted into the 1990s in the publications of national organizations. Newsletters distributed by the Eagle Forum, headed by Phyllis Schlafly, have included such headlines as "Teachers Sue Parents Who Raise Objections" (March 1986), "Michigan Parents Defeat State Grab for Power" (March 1989), "The Anti-Parent Policies of the NEA [National Education Association]" (November 1989), and "Seminar Trains Schools How to Combat Parents" (January 1990).

Year after year, groups like the Eagle Forum advocate such intense animosity between parents and public schools, and such strong parental control of each individual child's curriculum, that if public schools tried to meet these demands they would become too fragmented to function. The collapse of public education as it now exists would open the door to a voucher system providing tax dollars for private religious schools in which children would no longer be contaminated by what some fundamentalists see as the humanistic, communistic, amoral, liberal ideas taught in schools of education and promoted by the NEA.

In accordance with a recommendation in the Gablers' handbook on humanism, Wilson and Frost formed a group called Citizens Organized for Better Schools (COBS). Another parent, Bob Mozert, became the group's director. Mozert, an ordained fundamentalist minister, later founded the Abundant Living Christian Fellowship School, which some of the protesters' children attended. He was also the only man actively involved on the protesters' side of the controversy. Other husbands supported the protest in a general way, but they did not offer much testimony, read the Holt books, or even seem to understand some of the religious beliefs in question. Consistent with the traditional gender roles they advocated, they left the religious training of their children to their wives.

COBS circulated a written statement of belief that supported a moment of silence in public schools, the teaching of "factual truth with moral value and not nihilistic fantasy," public participation in school governance, and individualized instruction. The statement criticized the schools for failing to teach love of God and country and for teaching evolution and "secular humanism and other false religions." In a letter to the editor of the *Kingsport Times-News*, Mozert defined secular humanism as a "lethal religion" that denies God and moral absolutes. "The doctrines of humanism," he wrote, "include evolution, self-authority, situation ethics, distorted realism, sexual permissiveness, anti-Biblical bias, anti-free enterprise, one-world government and death education" (October 6, 1983).

COBS members put their principles into practice by pressing for changes in the public schools. They wanted the schools to revise or eliminate sex education courses and to institute a dress code that would clearly differentiate between the sexes. They demanded the removal of certain books from the senior high school library. Believing that alcohol is forbidden by the Bible, they wanted to prevent school buses from going near taverns, and they did not want children on field trips to stop for pizza because pizzerias usually sell beer. COBS also demanded that the Pledge of Allegiance be said in all classrooms and that outdated flags be replaced. The school board handed the list of complaints over to a subcommittee, and nothing happened for about two months. When the parents pressed for a reply, the subcommittee members consulted with other school officials and concluded, without explanation, "that our policy standards were up to anyone's standards and [the subcommittee] didn't feel they needed to change anything" (Board of Education Minutes, December 8, 1983).

The school board was within its rights in declining to remove library books or reroute school buses because of the protesters' interpretation of the Bible, but its refusal to explain its decisions left it open to charges of arrogance and arbitrariness. The board also failed to address more general complaints, such as the use of outdated flags in the schools. Like the protesters, the school officials were bent on demonstrating that they, and only they, were in authority.

As the tension between parents and educational authorities increased, some school personnel became extremely irritated by persistent criticism from people who were, for the most part, poorly educated themselves. School officials were also embarrassed by publicity associating their district with anti-intellectual, hard-line religious fundamentalism. In their frustration, they said things in public that came back to haunt them when the legal action started. The superintendent of schools, for example, stated that outside agitators must have been responsible for the controversy because the local protesters would not have been capable of organizing it themselves; and a school board member angrily rejected the possibility of attending a COBS function on the grounds that "he was not invited to this meeting, [and] did not want to be invited again because he was not interested" (Board of Education Minutes, November 10, 1983).

From a human point of view, the school officials' frustration was

understandable. They were being subjected to loud, unreasonable demands and to criticism that bordered on a smear campaign by people
who seemed determined to see them as the enemy. On the other hand,
their own behavior made them less and less approachable to taxpayers
who, whatever their opinions or tactics, had the right to challenge things
they did not like about the public schools. Seeing the protesters as relatively powerless antagonists without the sophistication or money to
create serious problems, the school authorities made the mistake of cutting off any possibility of settling the dispute locally.

When COBS failed to reach an understanding with the education officials, its members increased their efforts to persuade national groups
to bring pressure to bear on the Hawkins County schools. Concerned
Women for America eventually provided substantial help, but in the early
stages of the dispute the protesters' efforts were unrewarding. Frost, for
example, wrote to the magazine *American Rifleman* asking for support
against textbooks which, she stated, advocated gun control. Her letter
was forwarded to the National Rifle Association (NRA). The NRA replied
with a letter expressing opposition to the "anti-gun/anti-hunting senti-
ments which are being propagated in our school systems" and outlining
the NRA's efforts on behalf of "teachers who wish to promote the positive
attributes of hunting and gun ownership to America's students" (October
11, 1983). Would Frost, the NRA asked, send copies of the offensive
material in the Holt readers? She sent thirty to forty pages, but the NRA
did not reply and took no further action.

Some of the protesters' letters to outside authorities contained unproven and irrelevant accusations against the Hawkins County schools.
One letter to Governor Lamar Alexander complained that students were
being given academic credit for picking up food from the floor and for
bringing home-baked goods to the fall festival. Letters of that kind de-
lighted the school authorities, who used them to support their contention
that the protesters were cranks who wanted to discredit the school system
as a way of imposing their religious views on everyone.

All the time these events were taking place, some school principals
were still allowing the protesters' children to use old readers instead of
the Holt series. In November, when the controversy was not quite three
months old, the school board voted to forbid the use of alternate textbooks. Board members declared that they had selected the Holt books
and were determined that all Hawkins County public school children
were going to read them.

Most of the students who were using alternate readers were in Church
Hill Middle School, and the principal, James Salley, immediately called

a meeting of the protesting parents. He made it clear that the issue was no longer negotiable; no student would be permitted to use any reader other than the Holt books. The next day, he imposed three-day suspensions on all of the students whose parents refused to let them attend reading class. These included Marty and Rebecca Frost, Travis Mozert, and the children of five other families: the Couches, Crawfords, Eatons, Marshalls, and Whitakers.

Protesters and school officials alike saw the situation at Church Hill Middle School as a trial of strength for control of the children's education. In a newspaper interview, Bob Mozert asserted, "The children are obeying their parents. They are submitting to our authority" (*Johnson City Press-Chronicle*, November 16, 1983). Another interviewer quoted him as saying, "We have made our decision; our children will not be reading in that [Holt] reader" (*Kingsport Times-News*, November 15, 1983). On the other side, the assistant principal of Church Hill Middle School summarized the whole situation when he told a reporter, "It boils down to who is going to tell who to read what" (*Kingsport Times-News*, November 16, 1983).

Some of the children understood this battle of adult wills much better than they understood their parents' objections to the books. One boy could not define situation ethics, and he was not sure about the connection between gun control and his parents' religious beliefs. Nevertheless, he was clear about his parents' insistence that "they ain't going to make you read the books." He also recognized, accurately, that "[the school officials] was gonna make me read the books . . . they gave me the books and they told me, you're going to have to read it" (Deposition of Marty Frost, February 25, 1986, p. 26).

When the students returned to school after their three-day suspensions, they still refused to use the disputed readers, and Salley promptly suspended them for another ten days. Only one student, Steve Whitaker, returned to school after the second suspension and read the Holt books. Most of the other students were withdrawn from Church Hill Middle School. Those who remained—Marty and Rebecca Frost, Travis Mozert, Gina Marshall, and Brad Eaton—were suspended for another ten school days. Because of the Christmas holidays, this suspension would have lasted until January 6, 1984.

On December 12, Gina Marshall returned to school after Salley had called her parents. Although Steve Whitaker was being required to read the Holt books as a condition of remaining in Church Hill Middle School, Gina was allowed to use only reading skills worksheets that covered spelling, punctuation, grammar, and paragraph organization. She did not have to read the Holt stories themselves or answer questions about them. Because she was using no reader at all, she was technically observing the school board's ban on alternate textbooks.

By December 13, Salley had notified the other three families that the suspensions had been lifted and the children could return to school. He would not, however, promise that they would not have to read the Holt books. The parents felt that all of the children should have been offered the same instruction as Gina Marshall. They noted that her father regularly played golf with a school board member and a school principal, but they made no specific accusation. In fact, her arrangement became a point in their favor when they argued in court that it would indeed have been possible to accommodate their children. They also used Salley's lack of consistency to support their claim that school officials had treated them unfairly.

Unsettling as the events at Church Hill Middle School were, an even greater drama was unfolding at Church Hill Elementary School, where Jean Price was the principal and Sarah Frost was a second-grade pupil. Vicki Frost wanted to take over Sarah's reading instruction herself, removing the child from class every day but remaining in the building. The principal conceded that parents have the right to take their children off the grounds altogether, but she refused to allow Frost to teach Sarah from an alternate reader on school property. She also pointed out that second-graders have long reading periods, which meant that taking Sarah out of class for that length of time every day would soon have added up to a violation of the attendance rules.

One morning in late November, Frost went to Sarah's reading class, beckoned to the child, and started toward the school cafeteria with her. Price told Frost once again that she would have to take Sarah off the premises, but the mother and daughter went only as far as the family truck, parked in the schoolyard. Price called a police officer, who told Frost that she could not remain on school property. He also reminded her that Sarah would need a permission slip from the principal's office when she returned to school. Frost left, but when she brought Sarah back she had the child enter the school building by the door farthest from the office and go straight to class. She refused to fill out permission slips when removing or returning Sarah because, she felt, they impinged on her absolute authority as a parent.

Throughout the battle of wills over Sarah, Frost kept saying that the child would have to be expelled from school. According to Price's notes, Frost became "upset" when the principal insisted that Sarah had done nothing to deserve expulsion. Frost also said several times that she and Sarah might be taken to jail. Price later testified that Frost seemed to *want* her to take action against Sarah, but she did not know why.

On the evening following the parking lot incident, Frost telephoned Michael Farris, who was then head of the legal department of Concerned Women for America (CWA). Farris is also a fundamentalist minister and former head of the Moral Majority in the State of Washington. The protesters had begun corresponding with CWA early in the controversy, but it was Frost's telephone call that finally drew the organization into an active role.

CWA, headquartered in Washington, D.C., was founded in 1979 by Beverly LaHaye. Her husband, Tim LaHaye, is a fundamentalist preacher and writer. By the time the Hawkins County protest began, CWA had already filed a federal lawsuit, *Grove v. Mead School District No. 354*, over a textbook controversy in Washington State. In *Grove*, Farris represented a woman whose daughter, Cassie, had been assigned to read Gordon Parks' autobiographical novel, *The Learning Tree*. The book describes the experiences of an African American boy growing into manhood, and its language and situations offended Cassie, then a high school sophomore. When Cassie refused to read the novel, her teacher allowed her to substitute a different book. Nevertheless, CWA filed suit against the school district, alleging that *The Learning Tree* teaches the religion of secular humanism and should not be assigned to any public school student. Merely providing an alternate selection was not acceptable, since it stigmatized the child by suggesting that her religious views, not the book itself, were out of keeping with public school instruction. The district court eventually dismissed the case, and the appeals court upheld the dismissal, in part because Cassie had not been required to read the book. CWA was, therefore, especially interested in the Hawkins County controversy because the protesters' children were being forced to read the disputed texts if they wished to remain in public schools.

When Frost called Farris about the situation at Sarah's school, he made no promises about future support, but he did discuss the situation with her. The next morning, she went to City Hall and asked to have a police officer come with her to Church Hill Elementary School. She explained that she wanted the officer to witness that she was doing nothing wrong. No one was available to accompany her. She then went into the county clerk's office to photocopy two letters that she intended to give Price. According to the clerk, Frost requested prayers because she expected to be arrested that day.

Later that morning, Frost arrived in Price's office and asked for Sarah.

Price told her once again that she could take the child home if she wished, but she could not teach her from an alternate reader on the school premises. Frost then called the police. When an officer arrived, Frost gave Price two letters reminding her that the State of Tennessee encouraged parent volunteers in the schools. She interpreted the policy to mean that any parent who wanted to serve as a volunteer in any capacity had to be accepted, so Price had to allow her to teach reading to Sarah.

Price ordered Frost to leave the school with Sarah or without Sarah, just so long as she left. As far as the principal was concerned, there was nothing to say that had not already been said over and over, and she wanted to go back to work. When Frost refused to leave, Price handed a copy of a Tennessee state law to the police officer, Joe Ashbrook, and asked him to read it aloud. The law states:

> Persons improperly on school premises.—(a) In order to maintain the conditions and atmosphere suitable for learning, no person shall enter onto the grounds or into the buildings of public schools during the hours of student instruction except students assigned to that school, the staff of the school, parents of students, and other persons with lawful and valid business on the school premises.
>
> (b) Any person improperly on the premises of a school shall depart on the request of the school principal or other authorized person.
>
> (c) Violation of this section shall be a misdemeanor and punished as such. (Acts 1981, ch. 368, p. 1)

Price argued that, although Frost was the mother of a Church Hill Elementary School pupil, her "lawful and valid business" was over. She could take Sarah off the grounds, or she could allow the child to remain in school and leave the grounds herself, but she would have to do one or the other. Her business with Price was finished, and she was now trespassing. Frost maintained, and two judges later agreed, that the reference to "lawful and valid business" pertained to "other persons," not to parents, who had unrestricted access to the school.

After Ashbrook had read the trespassing law to Frost, he asked her to leave. When she refused, he took her into custody. She exclaimed, "Praise God!" and started to go get Sarah so that he could arrest her as well. Ashbrook restrained her with a hand on her arm and took her to the police station. In the meantime, the county clerk had received a telephone call from Jennie Wilson, asking whether Frost had been arrested yet. When Frost arrived at the police station, she telephoned Wilson, who in turn telephoned Farris and news reporters.

The school officials accused Frost and Wilson of deliberately staging a media event—and not for the first time. Only a week earlier, Salley had been startled when reporters showed up at his office to cover his suspension of the protesters' children. A month before that, Archie McMillan had begun receiving calls from reporters twenty minutes after the Wilsons had removed their grandchildren from Carter's Valley Elementary School. The common thread in all these events was the protesters' willingness to put their children into situations in which the school authorities had two choices: give the protesters what they wanted, or do something to the children that could be interpreted as hostile. Like the Far Right national groups that supported them, the Hawkins County protesters were convinced that school authorities were antagonistic to Christian children, and they did their best to prove their point. Price had the sense—and, perhaps, the compassion—not to take action against Sarah, which made the whole story much less sensational than it would have been if the little girl had been taken into custody.

At a hearing held about three weeks after Frost's arrest, a magistrate dismissed the charge against her on the grounds that the school trespassing laws did not apply to parents. Even though she was taking up hours of the principal's time by repeatedly demanding to defy the school board's order against alternate readers, there was no legal basis for arresting her for trespassing. She later initiated a successful civil suit against the school authorities, although she lost an appeal for substantial financial damages. The whole incident was yet another example of the dynamics that characterized the entire Hawkins County textbook dispute: persistent, authoritarian behavior on the part of the protesters, provoking an equally authoritarian reaction by school authorities, who were then open to the charge that they were violating the parents' rights over their children.

Throughout the controversy, the protesters had been talking about taking legal action against the school district. Around the time of Frost's arrest, CWA agreed to provide legal representation for a lawsuit in federal court. To kick off a fund-raising drive, the LaHayes and Michael Farris visited Hawkins County and held a rally which was attended by about eighty-five people. CWA also began to mail out letters to its members, requesting contributions. Its mailings clearly reflected the relationship between the Hawkins County controversy and CWA's own educational agenda, which promotes suspicion and hostility between schools and parents. "Already we have felt the heavy hand of the NEA (National Education Association)," one letter stated. "The teachers have, of course, rallied in favor of the school district's expulsion of the Christian students" (January 16,

1984). Later testimony refuted both the charge that children had been expelled and the allegation that Hawkins County teachers were antagonistic toward the protesters' children. The letter continued, "One of the students wrote us and said, 'I am a Christian. Is this why I am being kicked out of school?' That is a good question. We need your financial help to be able to bring quality legal work into Tennessee so that never again can it be said that children have been expelled simply because they were Christians." The letter also accused Price of denying Frost's right to take custody of Sarah, although Price had in fact refused nothing but permission to teach Sarah from an alternate reader on school premises.

Shortly after Frost's arrest, an anonymous COBS member wrote a letter alleging that public nudity and drug trafficking were common occurrences in the hallways of Volunteer High School. The nameless writer also complained that the girls' room at the middle school was dirty. No evidence was ever produced to support the charges of criminal activity, although school authorities did concede that the bathroom could use a cleaning. When the letter reached the superintendent of schools, Bill Snodgrass, he fired it off to the high school. There it was shared with faculty, staff, and students. The students, in particular, were outraged. They wrote letters to newspaper editors, spoke at Parent-Teacher Association (PTA) and school board meetings, and formed a new group, Students Against COBS (SAC). SAC T-shirts were sold in the school, and students whose parents belonged to COBS were harassed by other students. The COBS members were annoyed that students had been told about the letter, since, in their view, the whole textbook dispute was none of the students' business. The students' job was to obey their parents, period.

Thanks to the COBS letter, the December PTA meeting was considerably more dramatic than such events usually are. The *Kingsport Times-News* (December 6, 1983) estimated that about eight hundred people were present. Virginia Sue Eaton, one of the protesters who attended the meeting, later testified that a red-faced Superintendent Snodgrass had said that the protesters "could go to Texas or we could go to—I think he said Russia, and then he said, 'or they can go to,' and the crowd cheered, you know, and he said, 'Need I say anymore?'" (Deposition, January 30, 1986, p. 89). According to the *Kingsport Times-News*, Snodgrass also called the protesters "a wrecking crew" set on by "outside agitators with their fat wallets and attorney from Washington, D.C." Eaton concluded, reasonably enough, that "it wasn't your normal PTA meeting" (p. 91).

Immediately after the meeting, G. Reece Gibson, a juvenile court judge, took the podium. He announced the formation of a new organization, Citizens Advocating Right to Education (CARE), and presented a written declaration calling for freedom "from disruption, censorship by a fanatical minority and the imposition of the moral standards which would be imposed by minority groups." The declaration also defended "the integrity of the Hawkins County School System against false accusations, misleading statements and outright liable [sic] and slander." According to Gibson, approximately two hundred people joined CARE that night.

On December 10, the *Knoxville Journal* carried an interview with Judge Gibson that became one of the focal points of the controversy. He announced that if any of the protesters' children were brought into his court, he would disqualify himself from hearing their cases because of his own involvement in the textbook dispute. He would, however, suggest that his replacement try to persuade the school board to lift the suspensions, which were then still in effect. The reason for his recommendation was that if the suspensions *were* lifted and the protesters still did not send their children back to school, they could be taken to court. According to the newspaper interview, the judge said that restraining orders could also be obtained "against parents who try to excuse their children every day from the reading classes only."

The threat of legal constraint on parents was a very sensitive issue in Hawkins County. Frost had already defended her refusal to take Sarah off the school grounds by explaining that she was afraid of losing custody because of trumped-up truancy charges. Other protesters were also afraid of legal action and angry at the idea that the schools had any authority over them with regard to their children. Gibson later said that he had simply told a reporter what the law was when the reporter had asked him. All the same, when a judge became involved in the controversy and talked in public about legal sanctions against parents, the emotional climate became several degrees hotter.

Gibson's authority as a judge put neon lights around anything he said, but he was not by any means the only Hawkins County resident to react publicly to the protesters. On the contrary, the controversy dominated the "Letters to the Editor" section of the local paper. One angry mother wrote:

> I'm tired of you [COBS] coming into the school here and upsetting the classes my children attend. I send them to school for an education, and so far all they can get is confused, and it is your fault. Stop playing with my children's minds.... You live, think and raise your children the way you want and I'll do the same with mine.

So COBS, keep your fanatical beliefs within your own group and stay out of my children's education. (November 25, 1983)

Another Church Hill resident expressed mock horror that the geography textbooks

> had pictures and texts which were teaching these poor, innocent, open-minded students that the world is round. This is obviously not true as anyone who has ever been to Kansas will tell you. It is obvious that if the world is round, then those people who live on the bottom part would fall off. I believe that this teaching of round earth material is simply designed to encourage disrespect by children against their parents and an attempt to cause children to think for themselves instead of believing what we teach them. (December 9, 1983)

The protesters complained that people who disagreed with them did much more than just write to the newspapers. Frost's husband said that someone had written "Vicki Frost is a whore" on the wall of a Sears rest room, and that people had threatened to burn down the Frosts' house, slash their tires, and bomb their church (Deposition of Roger Frost, May 14, 1986, p. 38). Another protester, Janet Whitaker, testified that her son had been physically threatened by other students at Volunteer High School (Deposition, February 2, 1986, pp. 87–91). The protesters' opponents denied all of the allegations.

In the midst of this highly charged atmosphere, thick with accusations and counteraccusations, the actual filing of the lawsuit was almost an anticlimax. *Mozert v. Hawkins County Public Schools* came into existence on December 2, 1983, when Michael Farris filed a complaint in the United States District Court in nearby Greeneville, Tennessee. The case was assigned to Judge Thomas G. Hull and was heard without a jury. It was called *Mozert* rather than *Frost* because, as director of COBS, Bob Mozert's name headed the list of plaintiffs.

In addition to the Frosts, Mozerts, and Bakers, the complaint listed six families as plaintiffs: the Couches, Meades, Eatons, Marshalls, Owenses, and Arnolds. The last three later withdrew. The defendants in the case were the Hawkins County Board of Education, Superintendent Snodgrass, and four school principals, including McMillan, Salley, and Price.

When the lawsuit was first filed, the defendants were represented only by local counsel, but People for the American Way had already begun to take an interest in the case. PAW is a national liberal organization founded by television producer Norman Lear (*All in the Family*). Its offices are in Washington, D.C., not far from CWA headquarters. PAW agreed to pay the expenses of attorneys from the prestigious Washington law firm Wilmer, Cutler and Pickering, which undertook the case pro bono. The lawyer assigned to lead the defense was Timothy Dyk, who later represented news organizations in petitioning for the release of classified documents during the trial of Oliver North in 1989.

Shortly after *Mozert* was filed, PAW opened fire on anti-humanist forces by publishing a booklet entitled *The Witch Hunt Against "Secular Humanism,"* by David Bollier. The Reverend Dr. Charles Bergstrom, a Lutheran minister sitting on the board of PAW, contributed an introduction beginning:

> "Secular humanism" is the bogeyman of religious right wing groups who have taken for themselves such lofty-sounding names as the Moral Majority and the Christian Voice. Reading their religio-political tracts and listening to their sermons on radio and television, one might almost be persuaded that great hordes of "secular humanists" have indeed banded together to wreak havoc on America. But it is difficult to believe that those who scream about "secular humanism" believe their own words. Their attacks on Christians and other citizens who dare disagree with them on a variety of issues are designed to intimidate dissenters and stifle debate, and their dire predictions about the coming invasion of "secular humanists" are carefully calculated to generate millions of dollars in contributions from frightened citizens. (p. 1)

Throughout the lawsuit, PAW and CWA continued to assail one another's positions—and to solicit funds—with this kind of ringing rhetoric.

As soon as CWA and PAW entered the picture with their deep pockets and Washington lawyers, *Mozert* turned into a national event reaching far beyond the original dispute between Hawkins County parents and school authorities. The case became a clash between two well-funded and highly politicized national organizations, each fighting to set a legal precedent that would support at least part of its educational agenda. CWA experts refined and expanded the plaintiffs' objections to the Holt readers until it became painfully obvious that the Hawkins County parents did not even understand some of the concepts their case had come to represent.

The protesters originally tried to get the Holt series out of the public schools altogether. When the school board flatly refused to remove the books, they switched to demanding alternate readers for their own children, and that was the focus of their legal complaint. As they saw the situation, the Hawkins County public schools were forcing their children either to read books that violated their religious beliefs or to give up their right to a free public education. From the school authorities' perspective, selecting textbooks, even alternate readers, on the basis of certain students' religious beliefs would violate the separation of church and state. Besides, providing students with such a limited, parochial education would do them a disservice. As Superintendent Snodgrass explained in one of his calmer moments, "Reality consists of a myriad of conflicting values and differing religious beliefs. A reading program could not go much beyond 'See Dick run.' if the materials used contained no expressions of values whether religious or otherwise. The textbooks adopted by the Hawkins County School System teach and promote reading not values and religion." (Supplemental Affidavit, January 3, 1984, p. 6).

The plaintiffs' complaint listed nine reasons for objecting to the Holt books. Judge Hull promptly dismissed eight of them because the First Amendment does not guarantee freedom from ever hearing ideas that conflict with one's religion. The arguments he dismissed said that the reading series promoted disrespect for parents, the Bible, and Jesus Christ, and that it advocated witchcraft, situation ethics, idol worship, humanistic values, and evolution. The one objection that the judge wanted to hear more about stated, "The books teach that one does not need to believe in God in a specific way but that any type of faith in the supernatural is an acceptable method of salvation. The Bible teaches that Jesus is the Way, the Truth, and the Life and that no man may come unto the Father except through Him" (First Amended Complaint, December 19, 1983, p. 6). Hull ruled that this argument, unlike the eight that he had dismissed, had the potential to justify a First Amendment lawsuit. He wrote, "Only if the plaintiffs can prove that the books at issue are teaching a particular religious faith as true (rather than as a cultural phenomenon), or teaching that the students must be saved through some religious pathway, or that no salvation is required, can it be said the mere exposure to these books is a violation of free exercise rights" (Memorandum and Order, February 24, 1984, p. 5).

The CWA reply to Judge Hull's ruling focused on "More Than Reading," by Thomas J. Murphy, a senior vice president at Holt. Murphy's essay, which appeared in the teachers' editions of the Holt readers, encouraged respect for a wide range of cultures and ideas. The plaintiffs objected to the essay because they saw respect for non-Christian societies as an attack on their absolute faith in Jesus Christ as the only means to salvation.

Murphy's essay also suggested that students should "have a sense of themselves as individuals and as participants in a national and world community." The essay described this goal as "a noble idea and a sign of growth in the idealism that is part of our people" (Bernard Weiss et al., *Riders on the Earth* [New York: Holt, 1983], p. T–795). The plaintiffs mocked the term *noble idea,* which they considered ironic because of their strong opposition to world community and the religious tolerance it would require. "Those who cling to Judeo-Christianity reject the whole concept of world-community, one-world-government, or human interdependency as the concept is variously labeled," they maintained (Memorandum Regarding Stories on Issue of Salvation, p. 2). The memorandum continues:

> By convincing Christian children that "all religions are the same" the claim of Jesus Christ to be the exclusive way of salvation, both for individuals and for the world as a whole, is negated. It must be negated for the noble idea [world community] to take root in the child's mind. The Hindu concept, that 'All religions are merely different roads to God' must be transplanted into Christian children to create good world citizens. This attacks the very essence of the Christian doctrine of salvation. (p. 3)

While attacking globalism and multiculturalism as concepts, the plaintiffs also opposed specific examples of cultural diversity and religious tolerance. One of their targets was a dramatized version of *The Diary of Anne Frank* in the eighth-grade Holt reader, *Great Waves Breaking.* They were especially disturbed by a part of the play in which Anne says to a friend, "Oh, I don't mean you have to be Orthodox . . . or believe in heaven and hell and purgatory and things . . . I just mean some religion . . . it doesn't matter what. Just to believe in something!" (p. 387). From the plaintiffs' viewpoint, it matters very much what religion one practices, and they did not want their teenage children to know that not everyone sees life that way.

Besides presenting the idea that all religions are equally meritorious, the Holt readers included material that the plaintiffs interpreted as meaning that all religions are without merit. In "The Blind Men and the Elephant: A Hindu Tale," a poem by John Godfrey Saxe, six blind men set out to discover what an elephant is like. Each man encounters a different part of the beast: side, tusk, trunk, knee, ear, and tail. Naturally, each blind seeker draws a different conclusion about elephants. The last two stanzas of the poem particularly offended the plaintiffs:

> And so these men of Indostan
> Disputed loud and long,
> Each in his own opinion

Exceeding stiff and strong,
Though each was partly in the right
And all were in the wrong!

MORAL

So oft in theologic wars,
The disputants, I ween,
Rail on in utter ignorance
Of what each other mean,
And prate about an Elephant
Not one of them has seen!
(*Great Waves Breaking*, p. 408)

The plaintiffs charged that the poem's ending demeans religion by suggesting that "all religious leaders are no more than the blind men feeling the elephant" (Memorandum Regarding Stories on Issue of Salvation, March 12, 1984, p. 6).

Throughout their analysis of the Holt series, CWA and the Hawkins County protesters saw no difference between mentioning that an idea exists and promoting that idea. Consistent with their literal reading of the Bible, they interpreted all printed material as an attempt to compel belief. As a result, they were opposed to allowing their children to learn anything about ideas or cultures other than their own, which raised serious questions about the role public schools could legally play in imposing such stringent limits on the children's horizons. PAW and the Hawkins County school authorities took the position that parental rights are, and should be, sacred in a nontotalitarian state. Nevertheless, they argued, the reason all citizens pay for public schools is that the education of future generations is of concern to the whole society. Leaving children ignorant of, and hostile to, any ideas except those of a single religious group is not consistent with the common good. Accordingly, the school authorities tried to fend off the plaintiffs' accusations by contending that promoting tolerance for diversity is a compelling state interest sufficient to justify teaching something opposed by individual parents.

After reading briefs submitted by CWA and PAW attorneys, Judge Hull dismissed the case without a trial on the grounds that the plaintiffs had no basis for a lawsuit. He agreed that the Holt series portrayed religious tolerance and world community favorably, but he did not see how that could conceivably violate anyone's constitutional rights:

> This Court must reassert what it indicated in the previous memorandum, that the First Amendment "does not guarantee that nothing

offensive to any religion will be taught in the schools" *Williams v. Board of Education of the County of Kanawha*. What is guaranteed is that the state schools will be neutral on the subject, neither advocating a particular religious belief nor expressing hostility to any or all religions. (Memorandum and Order, March 15, 1984, p. 5)

In his view, the Holt books not only presented religion in a neutral way, but were also "well calculated to equip today's children to face our increasingly complex and diverse society with sophistication and tolerance" (p. 5). The plaintiffs immediately announced that they would appeal his decision.

Both sides thought that the dismissal would be upheld, but the Sixth Circuit Court of Appeals surprised everyone by ordering Judge Hull to try the case. According to the appeals court, the only cases that should be dismissed without a trial are those that include no major disputed issues. *Mozert,* however, included two such issues: whether forcing the plaintiffs' children to use the Holt readers burdened their religious rights; and, if so, whether any important state interest justified the burden. Since the appeals court had, in Judge Hull's words, "sent this thing screaming back down here again," both sides began preparing for the trial that was scheduled to take place the following year.

CHAPTER THREE

A Clash
of Symbols

*And they mainly want to teach them not to question, not to imagine, but to
be obedient and behave well so that they can hold them forever as children to their
bosom as the second millennium lurches toward its panicky close.*
—JEROME STERN

Before the *Mozert* trial started, the lawyers on each side interviewed the
other side's witnesses to find out what kind of evidence they were going
to give. In their pre-trial statements, called depositions, the Hawkins
County protesters presented more than four hundred objections to the
Holt reading series. Vicki Frost's testimony alone added up to 1117 pages.

The protesters, who described themselves as born-again fundamentalist
Christians, based their entire understanding of reality on their particular
interpretation of the Bible. In their way of looking at life, all decisions
should be based solely on the Word of God; using reason or imagination
to solve problems is a act of rebellion. Everyone should live in traditional
nuclear families structured on stereotyped gender roles. Wives should
obey their husbands, and children their parents, without argument or
question.

Regarding the world outside the family, the United States has, since
its inception, been the greatest nation on earth. Any criticism of its founders, policies, or history offends God and promotes a Communist invasion by discouraging boys from growing up to fight for their country.
Since war is God's way of vindicating the righteous and punishing the
wicked, anti-war material—and, by extension, criticism of hunting or

gun ownership—is unpatriotic, disrespectful to God, and detrimental to the moral fiber of American youth.

Pollution and other environmental concerns are humanist propaganda designed to provide an excuse for government interference in big business and for international cooperation, either of which is capable of destroying this country. Unregulated free enterprise represents God's will and the American way of life. International cooperation might lead to a one-world government, which would be the reign of the Antichrist and bring about the end of the world. Besides, world unity would have to be based on religious tolerance, which is unthinkable.

Christianity—that is, Protestant fundamentalism—is the one true religion and the religion on which the United States was founded. Fundamentalist children will only be confused by stories about people of other faiths, especially if textbooks do not explain that those beliefs are wrong. As for children of other religions, they should not be encouraged in their errors by seeing their beliefs represented in textbooks as if they were equal to the one true faith. The same holds for stories suggesting that some people have no religion.

In order to protect their children from ideas they considered harmful, the *Mozert* plaintiffs attacked every item in the Holt reading series that could conceivably start a discussion about world unity, nontraditional gender roles, family democracy, moral relativity, the brotherhood of man, nonreligious views of death, imagination, reason, neutral descriptions of religion, skeptical references to religion, critical views of the founders or policies of the United States, socialism, social protest, universal communication, magic, imaginary beings, environmentalism, kindness toward animals, vegetarianism, negative views of war or hunting, fear of nuclear war, disarmament, or gun control. Despite their variety, all of these objections share the same roots: dependence on biblical authority as opposed to any form of logic, creativity, self-reliance, or self-definition; and total commitment to one religious and cultural group, to the exclusion of globalism and multiculturalism.

This world view, while not representative of all fundamentalists, is by no means unique to the *Mozert* plaintiffs. It reflects the position of several national organizations, such as Citizens for Excellence in Education and the Eagle Forum, whose lobbying efforts target the same topics as *Mozert* and contribute to book bannings and alterations in textbooks. *Mozert* also combines in a single event all of the subjects discussed piecemeal in other recent textbook lawsuits.

The sheer scope of the protesters' objections to the Holt series shows that what they define as religion includes topics that are ordinarily considered political or personal. In fact, part of the school officials' defense was that it was impossible to come up with *any* ideas that the plaintiffs did not consider religious. The breadth of the religious beliefs of fundamentalist textbook activists creates a difficult situation for school officials all over the country. Public schools have the legal right to present information that does not conform to a particular religion as long as they do not teach it as religious truth, but, all the same, it is no small matter to demand that children either give up a free public education or learn material that offends their parents' faith. Parents have, and should have, a great deal to say about the upbringing of their children, especially with regard to religious training. Occasionally, however, someone in a school system has to decide whether a particular parental demand is so sweeping, and so far from anything that could possibly be considered secular thought, that public schools cannot go along with it. And that, of course, is when the fireworks begin.

The Hawkins County parents' request for alternate instruction might seem like a reasonable compromise, since it would accommodate their beliefs without affecting anyone else's children. The catch is that what they wanted was a little private school within the public school, where taxpayers' dollars would have been used to prevent the protesters' children from learning that other people think differently from their parents. Even in the context of individualized instruction, can a public school teach children that everyone who is different from them is inferior? Can it order little girls to grow up to be June Cleaver? Can it say that the United States should do nothing about acid rain falling in Canada because pollution does not exist and international cooperation is wrong?

General descriptions of a world view are all well and good, but the real impact of textbook activists comes from specific objections to specific textbook content. This chapter uses two approaches to describe what the Hawkins County protesters did—and did not—want to see in their children's readers. First, it shows how the different parts of their world view interact in their responses to three upper-grade stories, each of which generated twenty to twenty-five separate objections. Second, it gives short examples from all grade levels to show the scope of the plaintiffs' objections and the extent of the material affected by them.

The three stories the plaintiffs criticized most broadly were "The Forgotten Door," by Alexander Key (Grade 6), "Raymond's Run," by Toni Cade Bambara (Grade 7), and "To Build a Fire," by Jack London (Grade 8). In "The Forgotten Door" an alien boy named Little Jon falls through an opening between his world and Earth. He finds himself in the Smoky Mountains, on the border between North Carolina and Tennessee. The protesters identified with the rural inhabitants and were dismayed to find them compared unfavorably with Little Jon, who, they observed pointedly, was not even a Christian.

The first person Little Jon encounters is Gilby Pitts, a poacher whose only response to anything unfamiliar is knee-jerk hostility. Little Jon is upset when Pitts shoots at a doe, since the boy had just been chatting with her by telepathy. This opening scene, by itself, generated five separate objections. First, Pitts's suspicion of anything foreign seemed perfectly appropriate to the protesters, and they did not see why he should be ridiculed for it. Second, they accused the story of subtly promoting belief in evolution by showing communication with animals. Third, Little Jon's sympathy for the doe offended them because the Bible says that God created animals for humans to exploit, so nothing anyone does to them could possibly be wrong. Besides, since God demanded animal sacrifices in the Old Testament, teaching sympathy for animals might turn children against God. Fourth, objections to hunting violate the constitutional right to bear arms. They also promote pacifism, sapping the will of American youth to fight off Communists. Fifth, telepathy is a form of magic and therefore forbidden by the Bible. It is also dangerous because it breaks down language barriers and promotes tolerance for diversity.

Little Jon runs from Pitts and finds himself on a highway. When he senses friendliness in the occupants of an approaching truck, he signals to them, and they stop to help him. His rescuers, the Bean family, take him home and treat him kindly. He can read their thoughts but cannot speak to them until he learns English, which takes about two days. His ability to read minds offended the protesters because, Frost explained, "God alone can read the thoughts and the intents of the heart, and I believe that these mental exercises, you know, mental telepathy is an effort by man to lift himself to a higher level in an attempt to become his own god" (Deposition, April 3, 1986, p. 395).

Pitts circulates rumors about a "wild boy" who is "unnatural" and threatening, and in order to protect Little Jon the Beans invent a fake identity for him. The teachers' manual suggests asking students whether it is possible to be honest all the time. The protesters, who thought that Pitts's reaction to the telepathic alien was entirely proper, were offended to find him shown as the enemy. And why, they wondered, would the teacher ask whether it is possible to be honest all the time? The Bible says that lying is a sin, so it is not only possible but necessary never to lie. By suggesting that the details of a specific event have anything to do with right and wrong, the teachers' manual was promoting situation ethics, a tenet of the religion of secular humanism. In the protesters' view, the purpose of education is not to ask what children think about moral issues, but to teach right and wrong—that is, rules that apply in every circumstance.

Little Jon has never heard of war, and the Beans conclude that his society must be more advanced than our own. The story also includes a negative reference to the Korean War. The protesters responded with an impassioned defense of war in general and the Korean War in particular. Virginia Sue Eaton provided a scriptural basis for this point of view:

> And we do have the right to go to war as long as we're not the aggressors, but defensive wars, and the Bible even says that God will be on our side. . . . In this book, there's one place that says that money is what starts wars, and in a place called Korea nobody decided the right or the wrong of that war, and that's not true. It's as though that war is only done for money reasons or political reasons or whatever. . . . We do know that it was right because we were fighting a good cause in Korea. It's just that we decided to pull out. It was decided that it was right. That's presented in the wrong atmosphere. (Deposition, January 30, 1986, pp. 142–44)

In a scene the plaintiffs found particularly offensive, the Beans and their neighbors attend church with the poacher Pitts and another family made up of petty thieves and liars. The protesters saw the story as an attack on Christianity because the churchgoers include sinful people and because the Christian community of the Smoky Mountains compares unfavorably with the non-Christian world of Little Jon. In the alien culture, there are no locks on anything because people do not steal or commit violence. Little Jon has to be taught what lying means and is horrified to discover that some people try to get rich by cheating their neighbors. The contrast between worlds clearly suggests that Christianity and the free-enterprise system do not guarantee an ideal society, and the plaintiffs objected to exposing children to such a blasphemous and un-patriotic possibility. They did not address the question of whether the story's description of American life is true; they simply argued that it is not *right*.

Little Jon's mind-reading ability becomes public knowledge when the Beans are called into court to explain who he is. Frantic with fear of the unfamiliar, especially anything having to do with extrasensory perception, the neighbors vandalize the Beans' house and steal their cow. The plaintiffs protested that this portrayal of Christians committing unjustified and unnecessary violence was entirely inappropriate. To make matters worse, the neighbors are determined to kidnap Little Jon because his talent has commercial value, suggesting that capitalism generates greed.

After a long search, Little Jon finds the place where he fell into the Smoky Mountains. Shortly afterward, his family opens the passage from their side, and he is free to return home. He invites the Beans to cross over with him to escape from their neighbors, and they accept. Their decision disturbed the protesters, who disapproved of American Protestants defecting to an alien culture. Frost explained: "In this story the Beans are people who seem to have some type of religion, and they go to church, and in this setting it seems to be what I have told you [Protestant], and in the end they forsake their religion and all of this world's ideals to go live in another world where peace and harmony and the values of Little Jon are" (Deposition, April 3, 1986, p. 389).

The protesters were entirely correct in saying that "The Forgotten Door" criticizes people like themselves; it does. The main point of their lawsuit was that their children should be taught to fear and reject anything that differs from their own culture. The story not only attacks that idea head-on but also puts it into the mouths of people who share the protesters' heritage, speech, and lifestyle. The story avoids stereotyping church-going Protestant farmers because the broad-minded and compassionate Beans fall into that category too, but the protesters saw the Beans' behavior as a problem, not a redeeming factor. The Beans' attitude struck them as a betrayal of their culture, and they saw the Beans, not their neighbors, as the villains of the piece.

The protesters' reluctance to have their children read a story that portrays people like themselves in a negative light is perfectly understandable. If the question were asked in the abstract, "Should public schools present a story ridiculing a particular culture?" most people would probably say, "Of course not." On the other hand, the quality that the story targets is intolerance for diversity. Public schools are supposed to teach that intolerance is wrong, but how effectively can they do so without showing intolerant people behaving badly? Given the favorable portrayal of the Beans, the story does not say that rural Christian churchgoers are bad, but that people who automatically reject the unfamiliar are unjustified in doing so and create unnecessary difficulties for others.

If public schools have an obligation to teach acceptance of different cultures, the Hawkins County protesters asked, why were their own beliefs not included in this acceptance? The answer of education officials was that the protesters' endorsement of the kind of intolerance exemplified by the Beans' neighbors left the public schools only two choices: oppose the protesters' rejection of all ideas but their own, or tolerate intolerance.

The *Mozert* plaintiffs' opposition to stories about unfamiliar worlds extended to the urban setting of Toni Cade Bambara's "Raymond's Run." Their specific complaints about "Raymond's Run" were different from their objections to "The Forgotten Door," but the underlying problem was the same. They opposed whatever was foreign to them, especially if it stated or implied values that differed from their own. Bambara's depiction of the harsh life of a Harlem child fell into that category almost as much as Key's description of an alien planet did.

Stories by and about minorities are often set in the inner city and involve nontraditional family structures. The protesters considered these stories unwholesome and irrelevant. They did not live in inner cities themselves, and they saw no reason for their children to read about them. Better, they argued, to present upbeat stories that take for granted the rightness of mainstream American historical and social institutions. As for lifestyles, God has commanded everyone to live in traditional nuclear families, and that is all children need to know. It can only confuse them to learn that some of their contemporaries live in single-parent homes, blended families, or foster care. Children who do not live in traditional families should learn, by the omission of people like themselves from textbooks, that their lifestyles are substandard.

The protesters opposed stories that describe racism and social injustice because they were convinced that America offers boundless opportunity to everyone. If people are poor, homeless, or unemployed, it is because they are lazy. Criticizing American economic or social practices, past or present, promotes Communism and social revolution.

Squeaky Parker, the adolescent narrator of "Raymond's Run," tries hard to succeed at schoolwork and athletics. She also takes care of her mentally retarded brother, Raymond. When the city's May Day activities are announced, Squeaky decides to participate in the races, but she has no patience with the Maypole dancing. Her mother wants to buy her a frilly white dress and "new white baby-doll shoes," but Squeaky thinks that white dresses and white shoes are impractical, uneconomical, and affected: "You'd think she'd be glad her daughter ain't out there prancing around a Maypole, getting the new clothes all dirty and sweaty and trying to act like a fairy or a flower or whatever you're supposed to be when you should be trying to be yourself, whatever that is, which is, as far as I am concerned, a poor black girl who really can't afford to buy shoes and a new dress you only wear once a lifetime 'cause it won't fit next year" (Bernard Weiss et al., eds., *To See Ourselves* [New York: Holt, 1983], pp. 49–50).

Squeaky remembers with disgust that she once played a strawberry in a nursery school pageant "just so my mother and father could come dressed up and clap. You'd think they'd know better than to encourage that kind of nonsense. I am not a strawberry. I do not dance on my toes. I run. That is what I am all about" (p. 50). The plaintiffs were disturbed by her rejection of her parents' values, since one of the things they feared most was having their children grow up to be different from them. Besides, they asserted, the sassy, irreverent quality of Squeaky's narration is in itself evidence of rebelliousness and bad character.

Believing in traditional sex roles, the protesters considered Squeaky a bad example for children because of her tomboyish interest in competitive sports, her resistance to frilly clothing and traditional female pastimes, and her aggressiveness in defending herself and her brother. Judging from her behavior, she does not seem to have heard of the scriptural distinction between men and women.

Squeaky wins her race, but her real joy comes when she notices that her retarded brother has kept up with her all the way to the finish line. She realizes that she may be able to coach Raymond, who until now has been able to do very little, into becoming a winning runner in his own right. She and her runner-up smile at each other in mutual respect, and she reflects that real smiles are rare because "most everybody's too busy being runners, or flowers, or ballplayers, or strawberries instead of being something honest and worthy of respect . . . you know . . . like being people" (p. 54). Nevertheless, in his pre-trial deposition Bob Mozert dismissed the entire story as being "filled full of negativism, rebellion, bitterness, hatred" (January 27, 1986, p. 309).

Obviously, the protesters did not see eye to eye with Bambara on what constitutes goodness in a young girl. Squeaky's strength was, to them, not a virtue but a vice. Children, especially girls, should not have to fight; they should live in settled environments in which they can look to adults for protection. Stories about other kinds of neighborhoods do not belong in schoolbooks. The idea of an adolescent struggling to find her own identity and to separate from her parents was similarly unacceptable to them. In their world, adolescents are supposed to obey without question and echo their parents' views and lifestyle. Girls, in particular, should not be self-defining or rebellious because those qualities interfere with their development into obedient wives.

The protesters' failure to see any good in "Raymond's Run" reflects not only their opposition to cultural diversity but also their conviction that schools should teach students to conform to their parents' rules and values. School officials face a dilemma when parents want their children to complete twelve years of public education without being encouraged to think for themselves or solve their own problems. All taxpayers share the cost of public schools because the education of the next generation is considered the responsibility of all, and everyone has to live with the results. From that perspective, it is not by any means obvious that individual parents have the right to demand that public schools provide separate instruction to make sure that their children do not learn how to think.

Imagination, like independent thinking and tolerance for diversity, has no place in the Hawkins County protesters' world view. They alleged that the *process* of imagination, regardless of its content, distracts people from the Word of God. Once the mind is open to imagination, all kinds of alien thoughts may enter, and the soul may be lost. Moreover, using imagination to solve problems substitutes a human faculty for the absolute reliance on God that is necessary for salvation.

Jack London's "To Build a Fire" runs directly contrary to this. Its main character, a nameless man struggling along a Yukon trail on an icy winter morning, is described as having one fatal flaw: a lack of imagination. Although he knows that the temperature is more than fifty degrees below zero, this knowledge "did not lead him to meditate upon his frailty as a creature of temperature, and upon man's frailty in general, able only to live within certain narrow limits of heat and cold; and from there on it did not lead him to the conjectural field of immortality and man's place in the universe" (Weiss et al., *Great Waves Breaking*, p. 73).

The teachers' manual explains that the man's lack of imagination threatens his life because "[a] person with imagination can conceive of future dangers and comprehend human frailty" (quoted in Deposition of Vicki Frost, April 15, 1986, p. 162). This assertion of the power of imagination offended the plaintiffs, who maintained that physical survival, like spiritual salvation, depends entirely on God. "Man's survival," said Frost, "does not depend upon man's ability to create in his imagination solutions to problems. Man's survival is determined by God" (Deposition, April 15, 1986, p. 163).

By saying that the Yukon traveler could have saved his life if he had only recognized his danger soon enough, the story implies that humans have the potential to solve their own problems. This idea, above all others, defines what some fundamentalists mean by the religion of secular humanism. To them, hope of salvation comes only through Christ, not through human efforts. Developing the proper attitude of dependence on God requires relinquishing all sense of personal control over any aspect of life, including physical well-being.

As the man in "To Build a Fire" hikes along the snow-covered trail, he accidentally gets his feet and legs wet. They freeze instantly, and he needs a fire to thaw them out. Shortly after he gets the fire started, a load of snow falls from an overhanging spruce tree and puts it out. Since he should have had better sense than to build the fire under a snow-laden tree, the narrative describes the incident as "his own fault, or, rather, his mistake" (p. 81).

The plaintiffs protested once again that "To Build a Fire" teaches the humanistic tenet that survival depends on what people themselves do rather than on God's will. If the man is accountable for the bad consequences of building his fire in the wrong place, then he would also have been responsible for the good results if he had built it in the right place— in other words, if he could imperil himself, he could save himself. As a religious belief, the conviction that God is solely responsible for the physical survival of individuals, the human race, and the planet is protected by the First Amendment. As a matter of educational policy, however, it runs counter to one of public education's chief missions: to prepare citizens to accept responsibility and figure out how to solve problems. It is difficult to see how public schools could, even in individualized instruction, promote the idea that people must not take responsibility for their own welfare or use reason and imagination to solve problems.

The man in London's story struggles to find some means of warming himself but eventually realizes that his situation is hopeless. After a brief period of panic, he resigns himself to the inevitability of dying: "Well, he was bound to freeze, anyway, and he might as well take it decently. With this new-found peace of mind came the first glimmerings of drowsiness. A good idea, he thought, to sleep off to death. It was like taking an anesthetic. Freezing was not so bad as people thought. There were lots worse ways to die" (p. 87).

The plaintiffs objected to the story's description of approaching oblivion on the grounds that the only acceptable way to view death is in terms of heaven and hell. They also argued that the absence of any reference to eternal life promotes belief in evolution by describing the death of a man in terms that could be used to describe that of an animal.

The death scene itself consists of one sentence: "Then the man drowsed off into what seemed to him the most comfortable and satisfying sleep he had ever known" (p. 88). The protesters maintained that this description advances the religion of secular humanism by implying that there is no afterlife. Frost summarized the difference between the fundamentalist and humanist views of death:

> And of course, when the Christian dies, the born again Christian, he or she goes to be with the Lord. . . . For those who believe, their security is secured by Jesus Christ in heaven, but for the non-believer, those who have rejected the Lord Jesus Christ, that they will go to hell. . . . [T]he humanist believes that there is no God, no hereafter, no hope of the eternal, that maybe it's like in this story, you drift off into a sleep, good night, goodbye forever, you're gone (Deposition, April 15, 1986, pp. 166–67).

The plaintiffs also expressed concern that the peacefulness of the man's death could encourage suicide.

If textbooks omitted secular descriptions of death like the one in "To Build a Fire," one of two things would happen. Either children would be deprived of literature that mentions death, which would exclude virtually all of the classics, or they would read only stories in which death is discussed in terms of an afterlife. Some fundamentalists see no problem with either solution. Several Hawkins County parents told school authorities that they wanted their children to learn to read functionally, and that was all. In Florida, a school superintendent who described himself as a conservative Christian banned sixty-four books, including *Hamlet* and *King Lear,* with a single memorandum. The strict authoritarianism of their beliefs makes these fundamentalists radically anti-intellectual because reason and imagination threaten what they mean by faith. To them, the idea that certain literature is of value in itself is nothing more nor less than a temptation to place human accomplishments above the will of God. Similarly, people who believe that the only two ways to view the world are the religions of fundamentalism and secular humanism find it perfectly reasonable to demand that Christian beliefs about death be taught in public schools. After all, they argue, public schools are now teaching the religion of secular humanism, and there is no possibility of omitting religion altogether because every idea represents either divine or human faith. Given that view of reality, it makes no sense to choose creatures over the Creator.

The objections that the Hawkins County protesters raised to "The Forgotten Door," "Raymond's Run," and "To Build a Fire" appeared over and over in their testimony about the Holt series. One challenge involving non-Christian views of death was aimed at a short story entitled

"Benjamin Franklin Flies His Kite" (Grade 7), which, they said, teaches that Franklin was a Hindu. The confusion arose because of the imagery in Franklin's epitaph, which is quoted in the story: "The Body of B. Franklin, Printer, Like the cover of an Old Book, Its contents torn out and stript of its lettering and gilding, lies here, food for worms. But the Work shall not be lost: For it will (*as he believed*) appear once more, In a new and more Elegant Edition, Revised and Corrected by the Author" (Weiss et al., *To See Ourselves*, p. 534; this version is slightly different from the original).

A reporter in the story, commenting on the epitaph, asks whether Franklin believed in reincarnation. The protesters did not distinguish between what a fictional character says and what the story is "officially" promoting, nor did they see any difference between asking *whether* something is true and teaching that it *is* true. They therefore concluded that children were being told that reincarnation is an acceptable view of death and that Franklin believed in it. As Janet Whitaker explained, "They are talking about, you know, Mr. Franklin, you know, believes in reincarnation, you know, they ask that question, and the Bible plainly states that, you know, we are not going to come back as anything when we die, you know, that when the time comes that our bodies will be resurrected and joined with the soul, but when you are put, you know, when your body is put in the ground that you are not going to be reincarnated as something else" (Deposition, February 2, 1986, p. 144). The protesters went on to claim that "Benjamin Franklin Flies His Kite" was designed to lessen the children's pride in their country by convincing them that one of its founders was a Hindu. Besides missing the point of the story completely, this interpretation assumes that children will inevitably lose respect for Franklin if they become convinced that he was not a Christian.

One of the best-known stories challenged in *Mozert* was *The Wizard of Oz* (Grade 6), which, like "To Build a Fire" and "Raymond's Run," promotes self-reliance and personal responsibility. At the beginning of the story, the Lion wants courage, the Tin Man wants a heart, and the Scarecrow wants brains. Then, as the story goes on, the Lion acts bravely, the Tin Man shows compassion, and the Scarecrow behaves intelligently. None of these creatures prays to God, so, presumably, either the desired qualities were within them all the time or they developed the abilities themselves. The protesters testified that *The Wizard of Oz* offended them by advocating the religion of secular humanism in opposition to their own belief that goodness in this world and salvation in the next come only through Christ, not through human effort.

According to the protesters, *The Wizard of Oz* not only models sinful self-reliance, but also promotes Satanism. The Bible says that all witchcraft is the work of the devil, but the good witch Glenda helps Dorothy, which means that the story encourages children to worship the devil. The same is true of "Cinderella" because of the fairy godmother. Frost testified that when a neighbor gave her children a recording of "Cinderella," she took it away from them. She also rejected Santa Claus and the Easter Bunny as sinful fantasies that lure children from the worship of God.

Besides violating the scriptural prohibition against witchcraft, magic creatures stimulate imagination. The protesters explicitly stated, in opposing "To Build a Fire," that imagination should not be used to solve problems. They also objected to it because imagining how someone else feels might lead children to change their own beliefs, feel dissatisfied with themselves, or tolerate diversity and mediocrity. As Frost testified, imagining how another person might feel is also dangerous because if children became too sensitive to the feelings of others, they might lie to avoid causing pain. She gave an example involving a woman who made her own clothes but was not very good at it. A child who imagined the dressmaker's feelings might avoid "telling her how ugly, you know, her clothes were.... There wouldn't be an occasion where you would distort the truth or tell a lie simply because of another person's feelings" (Deposition, April 15, 1986, pp. 70–71).

Another use of imagination that troubled the protesters was fantasy. They rejected all fairy tales and folk tales on the grounds that anything involving magic castles, enchanted forests, dragons, spells, unicorns, wizards, trolls, and the like promotes witchcraft and encourages children to create worlds inside their own minds instead of concentrating on the Word of God. Apart from the specific content of any particular fantasy, thinking imaginatively is wrong in itself because it tempts people to substitute their own ideas for God's. As Frost testified, "The imagination or the thoughts of a child, and the thoughts are to be captive to the obedience of Christ. Their thoughts are not to go outside the realm of scriptural authority. There are several scriptures that deal with man walking after the imagination of his own heart, and a man's imagination can lead him away from God" (Deposition, April 3, 1986, p. 315). She concluded that schools should confine themselves to "the domain of knowledge and facts educationwise" (Deposition, April 15, 1986,

p. 69) and not incorporate imagination or feelings into the reading curriculum.

The main reason for the protesters' opposition to imagination, independent thinking, and problem solving was that they expect children to obey unquestioningly. As they see the world, no good can come from developing one's own identity or learning to think for oneself because God makes all decisions and virtue consists of obedience. Children, in particular, should be trained to consider only one question in making any choice: Does the act I am considering conform to the Word of God and/ or the commands of my parents?

Frost's comments on an excerpt from the second-grade teachers' manual summarizes her view of child-rearing. As she testified,

> [The manual states,] "Seven year olds are beginning to develop an ethical sense. Seven is a responsive age, and it is easy to impose on the child's eagerness to please. It is up to adults to steer the middle course that gives the seven year old the support, encouragement, guidance he or she needs, while at the same time encouraging the child to become independent and self-reliant." And the philosophy on this page is a religious violation of how that I teach my child from a biblical standpoint. My child is to—my children are to listen to the ways of their mother and their father as unto the Lord, and they are to receive my instruction and my guidance, not to rebel and want to go their own way (Deposition, March 19, 1986, pp. 133–34).

Shel Silverstein's humorous poem "Sarah Cynthia Sylvia Stout Would Not Take the Garbage Out" (Grade 4) was one of many Holt selections cited for promoting disobedience. Sarah Cynthia ignores her parents' orders to dispose of the trash until it spreads all over town. The plaintiffs were not amused. They interpreted the poem as a serious attempt to undermine parental authority by showing a disobedient child, and they objected to a suggested discussion question involving the students' own feelings about household chores. Children have no right to form opinions about their parents' orders, so questions about how they feel or what they like are invitations to sin. Such questions could also, in Frost's words, "create an alienation between parent and child" (Deposition, April 3, 1986, p. 276) by fostering rebellion as children verbalize their own views and, worse, as they find out from listening to other children that some households are run differently from their own.

As part of their crusade against what they considered permissive child-rearing practices, the *Mozert* plaintiffs also wanted to eliminate stories in which naughty children get away with misbehaving. Such stories, they claimed, weaken the association between wrongdoing and punishment. One of the selections criticized for this reason was "Goldilocks and the Three Bears," in which Goldilocks gets away scot-free after committing illegal entry, petty larceny of porridge, and vandalism of Baby Bear's stool.

Since the protesters kept saying that reading the Holt series might affect their children's behavior, the defense lawyers naturally asked them whether their children had in fact become rebellious. Two of them said yes. Frost testified that her daughter Sarah had begun to "demand her way" after reading some of the second-grade stories and hearing class discussions. Pressed for a specific example of misbehavior, she said that Sarah, who until then had been "the meekest of my children" (Deposition, April 3, 1986, p. 251), had complained because she did not like what her mother had prepared for dinner.

Alice Mozert told about a similar incident involving her second-grade daughter, Sundee. The child had been selling candy bars as part of a fund-raising drive, and she ate one of them without asking permission. When her parents scolded her, she said that she had bought the candy with her own money. The Mozerts blamed the Holt readers for the little girl's self-will and independence.

For all their authoritarianism, the Hawkins County protesters were not monsters; they were parents who wanted what they believed was best for their children. They themselves had been brought up in the way they wanted to rear their children, and they genuinely believed that their religion is the one true faith and the only hope of eternal salvation. That is why they were so convinced of their obligation to micro-manage what their children did, what they knew, and when and how they thought. That is also why the knowledge that other influences were operating on their children infuriated them. All the same, as the school officials argued, parents of public school students cannot be authoritarian to the point of closing the children's minds to any fact or idea with which they disagree. This aspect of the Hawkins County dispute was not really about whether parents have rights over their children; both sides agreed that they do. The problem was that the protesters' definition of parental authority was so broad that school officials could not honor it without turning the children's instruction into a series of religion lessons designed to prevent them from developing judgment and personal responsibility.

The type of fundamentalism practiced by the *Mozert* plaintiffs is a Bible-based absolutism governing every aspect of life—so much so that simple knowledge of any other way of doing things is considered sinful in itself. Just as the Hawkins County protesters believed that there is only one right answer to every moral dilemma and one right way to rear children, they were convinced that there is only one right way to live: in a traditional nuclear family with a father who is the head of the house and goes out to work, a submissive wife who is a full-time homemaker and mother, and obedient children. The worst threat to this way of life, as they see it, is "sex role reversal." When women seek jobs outside the home, leadership roles, or public recognition, they offend God and jeopardize the entire fabric of American family life.

The plaintiffs' opposition to nontraditional roles for women was so strong that they condemned a short poem, "I'll Tell Emily" (Grade 2), for describing a little girl who likes worms, mice, and snakes. A picture of a girl petting a worm appears just before a picture of a boy holding a frog, and the protesters saw the juxtaposition of the two pictures as an attempt to blur the distinction between masculine and feminine roles. They labeled the picture of the girl "anti-family" because encouraging girls to believe that they can enjoy stereotypically male activities threatens the traditional family structure. Phyllis Schlafly supported the protesters' opposition to "I'll Tell Emily" by editorializing in an Eagle Forum newsletter against "pictures of girls playing with snakes" (*Phyllis Schlafly Report,* March 1986, p. 3) and other enticements for girls to behave like boys, which ultimately leads to women working outside the home.

Once women are married, it is their sacred duty to obey their husbands in all things. As Frost explained, "In Genesis, when man failed, he [God] identified Adam would have rule over Eve. After Eve submitted to Adam and there are set roles in Proverbs, Ephesians, Titus, there are set roles for men and women. She's to be a keeper, you know, to love—take care of the children, love the children and her husband and the man was to— in Genesis to work by the— to be the protector of the family and be the strong man of the house" (Trial Transcript).

Two of the plaintiffs, Sandra and John Couch, provided a personal example of the appropriate relationship between husband and wife. When a defense lawyer asked John whether he had known that Sandra was active in the textbook controversy, he replied that he had given his permission for her to participate for the sake of the children. She agreed with his account of their conversation, affirming that men "are to have the authority to make the final decisions, which does not mean—which does not degrade or lower the place of women" (Deposition, January 30–31, 1986, p. 229).

The conviction that God wills females to obey males motivated the protesters to oppose stories like "Raymond's Run" that show girls or women with minds of their own. They were particularly offended by "The Revolt of 'Mother'" (Grade 7), in which a nineteenth-century New England farm wife takes the initiative of moving her family into a sound new barn after her husband has refused even to discuss the dilapidated state of their old house. The protesters observed that the woman is a Bible-reading Christian, which makes her even more guilty for doing something about the condition of the house after her husband has indicated that he does not wish to discuss it. She should, they asserted, have known better.

The plaintiffs' concern about sex role reversal was not limited to girls. In a seventh-grade Holt story entitled "The Wall," a girl is an athlete and her brother is a musician. The plaintiffs contended that reading stories like "The Wall" violated their religion not only by encouraging girls to reject traditional sex roles but also by providing inappropriate models for boys. Softened by these examples of sex role reversal, their sons might not grow up to be the strong heads of households that God intended them to be. The protesters also believed that showing boys and girls sharing common interests would destroy the necessary barriers between the sexes. To Frost, "My Teacher the Hawk" (Grade 7) is objectionable because a boy comes to view a girl "as a human being, not just as a girl" (Deposition, April 15, 1986, p. 125).

The protesters' attitudes toward women, minorities, and non-Christians presented a problem for the Hawkins County schools. Even if parents teach their children at home that certain groups—whites, Christians, men—are naturally superior and have the right to impose their decisions on others, public schools cannot endorse any such idea. The teachers in Hawkins County were prepared to allow the protesters' children to answer questions in accordance with their religion, so that a child who said that the wife in "The Revolt of 'Mother'" should have submitted to her husband would not have been marked wrong. The difficulty arose because the protesters did not want their children to hear other children's ideas or to know that anyone considers non-Western ideas important or egalitarian marriages acceptable.

One solution the *Mozert* plaintiffs proposed was to eliminate "controversial" topics from public school instruction: that is, to exclude areas in which their home training was likely to conflict with ideas contained in their children's textbooks or with opinions expressed by other children. Following that suggestion with regard to minorities, non-Christians, and women would mean that children would learn only about white Christian men and their wives. Children who are non-Christian or nonwhite, and children who do not live with or intend to become full-time homemakers, would get exactly the idea the protesters think they should get: that they are departures from the norm and not very important anyway.

By the time the Hawkins County protesters filed their lawsuit, they had given up the idea of getting the Holt readers out of the schools altogether and were asking only for alternate textbooks for their own children. Even in individualized instruction, however, today's public schools could not possibly endorse ignorance or intolerance of any group. An important part of the mission of public education is to provide children of all backgrounds with representation in textbooks and with non-judgmental information about different kinds of people. Parents may choose to live a particular lifestyle themselves and may recommend it to their children, but public schools cannot cooperate in teaching children that anyone who thinks or lives differently from their parents is wrong.

The *Mozert* plaintiffs' deep commitment to Bible-based absolutes and their resulting intolerance for diversity has global as well as social implications. Recognizing that world unity cannot be achieved without breaking down cultural and religious barriers, and believing that there is no goodness or salvation except through Jesus Christ, they rejected the notion of interacting with people they consider heathens. They also feared that their children would learn the "error of equivalence," which the *Phyllis Schlafly Report* (March 1986) defines as "the falsehood that other nations, governments, legal systems, cultures, and political and economic systems are essentially equivalent to ours and entitled to equal respect. This hypothesis is false, both historically and morally" (p. 3).

To the protesters, the notion of a common humanity uniting the people of the world is evil in itself and can only produce more evil. They even objected to the title of *Riders on the Earth*, the Holt sixth-grade reader that had started the controversy. The title comes from "Fitting Parts into a Whole," by Archibald MacLeish: "To see the earth as it truly is, small, blue, and beautiful in that eternal silence where it floats, is to see ourselves as riders on the earth together, brothers on that bright loveliness in the eternal cold—brothers who know they are truly brothers" (p. 520). As Frost explained, "All men are not brothers. In the Christian belief, brothers are those who have received Jesus Christ as their Savior, who have been born again, are of the family of God. That's what makes us brothers. We are not brothers of every religion" (Deposition, April 15, 1986, p. 58).

The most drastic consequence of world unity would, the protesters predicted, be nothing less than Armageddon. If nations begin working together and respecting religious and cultural differences, then a single global government might be formed. According to the plaintiffs' interpretation of the Bible, a one-world government not ruled by Christ represents the reign of the Antichrist, which will bring about the end of the world. As Mozert testified,

> The system of the Antichrist will give rise to the one world government and there will be—that will be an ungodly government. It will be a government that opposes God....It relates to me that taking this also, the Scriptures given in the book of Revelation that anyone who receives the mark, the number or name of the Beast, which is the Antichrist, the one world government, shall not have eternal salvation, but the same who endures to the end shall be saved. (Trial Transcript)

Apart from anticipating the end of the world, the Hawkins County protesters gave two other reasons for objecting to stories involving non-Christian cultures. First, describing a variety of religions in a nonjudgmental way is disrespectful to the one true faith—their own—which cannot be regarded as just one religion among many. Second, their children should know as little as possible about other religions because such knowledge could only confuse them and lead them into temptation.

Among non-Christian religions, the protesters included any faith that is not based exclusively on a literal interpretation of the Bible, even if members of that religion think that they are Christians. Catholics, for example, believe that the body of the Virgin Mary, after her death, was taken into heaven along with her soul. That idea comes, not from the Bible, but from the teaching authority of the Catholic Church itself. As far as the *Mozert* plaintiffs are concerned, belief in such doctrines means that Catholics are not Christians, no matter what the pope says.

Combining their objection to other religions with their rejection of minority cultures, the protesters did not want their children to read stories by or about Hispanics. Even if a particular story does not mention religion as such, they argued, everybody knows that most Hispanics are Catholics. To convey his clients' attitude toward one Hispanic story, "The Hunchback Madonna," a CWA lawyer kept calling it "The Taco Madonna" until the PAW lawyers prevailed on him to stop.

Besides opposing stories about Catholics, the plaintiffs rejected selections involving Asians or Native Americans on the grounds that they are pantheists. The protesters also attacked classical mythology because it talks about false gods and because heroes like Ulysses and Hercules promote the humanistic belief that people can save themselves. More generally, they rejected all myths, legends, and folk tales, regardless of their source, for fear that children might start wondering whether the stories in the Bible are any more literally true than the tales of other cultures.

At the Tower of Babel, the protesters asserted, God made different people speak different languages to protect American Christians from the vile ideas of foreign cultures. Humanistic attempts to circumvent God's will by improving international communication or, worse, by bringing about universal communication can only lead to disaster. This topic was one of the first to arise in the Hawkins County controversy, since Frost's immediate reaction to the use of telepathy in "A Visit to Mars" included fear of what would happen if everyone were able to understand everyone else. For the same reason, the protesters opposed attempts to develop a single worldwide language. Frost stated,

> But it's the philosophy behind one world language. If all the people in the world speak the same language, my child is still a part of the world, but it's the philosophy of one world language which brings all the people together. And to the Christian, he cannot be enjoined with other peoples in the world in the same way. To the Christian, he is a separate people unto God. God scatter [sic] the peoples. We are not to be in fellowship with nonbelievers in a sense that we have much common ground. Heathen nations and nations which honor God are not to come together in a one world government. Nations which reject God, according to God Himself, will be turned into hell. He will separate the sheep nations from the goat nations, those who honor him or those who do not. (Deposition, April 3, 1986, pp. 378–79)

One Holt selection advocating a universal second language was Margaret Mead's "Unispeak" (Grade 8). A composition topic at the end of the essay asks students, "Play devil's advocate and write a reasoned argument *against* the universal second language" (Weiss et al., *Great Waves Breaking,* p. 459). The plaintiffs, who interpreted the term *devil's advocate* literally, were enraged by the suggestion that people who "opposed a universal second language ... would be on the devil's side" (Vicki Frost Deposition, April 16, 1986, p. 204).

The *Mozert* plaintiffs' opposition to world community led them to reject stories describing an increasingly complex world whose survival depends on international cooperation. They were convinced that humanists use scare tactics to deceive children into thinking that worldwide human efforts are necessary to save the planet. The teachers' manual entry for "No Swimming" (Grade 2), for example, suggests that human beings may be an endangered species because of overpopulation, pollution, and the depletion of natural resources. As Frost explained,

> This is contrary to the Word of God. The Lord is creator of the earth. I personally do not believe that there is a shortage of resources, and I believe that the intention of the Holt, Rinehart, Winston Reading Series is the perspective to place as early as possible upon these children the need to—planetary problems that have to be worked out on a planetary basis; that the world's got to come together as quickly as possible because we are an endangered species; man is going to run out of land, mineral *[sic]* and food; we're going to pollute all of our environment. This is a humanist—this is a view of life from a humanist standpoint, which is in direct contradiction to the Word of God. A child is not to be anxious. They are to trust in the Lord, lean not to their own understanding, cast all their cares upon him. The Lord has said that he'll supply all their needs according to his riches and glory. Throughout the scriptures, we are to trust the Lord for all of our needs. (Deposition, March 19, 1986, p. 164)

Throughout *Mozert,* the plaintiffs kept asserting that planetary problems do not exist or that if they do exist, God will solve them. Attempts to save creatures like whales or owls are both useless and sinful because, if God wants something to survive, God will either preserve it or re-create it. If God does not want it to survive, then human efforts are doomed, as are the souls of those who dare to oppose God's will. The same is true of pollution and the depletion of natural resources. God created the earth for the use of humans, and, if we pollute it or use up all its resources, God will either undo the damage immediately or transform the earth into paradise in the Second Coming.

As a matter of religious faith, people undoubtedly have the right to believe that God will re-create extinct species and fossil fuels, and that polluting the environment is not a problem because God will clean it up again. Public schools, however, are compelled to consider what Frost called, in another context, "the domain of knowledge and facts educationwise" (Deposition, April 15, 1986, p. 69). Even in individualized instruction, it is difficult to see how public schools could teach material that is indefensible except on the grounds of sectarian religious faith: that pollution does not exist, or that prayer is the only solution to the depletion of natural resources.

Besides opposing lessons on conservation, the plaintiffs charged that the Holt reading series, in its concern about overpopulation, advocates abortion. Margaret Mead observes in "Unispeak" that language is what distinguishes humans from animals. But, the protesters pointed out, newborn infants cannot speak. Mead's essay is therefore saying that newborns are not human, which means that fetuses must not be human, either. So, the protesters charged, "Unispeak" is subtle propaganda aimed at promoting abortion.

Along with overpopulation, pollution, and the depletion of natural resources, the plaintiffs dismissed the threat of nuclear war as a humanist scare tactic designed to promote one-world government. Dread of war could, they argued, encourage disarmament and intimidate Americans into allowing this country to be conquered easily. Promoting nonviolence could also encourage gun control. According to their reading of the Bible, pacifism, disarmament, and gun control violate the will of God, who ordered the Chosen People to fight wars against the wicked.

The plaintiffs objected not only to verbal anti-war messages but also to pictorial ones. The Holt sixth-grade teachers' manual contains a reproduction of Picasso's painting *Guernica,* a graphic portrayal of the brutality of war. In explaining her objections to *Guernica,* which, as the protesters pointed out, was painted by a Communist, Frost said, "War is an honorable thing when it secures the blessings of liberty, and to suggest to a child that, for example, that the war which was fought in this country, the Revolutionary War, which secured us the right to have a free country, to suggest that the blood that was spilt was an unworthy thing is not acceptable. And it's a philosophy that is not consistent with the Word of God" (Deposition, April 15, 1986, pp. 16–17). Under questioning, she conceded that *Guernica* has nothing to do with the American Revolution. Nevertheless, she and the other plaintiffs felt that the Holt series' anti-war message was unpatriotic in terms of the past as well as the future. They feared that children would learn disrespect for the military heroes of American history, as well as becoming weak and passive in the face of future enemy attacks.

In August 1983—the month Rebecca Frost began using her new Holt reader—the Eagle Forum's *Phyllis Schlafly Report* accused public schools of infusing fear, guilt, and despair into students in order to further a liberal political agenda including pacifism and nuclear disarmament. According to the *Report,* "The goals of the nuclear war curricula are (a) to promote U.S. nuclear disarmament, (b) to belittle the Soviet threat, and (c) to propagandize for federal spending for social goals at the expense of national defense" (p. 2). Two years later, the Eagle Forum included education about nuclear war in an article entitled, "The Radical Agenda of the NEA" (*Phyllis Schlafly Report,* February 1985). Another article, "Parents Speak Up Against Classroom Abuse" (June 1985), accuses the schools of needlessly frightening students with horror stories about the devastation that would be caused by nuclear war. The Hawkins County protesters were, therefore, by no means alone in their opposition to anti-war educational material, which continues to be a prime target of national organizations like the Eagle Forum.

The Holt readers, particularly those intended for younger children, included several stories about kindness to animals. Such stories, the plaintiffs warned, could bring about the end of the world. The PAW defense lawyers already knew that the protesters opposed kindness to animals on the grounds that God had created animals for human use, so we can do whatever we like to them. That issue had come up several times, notably in the protesters' objections to Little Jon's tenderness toward animals in "The Forgotten Door." The connection between kindness to animals and the end of the world was not, however, immediately obvious to the defense lawyers. When they pressed for an explanation, the protesters pointed out that animals are *different* from people. Urging kindness to animals is, therefore, yet another way of promoting tolerance for diversity, which could lead to religious tolerance. Without religious barriers, world unity could become a reality, producing the one-world government that will be the reign of the Antichrist and lead to the destruction of the world. And that, the protesters concluded, is how teaching children to be nice to animals could bring about the end of the world. A less apocalyptic reason for the protesters' opposition to kindness to animals arose from their general discomfort with promoting nonviolence. They saw empathy toward animals as a means of softening children, especially boys, thus discouraging hunting, war, and violence in general. As Frost explained, "When you say disarmament, please include that in one world government. All of this comes under the concept of one world government, disarmament, don't kill the animals" (Deposition, April 2, 1986, p. 28). She also observed, "If you think it's wrong to kill an animal for food, then the inference could be made that it is wrong to kill a person in war" (Deposition, March 19, 1986, p. 107).

One of the many Holt stories challenged for promoting empathy toward animals was "Freddy Found a Frog" (Grade 2). As the title suggests, a boy named Freddy finds a frog, which he puts in his pocket. On his way home, he asks a woman and a man what they would do if they had a frog: the woman says that she would cook the frog's legs, and the man says that he would use it as bait. Appalled, Freddy runs home to his mother, who allows him to keep the frog in the pond in their backyard. In the plaintiffs' view, the story promotes an excessively empathetic, pantheistic, non-Christian, non-utilitarian view of animals. They were especially disturbed by a teachers' manual entry suggesting that the students role-play how the frog might have felt about the possibility of being used as food or bait. Frost testified, "I do not want my children sitting down to the dinner table trying to feel like a cow and trying to think when they're eating a hamburger. See, inference is made here. The frog is just an example" (Deposition, March 19, 1986, p. 102).

The *Mozert* plaintiffs repeatedly called for balanced treatment of controversial topics, and, taken at face value, their request appears reasonable. Giving them what they meant by balanced treatment would, however, have brought about the exclusion of anything with which they disagreed. In accusing the Holt readers of presenting only nontraditional views of women, for example, they ignored the many stories and pictures showing women in traditional domestic roles. What they were really looking for in the name of balanced treatment was books presenting nothing but their own viewpoint. Giving only one side of any issue would be damaging enough to education, but giving only a side based on the beliefs of a particular religion—even in the context of individualized instruction—is inconsistent with public education in a secular nation.

Apart from the way it is applied, the balance argument is problematic because it is based on the idea that there are only two ways to look at reality—Biblical absolutism and secular humanism—and that both are valid to the same degree and on the same terms. Whenever textbook activists can pressure school boards or publishers into acting on this premise—and, as later chapters show, they sometimes can—it suddenly makes sense to teach their brand of Christianity in public schools in order to balance the "opposing view." What sometimes gets lost in the shuffle is the fact that their claims are not valid unless fundamentalism really is at least as important as everything else put together—and that premise is in itself a tenet of a particular religion. There is no externally verifiable evidence to show that everything other than an absolutist interpretation of the Bible can be grouped into some hypothetical "other" religion. Trying to do so leads to countless absurdities. In the name of tolerance for one religion, public schools are pressured into not only permitting but also fostering intolerance for all other religions, cultures, and life-styles. Institutions of learning are urged to teach children that thinking for themselves is wrong, and that there is only one right way to live and only one solution to every dilemma. Public schools are asked to limit the teaching of topics that the vast majority of Americans would define as secular because a single sectarian faith says that they are religious.

Although this chapter is one of the longest in the book, it covers only the most significant of the Hawkins County protesters' objections to the Holt series. Other topics that could have been discussed include alcohol use, laziness, skeptical views of religion, disrespect for the Bible, vege-tarianism, and negative portrayals of Protestant ministers and mission-aries. Once people accept two central beliefs—that education should teach intolerance for diversity and that it should not promote imaginative, independent thinking—the range of individual subjects open to attack becomes limitless.

Each topic treated in this chapter is illustrated by only one or two of the many examples available, and only a few sections include material from national groups. All the same, this selection of general beliefs, specific objections to the Holt readers, and nationally organized lobbying makes it clear that Far Right activists have a wide-reaching educational agenda that would, if accepted, signal the end of public education as it now exists. Their chances of total victory are slim, but, as the following chapters show, they do win a surprising number of skirmishes—enough to produce an unmistakable and documentable effect on nationally mar-keted textbooks and, thus, on American education.

CHAPTER FOUR

Judgment Day

Congress shall make no law respecting an establishment of religion,
or prohibiting the free exercise thereof...
—THE FIRST AMENDMENT TO THE U.S. CONSTITUTION

The *Mozert* trial began on July 14, 1986, almost three years after Rebecca Frost first drew her mother's attention to *Riders on the Earth*. The lawyers on both sides wrote lengthy briefs and summoned witnesses whose testimony filled sixteen volumes. The key issues that emerge from these towers of paper are central to all of the textbook lawsuits that have taken place since 1980. How far may, or must, public schools go to accommodate individual parents' religious beliefs? For that matter, what *is* a religion? How broadly can the word be defined before it becomes meaningless? Is secular humanism a religion, and if so, is it being taught in public schools in violation of the First Amendment?

The *Mozert* plaintiffs and the school officials they were suing had very different ideas about what the right to a free public education means. The plaintiffs argued that children must be instructed in accordance with their religious beliefs, while the school authorities said that public schools can offer nothing more or less than a mainstream secular education that is neutral on the subject of religion. The plaintiffs rejected the option of private religious schools on the grounds that parents should not be forced to choose between public education and the free exercise of their religion. The defendants disagreed; as they saw it, the option of sending children to private schools is an affirmation, not a denial, of the right to practice one's religion.

The subject of private religious education comes up in almost every textbook dispute. Sooner or later, school officials or parents who oppose the protesters ask, "Why don't you send your kids to private schools?" Fundamentalist activists find the question offensive. In their way of looking at things, they represent the norm or standard, and the secular humanists who have taken over the school system represent the aberration. The protesters resent the suggestion that they should pay taxes to support public schools and then spend their own money to buy their children the kind of education that is theirs by right. What *should* happen, they believe, is that public schools should recognize that the United States is a Christian country and shape the curriculum accordingly. Secular humanists, whom the protesters see as a small minority of Americans, could then pay to send *their* children to schools that accommodate their beliefs. Apart from saving money, these protesters want to use public education as a way of establishing that they are the "real" Americans, and those who oppose them are the ones outside the mainstream.

When the appeals court overturned Judge Hull's 1984 attempt to dismiss *Mozert* without a trial, it instructed him to determine two things: whether the enforced use of the Holt series imposed a burden on the plaintiffs' religious rights; and if so, whether there was any compelling state interest to justify the burden. Accordingly, the plaintiffs set out to convince Hull either that the Holt readers promoted the religion of secular humanism, or that the act of reading the books violated their own religion, or both. The school officials tried to show either that the use of the Holt readers involved no more than simple exposure to ideas, or that the ideas in the books were not religious, or both.

Just in case the judge accepted the plaintiffs' arguments, the school authorities also asserted that the state had compelling interests in using the Holt readers. The interests they mentioned included teaching children to read, upholding the authority of school officials to determine curriculum, saving the expense of providing alternate reading instruction, and avoiding excessive entanglement with religion.

When the plaintiffs were asked what religion they practice, they did not mention specific denominations; rather, they identified themselves as "fundamentalists" or "born-again Christians." Nevertheless, because they attended Baptist, Methodist, and Presybterian churches, the defense called expert witnesses from these denominations to testify that some of the plaintiffs' objections to the Holt readers represented their personal or political views rather than the creed of any particular religion. The chief defense witness in this area was Dr. J. Gordon Melton, director of the Institute for the Study of American Religion and author of an encyclopedia of religion. Melton testified that "apart from the doctrine of evolution, creation and the creation/evolution controversy that the objections to the books fall in that area outside the central beliefs of these churches [to which the plaintiffs belonged]" (Trial Transcript).

Having presented Melton's testimony, the defendants maintained that the right to free exercise of religion is limited to the central beliefs of one's denomination. They supported their argument with Supreme Court precedents, such as *Sequoyah v. Tennessee Valley Authority* (1980), in which Cherokee Indians objected to the proposed flooding of their sacred land. The Court found that the land was neither central to the Cherokees' religion nor indispensable to their way of life. Based on such precedents, the school authorities argued that the protesters' objections to the Holt series represented their personal opinions, not the central beliefs of any religion. Indeed, the defendants stated, "It is often difficult to determine the relationship between the stories to which the plaintiffs object and the religious beliefs alleged to be violated" (Defendants' Pretrial Brief, July 3, 1986, p. 29).

The plaintiffs attacked this line of argument head-on. The school authorities wanted to limit the word *religion* to the beliefs of a particular church, but the plaintiffs thought in much broader terms. To them, every idea was in some way religious. They changed denominations often and did not even know that there are any doctrinal differences among the Baptist, Methodist, and Presbyterian faiths. As far as they were concerned, all Protestant churches are pretty much the same, and their own allegiance was to their particular interpretation of the Bible. The case should, they argued, rest solely on the extent to which their objections to the Holt readers were "rooted in religion." The CWA lawyers wrote, "Courts are not authorized to weigh the relative importance of the various religious beliefs of an adherent of a faith, rather the centrality inquiry consists of an examination to see if the actions in question are appropriately related to a religiously-based belief" (Plaintiffs' Trial Brief, July 3, 1986, p. 5). In short, their position was that they did not have to prove anything at all about their beliefs except that they were religious.

The *Mozert* plaintiffs and their expert witnesses testified that certain articles of faith, such as the divinity of Christ, are nonnegotiable. In other areas, however, individual believers may emphasize different aspects of the Bible and draw different conclusions from it. This discretionary power is called "the priesthood of the believer." One witness, a fundamentalist pastor named Gary Brent Bradley, explained how some religious principles can be more basic than others:

> ... those things having to do with one's salvation and personal relationship to God through Jesus Christ the certainty of judgment, before Him, and all of those, all of those things having to do with the person and the work of Christ and the—and His Word are absolutely crucial. There are other issues which are essential for our understanding and living in a way that is pleasing to God [that] are not standards upon which church membership is based, and it gets to be a difficult thing because even some of those peripheral issues can become major issues, depending upon the way in which they are handled and the attitude with which they are approached. (Deposition, March 4, 1986, pp. 32–33)

The plaintiffs used Bradley's testimony to show that whatever choices individuals make about optional matters carry the force of religious conviction for those individuals. From then on, whenever the defendants challenged a belief on the grounds that it was not central to the plaintiffs' religion, the plaintiffs replied that the topic fell into the domain of the priesthood of the believer.

The school officials protested that their opponents were playing both ends against the middle, defining religion in whatever way suited them in each situation. Whatever the plaintiffs believed as a group was etched in stone; but wherever differences existed among them, they fell back on the priesthood of the believer. By this reasoning, the defendants could not possibly win. If they said that a particular belief is religious and therefore cannot be taught in public schools, the plaintiffs would reply that it should be taught as a balance to the religion of secular humanism. If, on the other hand, the school authorities argued that a particular belief is *not* religious, the plaintiffs would invoke the priesthood of the believer. The defendants protested that trying to pin down what their opponents meant by religion was like trying to nail Jell-O to the wall, and that such a vague definition could not possibly merit First Amendment protection. "And the Constitution does not protect every belief," they contended, "just because someone views her life and national life in religious terms" (Trial Transcript).

In addition to emphasizing religious centrality, the defendants argued that using the Holt readers did not burden the plaintiffs' free exercise of religion because of the distinction between indoctrination and simple exposure to ideas. Quoting several of the protesters' objections to the series, the school authorities accused them of failing to distinguish between mentioning an idea and teaching it as truth. The school officials also believed that the topics covered in the Holt readers are common in contemporary American society, and they challenged the plaintiffs' right to pressure public schools into avoiding subjects that all children encounter outside of school.

The school authorities wound up their case by saying that, even if the plaintiffs succeeded in showing that the Hawkins County schools were teaching material that conflicted with their religion, they would still lose. The Supreme Court has repeatedly ruled that public education cannot function in a pluralistic culture if it has to avoid everything that might be offensive to any religion. In *Williams v. Board of Education of the County of Kanawha* (1975), for example, the Court said that "the [First] Amendment does not guarantee that nothing about religion will be taught in the schools nor that nothing offensive to any religion will be taught in the schools."

The plaintiffs answered their opponents' arguments by saying that the act of reading the controversial stories—opening the book, moving one's eyes across the pages—was forbidden by their religion. Requiring their children to read the Holt books was, they argued, the same as forcing Orthodox Jewish schoolchildren to eat ham sandwiches. They also pointed out that theirs was not the first religion to decide that reading a book can be sinful in itself; the Catholic Church had only recently abolished its *Index of Forbidden Books*.

By shifting the focus of the argument from internal beliefs to external acts, the plaintiffs were able to introduce their own selection of Supreme Court cases. *Sherbert v. Verner* (1963) concerned a Seventh-Day Adventist who was fired for refusing to work on the Sabbath. She was later denied unemployment benefits on the grounds that her dismissal had resulted from her own actions. The Supreme Court ruled that government benefits could not be withheld from her as a consequence of her refusal to commit an act that violated her religious beliefs. Another case, *Thomas v. Review Board* (1981), also involved the denial of unemployment benefits, this time to a Jehovah's Witness who had refused to make armaments. The Supreme Court ruled that withholding unemployment benefits from Thomas violated his right to the free exercise of his religion.

Based on *Sherbert* and *Thomas*, the plaintiffs argued that they could not be forced to forfeit a government benefit—free public education—as a consequence of their refusal to commit an act forbidden by their religion. They wrote, "Plaintiffs believe that it is a violation of their religion for their children to read the Holt books. The government schools have responded by saying: If you don't read these books, your children cannot attend our schools. This is a clear case of compelling people to choose between the exercise of a First Amendment right and participation in an otherwise available government program" (Plaintiffs' Trial Brief, July 3, 1986, p. 11).

Throughout the trial, both sides knew that even if the plaintiffs convinced Judge Hull that the Holt books burdened their free exercise of religion, the school officials could still win if they could show even one compelling state interest to justify the burden. They came up with four: teaching children to read, regulating public education in an orderly way, avoiding unusually expensive and burdensome educational procedures, and avoiding excessive entanglement with religion.

The plaintiffs agreed that the state has an interest in teaching children to read, but they maintained that uniform textbooks are not necessary and denied that special instruction for their children would burden the school district. More importantly, they challenged the whole idea that the existence of a compelling state interest would mean victory for the school authorities. The right to act on one's beliefs may be restricted by state interest, but the right to believe is absolute, and "the use of these textbooks involves the direction or manipulation of what children believe" (Plaintiffs' Trial Brief, July 3, 1986, p. 23). In their view, class discussions, assignments, and tests would reinforce the ideas in the readers enough to affect the children's thinking.

On October 24, 1986, Judge Hull ruled in favor of the plaintiffs. He noted that they did not ask that the public school curriculum be changed, but only "that they should not be forced to choose between reading books that offend their religious beliefs and foregoing a free public education" (Memorandum Opinion, p. 2). He agreed with the plaintiffs that centrality of belief is irrelevant and that the Holt books teach certain ideas rather than simply exposing children to them.

> The plaintiffs believe that, after reading the entire Holt series, a child might adopt the views of a feminist, a humanist, a pacifist, an anti-Christian, a vegetarian, or an advocate of a "one-world" government.
>
> Plaintiffs sincerely believe that the repetitive affirmation of these philosophical viewpoints is repulsive to the Christian faith—so repulsive that they must not allow their children to be exposed to the Holt series. This is their religious belief. They have drawn a line, "and it is not for us to say that the line [they] drew was an unreasonable one." *Thomas [v. Review Board]*, at 715. (p. 12)

Having determined that the plaintiffs' free exercise of religion had been burdened, Hull turned to the question of compelling state interest. He concluded that, although the state undoubtedly has an interest in teaching children to read, it does not have to require all students to use the Holt books. He did, however, agree with the school authorities that the plaintiffs' beliefs were so sweeping and idiosyncratic that "any accommodation of the plaintiffs in the schools would have the effect of advancing a particular religion and would involve an excessive entanglement between the state and religion" (p. 22). Accordingly, he ruled that the plaintiffs could teach reading to their children at home, while their children continued to participate in the rest of the public school curriculum. Full-time home schooling had always been an option for the plaintiffs, but under Tennessee law children either attended school for the full day or were educated entirely at home. Hull's ruling extended the home-schooling concept to include partial "opt-out" arrangements. Nevertheless, he cautioned, "This opinion shall not be interpreted to require the school system to make this option available to any other person or to these plaintiffs for any other subject" (p. 24).

When Frost first brought up the idea of teaching Sarah herself, the school officials asked what credentials she had. She replied that she was a mother, and that that should be enough. The plaintiffs' anti-intellectualism, which strongly influenced their selection of instructional material, also prevented them from being concerned about teaching qualifications. They would have preferred to force the school board to shape a curriculum around their ideas, but failing that, they would settle for teaching their children at home in order to control the values, ideas, and information the children learned. The quality of education as such was much less important to them.

The Hawkins County protesters were not alone in their reasons for wanting home schooling or in their general attitude toward education. Almost every issue of the CWA monthly magazine features something about home schools, as well as articles opposing early childhood education, day care, and public education. One article promises that through home schooling "[p]arents can control destructive influences such as various temptations, humanism, and negative peer pressure" (*Concerned Women,* June 1989, p. 20). In addition to praising home schooling in principle, CWA assures parents that the process is not too time-consuming. Teaching children at home requires "only one-half to one hour for the early grades and work up to two hours of instruction and another one to one and one-half hours of independent study (by the student) for upper grades" (p. 21). Busy mothers are told that they need not use a "typical classroom curriculum" in which "the material is presented in such a manner that it has to be *taught*. Such material requires moms, consequently, to face the almost insurmountable task of having to teach material that requires constant adult attention" (p. 23). Instead, mothers can substitute

> the Biblical formula of line upon line and precept upon precept. Some educators call this the 'Rote Method.' It simply means that academic material is presented in such a manner that children learn by repetition; they repeat content line upon line. In other words, they drill, drill, drill until they *know* the material. They are not expected to understand it. They are expected to know it. A carefully designed curriculum will require *understanding* later as the child progresses through the publisher's scope and sequence. (p. 23)

States usually monitor the progress of home-schooled children by giving them standardized tests, and the rote method of learning might allow them to do quite well on multiple-choice questions. All the same, limiting study time to a maximum of three and a half hours a day and encouraging parroted answers are effective ways of circumventing meaningful education. If parents do not want their children to use reason and imagination to solve problems or to shape independent views, it would be hard to find a better way to insure those results than by confining education to mind-numbing memorization.

The CWA publication quoted earlier suggests that keeping children at home will protect them from "various temptations, humanism, and negative peer pressure." As the terms are used in CWA publications, *humanism* means anything that is not biblical absolutism, and *negative peer pressure* includes the awareness that some people hold views of which CWA disapproves. By these definitions, home schooling is a way of making sure that children learn biblical absolutism and nothing else. The *Mozert* plaintiffs made it clear that, if they had a choice, they would see that their children knew nothing about other races, religions, or ethnic groups except that they are inferior and wrong.

Hull's home schooling decision was a victory for the plaintiffs because of the principle it established, but it made no practical difference. By the time he issued his ruling, the children involved in the lawsuit were already settled in private religious schools, one of which was run by Bob Mozert, and their parents did not plan to move them. Apart from Mozert, the plaintiffs' witnesses included two headmasters who testified that the private schools they ran taught the values advocated by the Hawkins County protesters. Cross-examination by a PAW lawyer revealed that one witness was involved in a court action of his own because of alleged racial discrimination at his school. So, even though the *Mozert* plaintiffs failed to force the public schools to accommodate their beliefs, the kind of education they want is available to them through home schooling or selected private schools. But should it be?

Assuming that the community at large has a legitimate interest in its citizens' ability to respect reason and tolerate diversity, home schooling and religious private schools are not ideal solutions to the tension between biblical absolutism and public education. All they do is get the conflict out of sight without addressing the issue of parental versus community rights. If parents deny their children necessary medical treatment, the state will step in, establishing the principle that parents' rights are not paramount over the child's welfare or the health of others who might be jeopardized by the child's illness. Nevertheless, even where physical health is concerned, it is no small matter to overrule parents, and the difficulty is even greater with regard to less tangible educational issues.

The whole question of parental rights is a knotty one. On the one hand, allowing children to be taught unthinking hatred and fear of everything that is different from themselves is not just irresponsible but downright dangerous in today's world. On the other hand, if the government starts telling parents which beliefs they can pass on to their children and which will be "deprogrammed" by the state, where does that stop? Who decides whose ideas are too crazy to survive another generation? These are not easy questions, but sooner or later our society is going to have to take a stand on the extent to which state-approved home schooling arrangements or private schools can be used to transmit anti-intellectualism and intolerance for diversity from one generation to the next.

Two months after handing down his decision, Hull conducted a separate hearing on the plaintiffs' claim to reimbursement for the expense of sending their children to private schools while the case was in progress. He had already ruled that the school district had violated their religious rights, and he agreed that they were entitled to compensation for private school tuition, transportation, books, and registration. He also awarded them reimbursement for wages that they had lost while attending the depositions and the trial. Following the principle that each plaintiff should be restored to "as good a position as he enjoyed prior to the violation"

(Judgment in a Civil Case, December 18, 1986, p. 6), the judge awarded the Mozerts $6,214.40, the Bakers $8,528.90, the Whitakers $524.00, the Frosts $12,949.94, the Couches $5,272.15, the Eatons $10,619.60, and the Meades $6,412.60. The defendants promptly announced their intention to appeal.

Hull's support of home schooling was one of the defendants' primary targets when the case went to the appeals court. They maintained that his establishment of a partial home-schooling option was illegal, and that allowing students to opt out of reading class could encourage religious divisiveness by preventing them from learning about ideas other than those taught in their homes. The school authorities also questioned whether Hull's ruling could be limited to one school subject and one group of parents. They predicted that other parents would make new demands for exceptions to the public schools' core curriculum, creating overwhelming practical problems and a chilling effect on the inclusion of controversial material in textbooks.

The plaintiffs replied that the defendants were in no position to talk about avoiding religious divisiveness, since it was the school officials' lack of respect for fundamentalism that had turned Hawkins County into a battleground in the first place. They also reaffirmed that what they most disliked about the Holt series was its attempt to "homogenize appellees' [plaintiffs'] children from their distinctive beliefs so that they will become 'critically thinking and tolerant citizens'" (Brief of Appellees, March 4, 1987, p. 50).

On August 24, 1987, ten months after Judge Hull had handed down his decision, the Sixth Circuit Court of Appeals overturned it by a vote of 3–0. The opinion of the court was written by Chief Judge Pierce Lively, with Judges Cornelia Kennedy and Danny Boggs offering concurring opinions. Because each judge emphasized a different aspect of *Mozert*, their votes concluded the case without resolving the issues it raised.

Judge Lively focused on the notion of "mere exposure" to ideas. He wrote,

> The only conduct compelled by the defendants was reading and discussing the material in the Holt series, and hearing other students' interpretations of those materials. This is the exposure to which the plaintiffs objected. What is absent from this case is the critical element of compulsion to affirm or deny a religious belief or to engage or refrain from engaging in a practice forbidden or required in the exercise of a plaintiff's religion. (p. 21)

He also disagreed with the plaintiffs' claim that the Holt books taught certain ideas rather than merely mentioning them. In his opinion,

> The plaintiffs did not produce a single student or teacher to testify that any student was ever required to affirm his or her belief or disbelief in any idea or practice mentioned in the various stories and passages contained in the Holt series. However, the plaintiffs appeared to assume that materials clearly presented as poetry, fiction, and even "make-believe" in the Holt series were presented as facts which the students were required to believe. Nothing in the record supports this assumption. (pp. 9–10)

Lively rejected the plaintiffs' argument that reading the Holt books was in itself an act forbidden by their religion. He therefore disagreed with Hull's acceptance of Supreme Court precedents involving people who had refused to make armaments or to work on the Sabbath. According to Lively, requiring students to read the Holt books "does not constitute the compulsion described in the Supreme Court cases, where the objector was required to affirm or deny a religious belief or engage or refrain from engaging in a practice contrary to sincerely held religious beliefs" (p. 15). He also agreed with the school authorities that the plaintiffs' definition of religion was too broad to be accommodated within public education:

> It is clear that to the plaintiffs there is but one acceptable view—the Biblical view, as they interpret the Bible. Furthermore, the plaintiffs view every human situation and decision, whether related to personal belief and conduct or to public policy and programs, from a theological or religious perspective. Mrs. Frost testified that many political issues have theological roots and that there would be "no way" certain themes could be presented without violating her religious beliefs. She identified such themes as evolution, false supernaturalism, feminism, telepathy and magic as matters that could not be presented in any way without offending her beliefs. The only way to avoid conflict with the plaintiffs' beliefs in these sensitive areas would be to eliminate all references to the subjects so identified. However, the Supreme Court has clearly held that it violates the Establishment Clause to tailor a public school's curriculum to satisfy the principles or prohibitions of any religion. (p. 11)

Whereas Lively's opinion emphasized "mere exposure," Judge Cornelia Kennedy's focused on compelling state interest. She agreed with

Lively that reading the Holt series did not burden the plaintiffs' free exercise of religion, but she added that even if a burden had existed it would have been justified by the state's compelling interest in teaching children to draw conclusions, express opinions, and deal with "complex and controversial social and moral issues" (p. 2). The plaintiffs, she wrote, did not want their children "formulating their own ideas about anything for which they believe the Bible states a rule or position" (p. 1). This goal violates a legitimate state interest in teaching critical reading skills. In order to develop such skills, "the students must read and discuss complex, morally and socially difficult issues. Many of these necessarily will be subjects on which appellees believe the Bible states the rule or correct position. Consequently, accommodating appellees' beliefs would unduly interfere with the fulfillment of the appellants' objectives" (p. 2).

Kennedy also agreed with the school authorities that public education has "a compelling interest in avoiding religious divisiveness" (p. 4). She saw important differences between segregating students for reading instruction on the basis of their religion and allowing them to leave regular reading classes for other reasons, such as participating in gifted or remedial programs. Religious segregation would, she argued, violate the state's interest in "'promoting cohesion among a heterogeneous democratic people'" (*Illinois ex rel. McCollum v. Board of Education*, quoted in Kennedy opinion, p. 4).

The third member of the appeals court panel, Judge Danny Boggs, saw the case differently from his colleagues. In his view, reading the Holt books was not "mere exposure" to ideas; it was an act forbidden by the plaintiffs' religion. Their religious rights were indeed burdened, and unnecessarily so, since the public schools could have accommodated their request for separate instruction without fostering their religion.

Boggs argued that the notion of teaching critical reading skills is too "muddled" and "slippery" to constitute a compelling state interest. There was also no evidence to show that children could not learn the same critical reading skills, whatever they are, in an opt-out program. Nevertheless, while disagreeing with the school board's decision to forbid alternate readers, he reluctantly affirmed their authority to make it. He wrote, "As we ultimately decide here, on the present state of constitutional law, the school board is indeed entitled to say 'my way or the highway'" (p. 3). He continued, "It is a substantial imposition on the schools to *require* them to justify each instance of not dealing with students' individual, religiously compelled, objections (as opposed to *permitting* a local, rough and ready, adjustment), and I do not see that the Supreme Court has authorized us to make such a requirement" (p. 18).

Boggs did not agree with his colleagues' assertion that the plaintiffs' beliefs were too broad to be accommodated by the Hawkins County schools. His interpretation of the case was that the naiveté of the plaintiffs and the shrewdness of the defense lawyers had created a false impression by confusing two distinct issues: what the plaintiffs were claiming as constitutional rights, and what they were merely mentioning as preferences. This confusion had, he argued, obscured the real issues that *Mozert* was meant to test:

> The extent to which school systems may constitutionally require students to use educational materials that are objectionable, contrary to, or forbidden by their religious beliefs is a serious and important issue. The question of exactly how terms such as "contrary," "objectionable," and "forbidden," are to be assessed in the context of religious beliefs is a subtle and interesting one. But this decision, as I understand it, addresses none of those questions. When a case arises with more sophisticated or cagey plaintiffs, or less skillful cross-examination, that true issue must be faced anew, with little guidance from this decision. (p. 5)

Despite the inconsistencies among the three judges' opinions, their unanimous vote reversed Hull's ruling and dismissed the plaintiffs' complaint. The Hawkins County school board could continue to forbid alternate reading instruction, and the school district did not have to pay the protesters any money. The plaintiffs petitioned the Supreme Court to hear the case, but their petition was denied. The case was over, and the plaintiffs had lost. Or had they?

Early in the Hawkins County dispute, the protesters contacted Texas activists Mel and Norma Gabler. The Gablers sent the protesters one hundred copies of a handbook on humanism, along with an unfavorable evaluation of the Holt readers. When the case came to court, they testified in favor of the plaintiffs' views on secular humanism in public education. They also confirmed that they had reviewed the Holt series when the State of Texas selected reading textbooks in 1980 and had been dissatisfied with its humanistic content. They had not reviewed the 1983 edition, which was at issue in *Mozert,* but Holt representatives testified that the two editions were very similar.

Just as *Mozert* was coming to trial in the summer of 1986, Texas was again in the process of selecting reading textbooks. The Gablers were pleased by what they considered the greatly improved quality of the books submitted by almost all of the publishers—not just Holt. According to Mel Gabler, most of the 1986 readers were "much more balanced" than previous editions had been (Deposition, July 8, 1986, p. 18). They not only avoided offensive topics, such as disrespect for authority, but also de-emphasized objectionable approaches, such as asking open-ended questions about values. "Now, one of the things where they have greatly improved the books," he said, "is the matter of questions. The older books had many, many value questions delving into the thoughts and the feelings of the children. And now the questions are directed to the stories that the children have read." When a defense lawyer asked, "So they don't go into the values of the student at all?" Gabler replied, "There is a great improvement in that area" (p. 19).

In a *Rutgers Law Journal* article, Keith Waldman mentions a *New York Times* story comparing the 1983 and 1986 editions of *Riders on the Earth* (Grade 6) and *People Need People* (Grade 2). The news story shows that passages opposed by the *Mozert* plaintiffs were removed from the 1986 Holt books. The 1983 edition of *Riders,* for example, includes a reference to the humanistic ideals reflected in the Declaration of Independence. That reference is missing from the 1986 edition. Waldman observes, "From a business standpoint, self-censorship makes sense. First, the practice represents an attempt to please the widest possible audience and to insure a wide distribution of texts. Second, the practice avoids the possibility of challenges, costly litigation and adverse publicity" (Note 138, p. 460). The self-censorship that Waldman describes was not, according to the Gablers, limited to the Holt readers; almost all of the 1986 readers were more acceptable to them than the 1980 editions had been. While it seems likely that *Mozert* had something to do with the change, it would probably not have had that effect if it had been a one-of-a-kind event. As the rest of this book shows, *Mozert* was representative of the overall climate of American textbook publishing in the 1980s.

The question "Who won *Mozert?*" is complicated by the textbook changes Gabler described. The plaintiffs failed to establish the precedent that public schools must accommodate religious objections to textbooks, but they did sustain four years of nationally publicized litigation that cost Holt and the school officials time, embarrassment, and money. If the *Mozert* plaintiffs' children attend public school, they now have to read the books school officials select. School officials, however, have to choose from what is on the market; they cannot buy books that do not exist. Since the textbooks produced by America's largest publishers were more in keeping with the Gablers' beliefs in 1986 than they were in 1980, it is not at all clear that the *Mozert* plaintiffs were on the losing side.

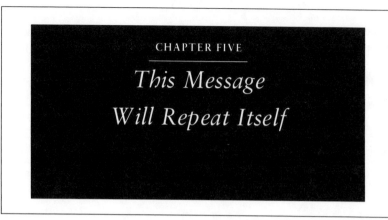

CHAPTER FIVE

This Message Will Repeat Itself

*Never before has a religion been created and
defined solely by its antagonists.*
—JOHN J. BUCHANAN

If *Mozert* had been an isolated incident, a lawsuit unlike any other in its decade, it would not have been particularly important. It included some dramatic moments, but it was ultimately decided on the basis of three well-established principles: first, freedom of religion is no protection against mere exposure to opposing ideas; second, the state has a compelling interest in promoting religious and social tolerance; and third, school boards have the authority to determine curriculum within very broad parameters.

Mozert was not, however, a unique event. It was typical of 1980s federal lawsuits which, in combination with the market forces discussed in chapters 8 and 9, have helped to shape today's textbooks. Textbook controversies generally begin as *Mozert* did, with a conflict involving protesting parents, school officials, and parents who disagree with the protesters. If a local dispute develops into a nationally publicized federal court case, it does so because of the financial support of one or more national organizations. Each of the lawsuits discussed in this book has a different emphasis, but all of them include the same central issues as *Mozert*: competition between parents and school officials over the control of children's education, conflicts over the role of religious beliefs in determining curriculum, and disagreements about the selection of social values to be taught in public schools.

One of the most important textbook lawsuits in the 1980s was *Smith v. Board of School Commissioners of Mobile County,* in which plaintiffs who described themselves as conservative Christians challenged the use of forty-five social studies, history, and home economics textbooks in the Alabama public schools. Unlike the *Mozert* plaintiffs, who asked for alternate readers, the *Smith* plaintiffs wanted the court to declare that secular humanism is a religion and should either be removed from the schools entirely or balanced by the inclusion of Christian teachings in the curriculum.

The lawsuit that became *Smith* began as a case called *Jaffree v. Board of School Commissioners of Mobile County.* In 1982, a non-Christian lawyer named Ishmael Jaffree filed a complaint in federal district court in Mobile, Alabama, contending that his children's teachers were violating the First Amendment by leading their public school classes in Christian prayers. School officials did not dispute Jaffree's description of what was going on in the schools, but, they pointed out, a 1982 Alabama state law permitted voluntary oral prayer led by the teacher.

Acknowledging that the Supreme Court has declared school prayer unconstitutional, Mobile County school authorities maintained that the Court had made a mistake. The establishment clause of the First Amendment says that "Congress shall make no law respecting an establishment of religion," but the State of Alabama is not Congress; therefore, the defendants argued, the First Amendment does not prevent Alabama from establishing religion.

The efforts of Mobile County school officials to keep prayer in the schools were supported by a group of parents and teachers who joined the case as defendant-intervenors. They asserted that Mobile County public schools were using secular humanist textbooks, which meant that Christian prayers could not be banned in the interests of religious neutrality while a competing religion was being promoted through state-approved books. Like the *Mozert* plaintiffs, the *Jaffree* defendant-intervenors defined secular humanism as the worship of humans rather than God, leading to the belief that humans should make their own decisions and solve their own problems.

Jaffree was tried before Judge Brevard Hand, who agreed that the Supreme Court had erred in applying the First Amendment to the states. Each state, he wrote, is "free to define the meaning of religious establishment under its own state constitution and laws" (p. 22). He also defined secular humanism as a religion that has "become so entwined in every phase of the curriculum that it is like a pervasive cancer" (p. 20). Since removing secular humanism from the curriculum would be almost impossible, the only alternative he saw was to allow Christianity to be presented in the schools as a balance. He therefore dismissed Jaffree's complaint with prejudice and ordered him to pay court costs.

Anticipating that his decision might be overturned on appeal, Hand summarized what he planned to do if a higher court ordered him to ban prayer from the public schools. He would not, he declared, simply end the case. Rather, he would realign it to allow Christian plaintiffs to sue the school authorities for using secular humanist textbooks. "If this Court is compelled to purge 'God is great, God is good, we thank Him for our daily food' from the classroom," he warned, "then this Court must also purge from the classroom those things that serve to teach that salvation is through one's self rather than through a diety [sic]" (p. 64).

To no one's surprise, the Eleventh Circuit Court of Appeals affirmed that the First Amendment does indeed apply to the states. Just as Congress is forbidden to establish a federal religion, the states are prohibited from establishing state religions. The Supreme Court agreed, striking down the Alabama school prayer law on the grounds that the Fourteenth Amendment makes the First Amendment applicable to the states.

Following the Supreme Court ruling, Hand kept his promise: instead of concluding the case, he reopened it for a new trial. Jaffree withdrew and was replaced by plaintiffs who opposed the use of textbooks which, they contended, promoted the religion of secular humanism. The defendants included not only the Mobile County school officials but also the state Board of Education, the state superintendent of education, and Governor George Wallace. The state defendants were added to the case because the challenged textbooks were on Alabama's state-approved list.

Douglas Smith, a biology teacher who argued that his right to free speech included discussing creationism in the classroom, headed the new list of plaintiffs. The name of the case was therefore changed from *Jaffree v. Board of School Commissioners of Mobile County* to *Smith v. Board of School Commissioners of Mobile County*. Nevertheless, at Hand's insistence it was not handled as a new lawsuit: the same case that had eliminated Christian prayer now provided the forum for a counterchallenge to secular humanism.

The National Legal Foundation (NLF), affiliated with the Christian Broadcasting Network (CBN) in Virginia Beach, Virginia, funded the new plaintiffs. According to the head of CBN, televangelist Pat Robertson, NLF is made up of seven hundred lawyers dedicated to opposing the ACLU.

Robertson preached about *Smith* on several episodes of his television program, *The 700 Club,* asking his supporters for prayers and financial contributions. *The 700 Club* also featured prominent guests, such as former secretary of education William Bennett, who assured Robertson's viewers that traditional religion is being systematically excluded from textbooks to make way for secular perspectives.

The ACLU and PAW, which was still providing representation for school officials in *Mozert,* joined in funding the *Smith* defense. The chairman of PAW, former United States congressman John Buchanan, and its president, Anthony Podesta, undertook speaking engagements and television appearances throughout the country to oppose the definition of secular humanism as a religion.

The battle between NLF and PAW heated up considerably when Pat Robertson announced his candidacy for president of the United States. PAW countered with a nationally televised program featuring clips from *The 700 Club,* pairing some of Robertson's comments about *Smith* with his claim to have deflected Hurricane Gloria away from his headquarters by prayer. The program also included ultraconservative Robertson statements on the United States Constitution, public education, and women's rights.

Robertson's association with *Smith* just as he was running for president underlined the political implications of such cases as nothing in *Mozert* could have done. Both lawsuits involved powerful organizations with well-developed political agendas, but Robertson's statements about *Smith* took on new significance in the context of his presidential ambitions. "The ultimate thrust of the new textbooks and the new learning," he warned, "is to move the United States into an international alliance with the governments based on the socialist model of the Soviet Republic" (Thomas Boyer, "Robertson Praises Ban on Textbooks," *Virginian Pilot,* March 8, 1987). "And the Alabama court case says if you can't have the Bible under the First Amendment, if that's going to be banned, well you're certainly not going to have taxpayers' money to teach evolution. I think that's fair" (March 9, 1987, *700 Club* broadcast; quoted in PAW memorandum, March 9, 1987). As these samples suggest, Robertson's goal, and the goal of his religious and political supporters, is to remove material they find objectionable from all students on First Amendment grounds. Robertson himself has never directly affected textbook content, but the topics mentioned in the two remarks quoted here—evolution and alliances with socialist countries—are often challenged by activists in the Texas textbook adoption process discussed in Chapter 9, leading to changes in books marketed nationwide.

On March 8, 1988, while *Smith* was still in progress, Robertson placed second or third in fifteen of the sixteen presidential primaries held on that day: second in Louisiana and Texas, and third in Alabama, Arkansas, Florida, Georgia, Kentucky, Maryland, Mississippi, Missouri, North Carolina, Oklahoma, Rhode Island, Tennessee, and Virginia. In the remaining March 8 primary, held in Massachusetts, he came in behind George Bush, Robert Dole, and Jack Kemp and ahead of Pierre duPont, "No Preference," Alexander Haig, and scattered write-in votes, in that order. The competition he faced varied from state to state, and in some states the number of votes he received was very modest. Nevertheless, few analysts had expected him to do as well as he did. He came nowhere near being nominated, but his surprising success in several primaries sent an unmistakable message to the politicians who *were* elected about the wisdom of taking the strength of the Far Right into account in public decision making.

In order to win, the *Smith* plaintiffs had to prove *both* that secular humanism is a religion *and* that textbooks used in Alabama public schools advanced this religion in violation of the First Amendment. The school authorities had to prove either that secular humanism is not a religion or that the challenged textbooks did not promote it. Despite differences between the two lawsuits in format and emphasis, the *Smith* plaintiffs were trying to set the same precedents as the *Mozert* plaintiffs. They wanted to prove that secular humanism is a religion, protest its dominance in American schools, encourage the inclusion of Christian teachings in the curriculum, and assert the absolute authority of parents over their children's education.

The *Smith* plaintiffs challenged thirty-nine history and social studies books and six home economics books approved for use in Alabama public schools. They argued that the history books favored nonbelief over belief by ignoring the role of religion in world events, and that the social studies and home economics books promoted self-reliance and personal decision making rather than obedience to God's will.

About a year before *Smith* came to trial, Governor Wallace took the other defendants completely by surprise by signing a consent decree stipulating that the religion of secular humanism should be excluded from public school textbooks under the First Amendment. He also alleged that omitting facts about religion from history books discriminates against religion and violates the students' right to receive information. Four months later, the Mobile County school commissioners signed a similar document.

Pat Robertson invited his *700 Club* television audience to celebrate: "The Governor of Alabama, George Wallace, said, 'I don't want to teach ungodly humanism in the schools where I'm governor,' and he said, 'Let's get 'em out of here.' " According to Robertson, the county board then said, " 'Well, we don't want to go to Court against you' " and agreed to take secular humanism out of the schools. "So that Alabama is a landmark move for religious freedom for Christian people and we are going to see that followed up in state after state because we can challenge those people in every single state they're doing it," he concluded (March 4, 1986, *700 Club* broadcast, quoted in PAW memorandum, March 5, 1986).

Wallace and the county commissioners were excused from the case. By the time the trial opened, the only defendants left were the state Board of Education and the state superintendent of education. They were supported by a group of parents and teachers who joined *Smith* as defendant-intervenors protesting the effort to remove state-approved textbooks from public schools to accommodate the beliefs of a particular religion.

The *Smith* trial lasted from October 6 through October 22, 1986. A few parents and teachers testified, but most of the witnesses were experts on religion or education, or both. By the end of the first week, their testimony had become so drawn-out and technical that Hand urged the lawyers on both sides to "discuss with your experts ahead of time so that when we ask them the time of day they don't tell us how to build watches" (Trial Transcript, pp. 1035–36).

The court reporter's version of the rapid flow of academic lecturing adds a Twilight Zone quality to the trial transcript. One witness allegedly testified, "Mare [*sic*] anarchy descends upon the world and the culture collapses whether before what Toynbee calls the external Bavarian, the foreign foe, or what he calls the internal Bavarian, the probitarian, the classes within the society which has ceased to believe in anything and which give nothing to the state but their bodies and their prodigy" (p. 1367).

Apart from problems caused by the witnesses' answers, the case suffered from the lawyers' overambitious questions. One state official was asked, "Are your duties persuant [*sic*] to the State statute that you implement these duties that you testified to?" (p. 1464). For once, a witness's response was brief and to the point: "Do I what?" Nevertheless, a few clear threads of argument emerged from the tangled web of expert and legal verbiage.

The plaintiffs in *Smith* wanted to define religion as broadly as possible in order to embrace secular humanism. Their witnesses testified that any world view involving moral choices is a religion, even if it does not include faith in a higher power. Since secular humanism promotes a form of moral choice—situation ethics—it is, they contended, a religion.

According to the plaintiffs, the chief prophet of secular humanism was John Dewey (1859–1952), a prominent educational philosopher who emphasized personal experience and scientific experimentation as the best means to knowledge. Dewey also signed *Humanist Manifesto I* (1933), which begins, "The time has come for widespread recognition of the radical changes in religious beliefs throughout the modern world." According to the manifesto, these "radical changes" should include acknowledgement of biological and social evolution and of moral relativity. Dewey's endorsement of the manifesto convinced the plaintiffs that his influence on American education had turned it into a training ground for secular humanists. The importance they placed on him was so great that one of the defendants, the state superintendent of education, was required to explain under oath why he had named his son "Dewey." The boy was named, the superintendent swore, "after his Granddaddy George Washington Dewey Jones" (p. 1673).

As an example of an officially recognized religion that promotes secular humanist thought, the plaintiffs' expert witnesses singled out the Unitarian Universalist Fellowship because of its emphasis on human reason, goodness, and responsibility. Unitarians accept atheists and agnostics as church members and tolerate a wide variety of individual religious beliefs. National humanist groups, such as the American Humanist Association, also fell under this definition of religion because they promote a particular philosophy of life. The experts' treatment of Dewey, Unitarian Universalism, and other people and movements representing world views of any kind was aimed at eliminating faith in a supernatural being as an essential ingredient of religion. Their goal was to show that ideas their opponents defined as secular—and therefore immune from challenge under the establishment clause—were in reality tenets of the religion of secular humanism.

Smith, with its legion of expert witnesses, included much more sophisticated testimony than *Mozert* did. Using statistics and documentary references, the *Smith* witnesses tried to provide a factual basis for ideas that in *Mozert* were expressed as simple statements of faith. All the same, both lawsuits were based on the same two premises: that every topic is in some way religious, and that any view that contradicts biblical absolutism is part of the religion of secular humanism.

Although the ideas underlying the two lawsuits were similar, the proposed applications were quite different. CWA and the Hawkins County protesters tried, by demanding separate instruction for the protesters' children, to establish the principle that they are entitled to have their religion taught in public schools. NLF and the *Smith* plaintiffs approached the same goal from a steeper angle, trying to prove that no public school student should use textbooks promoting the religion of secular humanism without a Bible-based "balance."

The practical implications of *Mozert* were not trivial: taken to an extreme, the "alternate instruction" principle could fragment public education into destruction. *Smith* went even farther, suggesting that all students should use textbooks purged of secular humanism. With secular humanism defined as whatever is not biblical absolutism, removing it from textbooks would—not potentially, but immediately—end public education by turning it into religious instruction. Both sets of plaintiffs said that they were seeking a balance between two competing religions; but, in practice, their testimony did not include any examples of secular humanist thought that they would have been willing to leave in their children's textbooks. Besides, the Alabama plaintiffs, like their Tennessee counterparts, based their whole balance argument on the notion that their religion and secular humanism represent the only two possible world views.

Since *Mozert* and *Smith* shared the same philosophical base, it is not surprising that they covered many of the same specific topics. One of the most important areas of overlap involved parental authority; both groups of plaintiffs wanted children and adolescents taught to obey their parents absolutely and without question. With this kind of upbringing, they argued, children will grow into adults who make decisions based on the will of God rather than on their own reason and preferences. One of the *Smith* plaintiffs' chief expert witnesses, Dr. William R. Coulson, emphasized this point throughout hours of testimony spread over five days.

Coulson, a licensed clinical psychologist, was instructed in humanistic psychology by Carl Rogers. His training was based on the idea that humans, who are fundamentally good, are capable of making their own decisions and solving their own problems. After several years of association with Rogers, Coulson became disenchanted with humanistic psychology and adopted a radically different set of beliefs. By the time he testified in *Smith*, he was convinced that self-reliance and personal decision making are the worst possible approaches to life.

Most of Coulson's testimony concerned home economics books intended for eleventh- and twelfth-graders, who are typically sixteen to eighteen years old. In addition to chapters on cooking and sewing, the books contained "family life" sections promoting a positive self-image, independent decision making, and personal responsibility. Coulson protested that the books might encourage juvenile delinquents, who do not deserve to have self-esteem, to think positively about themselves. He also argued that encouraging teenagers, whom he called "little children," to think independently violates parents' rights.

One reason for Coulson's opposition to the home economics books was their implication that some day students would grow up and choose their own careers. He testified that defining career selection as a natural part of growing up violates the rights of parents because "in a way it kind of undercuts that family's own enterprise for the book to say authoritatively: You must decide for yourself what role to take. I would imagine a father saying, not in this family" (p. 711).

"Is it wrong to tell a student that he can decide between right and wrong?" Coulson mused during his testimony. "I think it's a terrible mistake and an abuse of the child to tell him that" (p. 575). Asked whether teenagers who are offered drugs have to make a choice, he replied, "No, they don't have to make a choice. They can fall back on the commandments" (p. 644). When a defense lawyer asked whether teenagers who fall back on the commandments are making a choice, the psychologist asserted, "Not if they're well trained. If they're well trained, they have no choice. They cannot but do the right thing" (p. 644).

Coulson also maintained that high school students should not be told that their parents can make mistakes. Instead, teenagers should be encouraged to see their parents as God's representatives who "have some kind of additional—in the case of a believer, God-given assignment than just to be human" (p. 661). Democratic family structures violate God's will, and teenagers should not expect to play any role in family decision making.

Coulson's views were reinforced by another witness, Joan Kendall, former member of the Alabama State Textbook Committee and co-chair of the Eagle Forum Stop Textbook Censorship Committee. She was particularly offended by a home economics book that presented a favorable description of day care centers requiring clients to take classes in parenting skills. "What bothered me," she explained, "was I thought parents were autonomous. I found it problematic and troublesome to me that they [the authors] would espouse that [parental training] to tomorrow's voters. I think the very idea of requiring parents to come and learn how to be effective parents is outrageous" (pp. 2523–24). She also testified, "It's my understanding that parental autonomy is protected in this country. And I don't think we should even begin to undermine or chip away

at that and I can see that that book does that. I find it very bothersome"
(p. 2525).

Kendall mentioned a meeting, sponsored by the Eagle Forum, at which
she had heard Dr. Paul Vitz criticize history books for omitting facts
about religion. Vitz, a key witness for the *Mozert* plaintiffs, went on to
testify for the plaintiffs in *Smith*. Just as Coulson led the attack on home
economics books, Vitz, a psychology professor at New York University,
spearheaded their opposition to history books.

Vitz's testimony in both lawsuits was based on a study he had written
for the National Institute on Education. He analyzed social studies textbooks, basal readers, and American history books to see what, if anything, they said about religion. The *Smith* plaintiffs' strongest opposition
was aimed at American history books, and Vitz provided long lists of
examples to show that the books used by today's high school students
say very little about the role religion has played in the development of
this country. Events that were missing or, in his opinion, inadequately
treated included the religious motivation for the Puritans' settlement of
New England, the existence of Protestant missions to Native Americans,
the role of religion in the abolition of slavery and in the civil rights
movement, and the importance of religion in immigrant cultures. Vitz's
testimony supported the plaintiffs' contention that omitting or blurring
the role religion has played in world events denigrates it by suggesting
that it has not been influential in real life.

PAW and the Alabama school officials shared their opponents' dismay
at the omission of religion from history and social studies textbooks.
There were some differences between defendants and plaintiffs about
exactly what material should be included, but the absence of religion was
equally unacceptable to both groups. The best evidence of their concur-
rence was a paperback book entitled *Looking at History: A Review of
Major U.S. History Textbooks,* by O. L. Davis, Jr., et al. (1986). The
book deplores the neglect of religion in American history books: "Religion is simply not treated as a significant element in American life—it
is not portrayed as an integrated part of the American value system or
as something that is important to individual Americans" (p. 3). The
plaintiffs used the book to show that anti-religious liberals had intimi-
dated publishers into omitting religion from history books. Their point
would have been better taken if *Looking at History* had not been published by PAW.

The defense lawyers pounced on the irony of their opponents' using a
PAW book to argue that PAW and its allies could not possibly believe what
the book said. *Looking at History,* the defense asserted, just goes to show

how wrong the plaintiffs were in blaming secular humanists for the omission of religion from history books. According to the defendants, the real reason publishers leave religion out of their books is that they want to avoid controversy with militant religious groups as well as with atheist activists. The publishers' eventual response to *Smith*, summarized at the end of this chapter, suggests that the defense position was at least partially accurate.

Since the plaintiffs' case was couched in academic terms by scholarly witnesses, the defense replied in kind. Their experts challenged the plaintiffs' definition of religion, describing it as much too broad to merit First Amendment protection. They, like the Hawkins County school officials, also maintained that secular humanism is not a religion, and even if it were, using material that simply coincides with it is not unconstitutional.

The defendants' chief witness was Paul Kurtz, professor of philosophy at the State University of New York and a prominent member of the American Humanist Association. He testified about *Humanist Manifesto II,* which he had drafted in 1973. The earlier version of the manifesto, signed by Dewey, dismisses traditional religion as outmoded and insufficient for the needs of the modern world. *Humanist Manifesto II* attacks it head-on for being "harmful, diverting people with false hopes of heaven hereafter." No one disputed the obvious fact that *Humanist Manifesto II* expresses hostility to traditional theistic religion; the question was whether it is a sacred text of the religion of secular humanism. According to its preface, "Those who sign *Humanist Manifesto II* disclaim that they are setting forth a binding credo; their individual views would be stated in widely varying ways." On the basis of this statement, Kurtz testified that the document represents personal opinion, not religious dogma. He agreed that there is such a thing as secular humanism, but it is not a religion; it is a philosophy that has no transcendent element, no worship services, no body of doctrine, and no claim to absolute truth. Its only view of salvation has to do with pollution and other planetary problems.

Kurtz denied not only that Dewey's teachings continue to dominate American education but also that they can be equated with secular humanism. He saw secular humanism as "broader than the thought of Dewey because it expresses the whole of the modern philosophical outlook [of] which Dewey only represented one small part" (pp. 1699–1700). He also contradicted Coulson's testimony on the grounds that what Coulson condemned was a combination of humanistic psychology and progressive education, not secular humanism.

The testimony in *Smith* was long, rambling, and wide-ranging, but it kept coming back to two central questions: "Is secular humanism a religion?" and "Do the challenged books promote secular humanism in violation of the First Amendment?" Those were clearly the issues the judge's decision would have to address, and Hand had taken the unusual step of announcing his views in advance. In a 111-page decision, he expanded what he had said at the end of *Jaffree*. Secular humanism is indeed a religion, and it permeates public education in violation of the First Amendment. The challenged textbooks are therefore unconstitutional because they represent an establishment of religion in public schools. He ordered that all but one of them be removed from use immediately, except "as a reference source in a comparative religion course that treats all religions equivalently" (Findings of Fact and Conclusions of Law, March 4, 1987, p. 4). The remaining book, Boorstin and Kelly's *A History of the United States,* was spared because it was, in Hand's opinion, the least objectionable of the history texts.

Hand also warned teachers not to say anything to their students that might advance secular humanism. Borrowing an example from Coulson's testimony, he said that telling children not to lie because others might disapprove promotes the religion of secular humanism by offering a human reason for telling the truth, as opposed to saying that lying is forbidden by God. "The state may teach that lying is wrong, as a social and civil regulation, but if, in so doing it advances a reason for the rule, the possible different reasons must be explained evenhandedly" (p. 110).

Hand's decision was reversed by the Eleventh Circuit Court of Appeals, which found that the challenged textbooks did not violate the First Amendment. "Rather," the appeals court ruled, "the message conveyed is one of a governmental attempt to instill in Alabama public school children such values as independent thought, tolerance of diverse views, self-respect, maturity, self-reliance, and logical decision-making. This is an entirely appropriate secular effect" (Opinion, August 26, 1987, p. 9). The court's unequivocal statement that teaching those particular values does not advance a religion was a blow to the national effort to remove such ideas from public schools on First Amendment grounds.

Mozert and *Smith* shared so many common features that the two appeals court opinions almost had to coincide at some points. The Eleventh Circuit Court of Appeals, like the Sixth, held that the First Amendment does not protect individuals from mere exposure to ideas with which they disagree. It also ruled that public school instruction is not unconstitutional simply because it happens to coincide with ideas that the plaintiffs call humanistic, and that neutrality toward religion does not mean equal coverage of different beliefs. The appeals court therefore reversed Hand's judgment and sent the case back to him. Recalling what had happened when they reversed his decision in *Jaffree*, the appeals court justices took the precaution of specifying that they were remanding *Smith* "for the sole purpose of entry by the district court of an order dissolving the injunction and terminating this litigation" (p. 12).

When Hand first turned *Jaffree* into *Smith*, plaintiffs and defendants alike predicted that the case was headed for the Supreme Court again. Nevertheless, *Smith* ended quietly after the appeals court opinion. Petitioning the Supreme Court would have involved a great deal of publicity, and it is possible that Pat Robertson, whose presidential campaign was still going on, wanted to avoid reinforcing his public image as a religious rather than a political figure. Whatever the reason, the time period for filing an appeal to the Supreme Court passed without incident, and *Smith* was over.

NLF and PAW are unlikely bedfellows, but they united briefly in *Smith* to oppose history books that do not include fair coverage of the role religion has played in world events. Textbook publishers got the message that their policy was unacceptable to a surprisingly wide range of the public, so they gave news interviews promising to reform their textbooks. Their plans for improvement were greeted with enthusiasm until representatives of the Association of American Publishers explained their companies' proposals in more detail at a National School Boards Association conference.

Textbooks would, the spokespersons stated, include more information about the positive contributions religion has made to history. They would not, however, include any fact suggesting that the role of religion has ever been anything but benign. Conference participants protested that militant religion has been the motivating force behind persecutions, inquisitions, and wars, but the publishers' representatives remained firm. Associating religion with violence, they explained, does not sell textbooks. It may seem odd that publishers' representatives would reply in this way to an audience of school board members, since school boards make final decisions about textbook selection. The market dynamics of textbook publishing are discussed in detail in chapters 8 and 9; but briefly, the strongest influence on textbook content comes from state-level adoptions, particularly in very large states; local boards and state boards in smaller markets have much less to say. Protesters in Texas, in particular, have targeted negative depictions of religion so successfully for so many years that publishers are reluctant to include that kind of material.

The publishers' responses to *Smith*, like their actions following *Mozert*, illustrate two realities of textbook lawsuits. First, regardless of its legal outcome, a nationally publicized court case can have a direct effect on textbook content. Second, litigation, combined with market forces in large states, encourages publishers to produce textbooks based on avoiding controversy rather than on providing balanced presentations or up-to-date scholarship.

CHAPTER SIX

A Monkey's Uncle

*I am examining you on your fool ideas that no intelligent
Christian on earth believes.*
—CLARENCE DARROW TO WILLIAM JENNINGS BRYAN

In *Mozert* and *Smith,* the plaintiffs argued that American textbooks are
so saturated with secular humanism that public schools are being used
to establish a religion. The courts replied that, even if secular humanism
were declared a religion, using textbooks that happen to coincide with
the beliefs of a particular religion is not in itself unconstitutional. School
boards have the authority to determine curriculum, and their decisions
cannot be successfully challenged in court unless the materials they select
are chosen for primarily religious reasons or have a primarily religious
effect.

As groups like Concerned Women for America, the Eagle Forum, and
the National Legal Foundation realized that they were probably not going
to win textbook lawsuits in federal appeals courts, they gradually changed
their strategy. Instead of mounting legal challenges to school board decisions, they concentrated more and more on influencing school board
votes and state legislation in directions acceptable to them. When they
succeeded, it was their opponents, not they, who had to face the reluctance of American courts to interfere with school curriculum simply
because it coincides with the beliefs of a particular religion. Once a
decision has been made by local or state authorities, it will probably not

be reversed in court unless its religious motivation or effect is unmistakable.

Despite judicial resistance to moderating curricular disputes, there was one area in which opponents of Far Right textbook activists had a reasonably good chance of proving unconstitutional religious bias. The Supreme Court has repeatedly ruled that the history of anti-evolution lobbying by religious groups can be used to show that challenges to the teaching of evolution are religiously motivated. So, when the ACLU challenged a Louisiana state law regulating the teaching of human origins, a century and a half of religious controversy came into play. From this perspective, the events leading up to *Aguillard v. Edwards* began on November 24, 1859, when Charles Darwin's *The Origin of Species* was published.

One of the many ironies surrounding textbook censorship is the fact that Darwin, whose theories have incited such powerful religious opposition, did not deny the existence of a Creator. On the contrary, the final sentence of *The Origin of Species* affirms, "There is grandeur in this view of life, with its several powers, having been originally breathed by the Creator into a few forms or into one; and that, whilst this planet has gone cycling on according to the fixed law of gravity, from so simple a beginning endless forms most beautiful and most wonderful have been, and are being evolved." All the same, Darwin's account of the origins of life differs from the scriptural account of creation, and many of its supporters have not shared his belief in God. The concept of evolution has therefore been challenged by biblical literalists since it first appeared, and, by the time *Aguillard* began, opposition to evolution was already a familiar topic in American courts.

In 1919, sixty years after the publication of *The Origin of Species*, the World's Christian Fundamentals Association (WCFA) was formed to oppose the teaching of evolution in American public schools. Urged on by WCFA lobbyists, more than twenty state legislatures considered anti-evolution resolutions. The best-known of these, Tennessee's "monkey law," took effect on March 13, 1925. The law provided that "it shall be unlawful for any [public school] teacher to teach any theory that denies the story of the Divine Creation of man as taught in the Bible, and to teach, instead, that man has descended from a lower order of animals." The ACLU, then only five years old, offered to defend any teacher who violated it. A substitute biology teacher named John Thomas Scopes accepted the ACLU offer. He read chapters on evolution to his high school classes and was duly arrested and brought to trial.

The WCFA asked William Jennings Bryan, a three-time presidential candidate and one of the nation's best-known orators, to participate in prosecuting Scopes. Bryan, who had been influential in the adoption of the Tennessee statute, agreed. Clarence Darrow, a flamboyant liberal attorney, volunteered to join the team opposing Bryan. The ACLU kept its word by funding the defense, and the battle was on. *Scopes* immediately became a nationally publicized circus, with street vendors selling lemonade and stuffed monkeys. Self-proclaimed Holy Rollers exhorted the crowd to avoid education, which was the surest path to hell. According to one account of the trial, a preacher named Joe Leffew shouted,

> I ain't got no learnin' and never had none. Glory be to the Lamb! Some folks work their hands off up to the elbows to give their young-uns education, and all they do is send their young-uns to Hell ... I ain't let no newspaper into my cabin for nigh unto a year since the Lord bathed me in His blood ... I never sinned enough to look in one of these here almanacs ... I've eight young-uns in the cabin and three in glory, and I know they're in glory because I never learned 'em nothin'. (Quoted in L. Sprague de Camp, *The Great Monkey Trial* [New York: Doubleday, 1968], p. 170)

Early in the trial, news correspondent H. L. Mencken wrote, "it was obvious after a few rounds that the jury would be unanimously for Genesis" (quoted in Arthur and Lila Weinberg, *Clarence Darrow: A Sentimental Rebel* [New York: Putnam, 1980], p. 321); and he was right. After eleven days of testimony, Scopes was convicted. His conviction was later reversed on the technicality that the judge, not the jury, had imposed the $100 fine, but the anti-evolution law remained on the books until its repeal in 1967. Nevertheless, the news coverage of the trial and Darrow's scathing questioning of Bryan did so much damage to the creationist cause that only three other states—Mississippi, Arkansas, and Oklahoma—passed anti-evolution laws. (Oklahoma repealed its law within a year.) The *Scopes* "monkey trial," having met at least some of the ACLU's goals, went down in history as a national symbol of the struggle between science and religious fundamentalism.

It was not until 1968 that the United States Supreme Court issued a definitive opinion on state laws prohibiting the teaching of evolution in public schools. In *Epperson v. Arkansas,* the Court decided that there is no secular reason for banning the teaching of evolution, which means that anti-evolution laws violate the First Amendment by using government power to advance religious beliefs. *Epperson* did not end the movement to oppose the teaching of evolution in public schools; it simply motivated anti-evolutionists to try a new approach. Instead of eliminating the teaching of evolution, they focused on requiring instruction in creationism, which they defined as the theory that all life forms came into existence instantaneously through the action of a single intelligent Creator.

The Louisiana law that sparked *Aguillard* came about because of lobbying by a national organization called the Institute for Creation Research (ICR), based near San Diego, California. The ICR produced a model bill entitled the Balanced Treatment for Creation-Science and Evolution-Science Act and urged state legislatures, especially in the South, to pass it. The bill included a six-point description of the creationist theory that science teachers would be required to consider equally with the theory of evolution:

> Creation-science includes the scientific evidences and related inferences that indicate: (1) Sudden creation of the universe, energy, and life from nothing; (2) The insufficiency of mutation and natural selection in bringing about development of all living kinds from a single organism; (3) Changes only within fixed limits of originally created kinds of plants and animals; (4) Separate ancestry for man and apes; (5) Explanation of the earth's geology by catastrophism, including the occurrence of a worldwide flood; and (6) A relatively recent inception of the earth and living kinds. (Quoted in *McLean v. Arkansas Board of Education,* U.S. District Court Decision, January 5, 1982; 529 F. Supp. 1264 [1982])

The ICR's first success was in Arkansas, where a self-described born-again fundamentalist legislator, state senator James L. Holsted, sponsored the Balanced Treatment Act at the request of a group called the Greater Little Rock Evangelical Fellowship. Without consulting the Department of Education or the attorney general, and without sending the Holsted bill to any committee, the Arkansas state Senate passed it after only a few minutes of debate. The state House of Representatives sent it on to the Education Committee, which conducted a fifteen-minute hearing before recommending passage. During the brief debate in the House, picketers carried signs proclaiming, "Creation science will promote better scientific research, national productivity, and lower inflation" (*Chicago Sun-Times*, March 18, 1981; quoted in American Library Association, *Newsletter on Intellectual Freedom*, 1981, p. 72). On March 19, 1981, Governor Frank D. White signed the bill into law. Two months later, protesters led by the bishops of the United Methodist, Episcopal, Roman Catholic, and African Methodist Episcopal churches in Arkansas petitioned the federal district court to prevent the new law from being enforced. In their lawsuit, *McLean v. Arkansas Board of Education*, they contended that creation science, as defined in the Balanced Treatment Act, is a religious belief and cannot be taught in public schools without violating the First Amendment.

Like the plaintiffs in *Mozert* and *Smith*, the defendants in *McLean* argued that evolution is a tenet of the religion of secular humanism. Teaching creationism as well as evolution would therefore promote religious neutrality by presenting both of the possible views on human origins. Further, the defendants argued, creationism is as scientific as evolution and can therefore be taught as a secular subject.

The ICR attorney who had drafted most of the model Balanced Treatment Act asked permission to participate in the *McLean* defense. The Arkansas attorney general opposed the ICR request, conducted the defense himself, and lost. On January 5, 1982, the United States District Court for the Eastern District of Arkansas struck down the Balanced Treatment Act. According to the court, creationism is religion, not science; and evolution is science, not religion. The court rejected the notion that teaching both creationism and evolution would represent a balanced view of human origins. "The two model approach of the creationists is simply a contrived dualism which has no scientific factual basis or legitimate educational purpose," the *McLean* decision states. "It assumes only two explanations for the origins of life and existence of man, plants and animals" (529 F. Supp. 1266 [1982]).

When the district court struck down the Arkansas Balanced Treatment Act, the ICR and the Moral Majority of Arkansas pressured the state attorney general *not* to appeal. The reason for their concern was that Louisiana had passed a Balanced Treatment Act six months earlier, and the creationists believed that they had a better chance of defending the Louisiana act than the Arkansas act. They were therefore afraid that if the Arkansas attorney general lost again, the resulting Court of Appeals precedent might make it harder to defend the Louisiana law. The attorney general dropped the case, and *McLean* ended with the district court decision.

The Louisiana Balanced Treatment for Creation-Science and Evolution-Science Act, like its Arkansas counterpart, was based on the ICR model bill. Its sponsor was State Senator Bill Keith, whose support had been won by a national lobbying group called Citizens for Fairness in Education, based in Anderson, South Carolina. The stated purpose of the act was to protect academic freedom by prohibiting Louisiana public school teachers from discussing evolution without giving equal attention to creationism, and vice versa. School districts could ignore evolution and creationism altogether, but they could not teach one without the other. The act also provided for the development of creationist curriculum guides and barred discrimination against teachers who declared themselves creation scientists. There was no mention of curriculum guides for evolution or of protection for pro-evolution teachers.

Because of *McLean*, the specific examples of creationist beliefs provided by the ICR model were removed from the Keith bill to make it more general and, its supporters hoped, less vulnerable to legal attack. Despite the vagueness of the Louisiana legislation, there was no ambiguity about the association between creationism and religion. Edward Boudreaux, a prominent creation scientist, testified before the Louisiana state legislature that creation science is based on belief in a single, intelligent Creator. Keith himself told the legislature that he opposed evolution because it violated his religious beliefs and promoted secular humanism and atheism. Like the plaintiffs in *Smith*, Keith argued in favor of equal time for fundamentalist beliefs whenever ideas coinciding with secular humanism were presented in public schools.

The Louisiana state Senate passed the Balanced Treatment Act by a vote of 26–12. Support for the bill was even stronger in the state House of Representatives, which approved the act by a vote of 71-19. Governor David C. Treen signed it on July 20, 1981. Realizing that the law was certain to be challenged in court, the state Department of Education delayed implementing the new curriculum.

Shortly before the passage of the Keith bill, the ICR formed the Creation Science Legal Defense Fund (CSLDF). As its name suggests, the CSLDF was established to defend creationist legislation in the courts. When the ACLU threatened to challenge the new law, the Louisiana attorney general welcomed CSLDF help. He deputized CSLDF attorneys to represent state interests, and they tried to preempt challenges to the act by filing their own lawsuit against the Department of Education for its failure to implement the new curriculum. The suit, *Keith v. Louisiana Department of Education,* petitioned the United States District Court for the Middle District of Louisiana to declare the new law constitutional. The next day, lawyers provided by the ACLU filed suit on behalf of a group of Louisiana parents, teachers, and religious leaders opposed to the Balanced Treatment Act. Contending that the act violated the First Amendment by regulating public school instruction on the basis of religious beliefs, they petitioned the Court to declare it unconstitutional. Since the plaintiffs listed their names alphabetically, a teacher named Don Aguillard headed the list, and the lawsuit was entitled *Aguillard v. Treen.* David C. Treen, the first-named defendant, was governor of Louisiana when the suit was originally filed. When Edwin W. Edwards succeeded him as governor, the suit was renamed *Aguillard v. Edwards.*

With the involvement of the CSLDF and the ACLU, *Aguillard* became yet another tug-of-war between national organizations over the content of public education. The Louisiana clash was, however, especially poignant because of its historic overtones. Fifty-four years after *Scopes,* creationists and the ACLU once again faced each other in a legal battle over the presentation of human origins in American public schools.

The CSLDF lawsuit, *Keith v. Louisiana Department of Education,* was dismissed on the grounds that a federal court cannot be asked to determine the constitutionality of a law whose constitutionality has not been challenged. *Aguillard,* on the other hand, did challenge the constitutionality of the Balanced Treatment Act and was therefore heard by the United States District Court for the Eastern District of Louisiana. The ACLU plaintiffs, pointing to the Louisiana state legislature's debates on the Balanced Treatment Act, contended that its purpose was clearly religious and that its primary effect would be to advance a particular religion. If teachers chose to teach evolution, the law would force them to teach religion as well. If, on the other hand, they chose to avoid creationism by omitting evolution, the law would have had the effect of excluding legitimate academic material solely because it conflicts with the beliefs of a particular religion. The CSLDF defendants replied that the purpose of the Balanced Treatment Act was to promote academic freedom: Louisiana teachers had been omitting creationism from the curriculum because they were afraid that teaching it might be unconstitutional, so the new law would increase their freedom to present creationism without risk.

The district court granted the ACLU's request for summary judgment, ruling that the Balanced Treatment Act was so clearly unconstitutional that no trial was necessary. According to the *Aguillard* decision, "If the state cannot prohibit the teaching of evolution, manifestly it cannot provide that evolution can be taught only if the evolution curriculum is 'balanced' with a curriculum involving tenets of a particular religious sect" (634 F. Supp. 428 [E.D. La. 1985]). The CSLDF appealed the dismissal and lost because the Fifth Circuit Court of Appeals accepted the ACLU's historical argument. According to the appeals court opinion, "Since the two aged warriors, Clarence Darrow and William Jennings Bryan, put Dayton, Tennessee, on the map of religious history in the celebrated *Scopes* trial in 1927" (765 F. 2d 1253 [1985]), the opposition between creationism and evolution has been part of an ongoing religious controversy. "Indeed, the Act continues the battle William Jennings Bryan carried to his grave. The Act's intended effect is to discredit evolution by counterbalancing its teaching at every turn with the teaching of creationism, a religious belief" (765 F. 2d 1257).

The appeals court rejected the defense claim that the purpose of the Balanced Treatment Act was to promote the teaching of a previously neglected scientific approach. If that had been the intent of the act, the appeals court ruled, then the teaching of creation science would have been required whether evolution was taught or not. The court also rejected the defense argument that the Balanced Treatment Act promoted academic freedom, since its effect would have been to reduce, not to increase, teachers' choices. Therefore, having determined that the Balanced Treatment Act was religious in purpose, the Court of Appeals concluded that no further evidence was necessary to declare it unconstitutional.

The CSLDF appealed the case to the United States Supreme Court, which upheld the lower courts by a vote of 7–2. Justice William Brennan, writing for the majority, stated that the Balanced Treatment Act was clearly unconstitutional because its primary purpose was to further the beliefs of a particular religion. "Out of many possible science subjects taught in the public schools," he wrote, "the legislature chose to affect the teaching of the one scientific theory that historically has been opposed by certain religious sects" (p. 4864). After reviewing the legislative history of the Balanced Treatment Act and declaring that the language of the act itself could not possibly be interpreted as serving a secular purpose, he delivered the judgment of the Court:

> The Louisiana Creationism Act advances a religious doctrine by requiring either the banishment of the theory of evolution from public school classrooms or the presentation of a religious viewpoint that rejects evolution in its entirety. The Act violates the Establish-

ment Clause of the First Amendment because it seeks to employ the symbolic and financial support of government to achieve a religious purpose. The judgment of the Court of Appeals therefore is *Affirmed.* (*United States Law Week,* June 16, 1987, p. 4865)

The two Supreme Court members who opposed the majority opinion were Chief Justice William Rehnquist and Justice Antonin Scalia. They challenged their colleagues' use of the "*Lemon* test" (*Lemon v. Kurtzman,* 1971), which defines three conditions every law must meet in order to be consistent with the establishment clause of the First Amendment. "First, the legislature must have adopted the law with a secular purpose. Second, the statute's principal or primary effect must be one that neither advances nor inhibits religion. Third, the statute must not result in an excessive entanglement of government with religion" (p. 4861). The majority of the Supreme Court agreed with the lower courts that the Balanced Treatment Act failed the first *Lemon* requirement, the "secular purpose test," because its primary purpose was not secular. According to Scalia and Rehnquist, a law is constitutional if it has *any* secular purpose, even if its primary purpose is religious. Since the Louisiana state legislature claimed to have acted with a secular purpose—academic freedom—Rehnquist and Scalia argued that the Balanced Treatment Act passed the secular purpose test.

Rehnquist and Scalia did not merely disagree with the majority's understanding of the secular purpose test: they argued that the test itself is illogical and unenforceable, especially in view of the exceptions and limitations included in previous Supreme Court rulings. "Government," they mocked, "may not act with the purpose of advancing religion, except when forced to do so by the Free Exercise Clause (which is now and then); or when eliminating existing governmental hostility to a religion (which exists sometimes); or even when merely accommodating governmentally uninhibited religious practices, except that at some point (it is unclear where) intentional accommodation results in the fostering of religion, which is of course unconstitutional" (p. 4875). Considering all the difficulties and inconsistencies they saw in the secular purpose test, they recommended eliminating it altogether from arguments about the constitutionality of government actions.

Attacks on the *Lemon* test in recent Supreme Court opinions raise questions about the continuation of religious neutrality as it has been defined for the last two decades. Had the minority view prevailed in *Aguillard,* Louisiana public school teachers would now be required to present ideas based on the Bible as the scientific equivalent of evolution.

A precedent would also have been set for similar cases involving other topics that fundamentalist activists consider tenets of the religion of secular humanism. On March 19, 1991, the Supreme Court agreed to a request by the Bush administration to reexamine the entire *Lemon* test, which has been questioned not only by Rehnquist and Scalia, but also by Justices Sandra Day O'Connor and Anthony M. Kennedy. The votes of the newest members of the Court, Bush appointees David H. Souter and Clarence Thomas, are likely to determine whether the *Lemon* test will continue to dominate legal cases involving the establishment of religion.

CHAPTER SEVEN

Theme

and Variations

There must be some First Amendment recourse against the tyranny of board taste. Literary classics generally considered part and parcel of a liberal arts education cannot be constitutionally bannable because a board doesn't "like" them.
—ACLU BRIEF IN *VIRGIL*

When textbook protesters oppose the teaching of evolution, their religious motivation is obvious. As the Supreme Court has repeatedly asked, what secular reason could there be for excluding science from public school classes? Literature, however, is easier to challenge because the ideas it contains are often ambiguous or abstract, opening the door to a wide range of justifications for declaring particular literary works unsuitable for certain age groups. Public schools are, of course, expected to respect community moral norms, but the distinction between morality and religion is fuzzy enough to cause real difficulty in distinguishing between community values and religious beliefs.

Profanity is a good example of (and a frequent response to) this problem. Some textbook protesters assert that novels or short stories containing the word *damn* should not be taught in public schools because the word violates reasonable standards of morality. Their opponents reply that *damn* is objectionable only because it is offensive to certain religions; in itself, it is nothing more than a mild expletive. On a broader scale, one of the most common reasons for challenging literature is language that some parents define as vulgar or profane. If school boards vote to retain the books, they are accused of promoting secular humanism; if they ban them, they are accused of advancing fundamentalism.

Charges of violating the First Amendment were routinely hurled back and forth during disputes in the 1980s about literary works, but few controversies ever went to court because of the well-known reluctance of judges to interfere in educational decisions. One exception was a Florida case in which protesters convinced PAW that books were being banned for such clearly religious reasons that a lawsuit might succeed. The controversy began at Mowat Junior High School in Bay County, which had an innovative English program based on "young adult" literature—books written specifically for adolescent readers. In 1985, when the program had been in place for three years, the California Achievement Test reading scores of its students averaged two grade levels higher than the scores of students completing work at any other Bay County junior high school. Mowat's English program had also been designated a Center of Excellence by the National Council of Teachers of English. Only 150 secondary schools in the United States and Canada are Centers of Excellence, and Mowat was the only junior high school in Florida to be so designated. Some young adult novels discuss sexuality, family conflict, and drug abuse, so Mowat teachers required parental consent forms for any book that could be considered controversial. Alternate readings were available if parents or students objected to the assigned material. All the same, not everyone was pleased with Mowat's innovative approach. Late in 1985, Bay County superintendent of schools Leonard Hall received a letter from Marian Collins, grandmother of a Mowat Junior High School student. Collins said that a novel entitled *I Am the Cheese*, by Robert Cormier, included vulgar language and advanced "humanism and behaviorism" (Letter to Hall, November 14, 1985). Hall immediately ordered the principal of Mowat to ban the book without going through the district's review procedures. His action was especially controversial because the parents of ninety-one out of ninety-five students had already signed consent forms allowing their children to read the book.

I Am the Cheese, which had been part of the Mowat English program for three years, tells the story of a teenage boy whose father had testified against a criminal syndicate that had infiltrated the United States government. While the boy, Adam Farmer, was still too young to remember, the family had been given new identities through a witness protection program. Adam opens the novel by talking about being on a long-distance bicycle journey in search of his father, but it soon becomes clear that he is actually in a mental institution. In dialogues with a therapist/interrogator, he struggles to repress his memory of events that occurred when his family was found and attacked by a government agency still under the control of the crime syndicate. The title of *I Am the Cheese,* taken from the children's song "The Farmer in the Dell," refers to the cheese—Adam—standing alone at the end of the story.

When Cormier's novel appeared in 1977, it was listed among the *School Library Journal* Best Books of the Year, the *New York Times* Outstanding Books of the Year, and the American Library Association's Best Books for Young Adults. It also received glowing reviews in *Newsweek,* the *New York Times Book Review,* and the *Bulletin of the Center for Children's Books,* among others.*Booklist* said that "Cormier's theme of one person against overwhelming odds is developed here with stunning force in a novel which perceptive junior high readers can appreciate on its several levels" (May 1977). Nevertheless, Collins considered it an immoral book, and, two months after her original complaint, she wrote to Hall again. She thanked him for his intervention but pointed out that the novel was still being used at Mowat. She also wrote to the principal of Mowat, Joel Creel. When, she asked, was he going to comply with the superintendent's order?

Collins's daughter, Claudia Shumaker, had a daughter of her own in the seventh grade at Mowat. In response to a suggestion from Hall, Shumaker filled out a "Request for Reconsideration of Instructional Materials" form protesting the use of *I Am the Cheese.* She listed two types of objections to the book: first, she saw it, not as suspenseful, but as "morbid and depressing"; second, she objected to "crude and vulgar" language and sexual references (Request for Reconsideration, April 22, 1986). Attached to the request form were photocopies of four pages of the novel with a few sentences bracketed or underlined. One page describes a petting scene between Adam and an adolescent girlfriend. The others contain single references to breasts (Amy says, " 'Try lugging these things all over town every day' "), farts (" 'Look, Ace, don't let a few farts bother you' "), Kotex ("She abandoned [a shopping cart full of baby food] in front of the Kotex display"), and shit (" 'Shit on your old package' "). This time Creel sent the book to the District Review Committee, withdrawing it from classroom use while it was under consideration. A month later, the committee recommended that *I Am the Cheese* be reinstated. Hall did not respond, and the school year ended with the book still banned.

Two days after the review committee submitted its report, Shumaker's father, Charles Collins, became involved in the controversy. Collins, a prominent local real estate developer, had been a member of the Bay County School Board from 1954 to 1970. He agreed with his wife and daughter about the books used in the Mowat English program and expressed his views in a letter to the parents of all Mowat students. His letter, dated May 22, 1986, charged that novels used in the program contain "obscene language and sexual explicities *[sic]*." He amplified his views in a newspaper interview: "'There's no respect in this county any more,' Collins said. 'You cannot go down the halls of the high schools and junior highs without hearing the dirtiest language you ever heard in your life. I believe these filthy little books are the cause'" (*Bradenton* [Florida] *Herald,* May 31, 1987). He objected to *I Am the Cheese* in particular because "[s]ubversive teaching categorizing government officials as agents murdering parents and children is very unhealthy and disturbing to students in Jr. High School" (Open letter, May 22, 1986). Hall agreed, arguing that students should not be taught that a government department might be corrupt and unworthy of trust.

The Mowat English teachers called an evening meeting of all concerned parents, students, and teachers. Several hours before the meeting, Hall loudly berated the teachers, whom he blamed for the controversy. According to a complaint some of them later filed, he ordered them to exclude all students from the meeting and to tell the students that the exclusion was the teachers' idea. He also told them not to discuss the First Amendment with their classes or answer any student questions about the dispute. In a newspaper interview, he explained, "I think [the controversy] caused a lot of students to think about their rights and took their minds off their studies. We are here to educate the students, not to confuse them" (*Panama City News Herald,* June 11, 1987).

The meeting was held without students. A few of the three hundred participants expressed concerns based on Collins's letter, but the vast majority supported the Mowat English program. Ironically, Collins himself was not permitted to speak. After their encounter with Hall, the teachers had decided to limit participation to the parents of Mowat students, which disqualified Collins. Throughout the controversy, Hall wanted to allow all citizens to file protests against books taught in the public schools, whereas most of the teachers wanted to limit challenges to parents of public school students.

On the first day of summer recess, Hall not only rejected the review committee's recommendation to reinstate *I Am the Cheese* but also announced sweeping changes. From now on, all books except state-approved textbooks were removed from use pending a school board review. Even literary classics that had been taught in Bay County for many years were affected by the new policy, so English programs using novels or other book-length literary works rather than state-approved textbooks were out of business until the board had acted on each book separately. Teachers were required to write a rationale for each book, summarizing its plot and themes and explaining its value and the way in which it would be presented. Hall's action included not only books taught as part of the curriculum, but also "classroom libraries"—books, mostly paperbacks, that teachers kept in their classrooms to encourage voluntary student reading. Such libraries were particularly troubling to Shumaker, who protested to a reporter that walking into a Mowat classroom was "like walking into a B. Dalton with desks. There are books just lining the walls" (Peter Carlson, "A Chilling Case of Censorship," *The Washington Post Magazine*, January 4, 1987). Some classroom libraries contained over a hundred titles, and teachers were given the choice of submitting a separate rationale for each book or dismantling the library.

Hall proposed to the school board that all materials other than state-approved textbooks be reviewed according to a five-step procedure. First, the teacher would submit a detailed rationale for each book to be included in the curriculum or shelved in the classroom. Second, the principal would either reject the rationale or send it to the county instructional staff. Third, the staff would either reject it or send it to the superintendent. Fourth, the superintendent would either reject it or send it to the school board. Fifth, the school board would make a final decision. The board would also receive a list of rejected books. Rejection at any level would terminate the procedure, and teachers would not be able to appeal. Hall's proposal also included a procedure allowing any citizen who objected to a board-approved book to appeal to a school committee, then to a district committee consisting of four teachers and five laypeople, then to the school board. The proposal provided no appeal procedure for citizens who disagreed with a decision to reject a book.

Parents and teachers opposed to Hall's proposal protested that it was ham-fistedly authoritarian and heavily biased toward excluding, rather than including, material. They also objected to his requirement that all materials in classroom libraries or on English reading lists be treated as if they had never been used in Bay County, even if they had been in use for years. Seventeen of the twenty-five citizens who spoke at a stormy four-hour school board meeting in August opposed Hall's proposal. The board added a grace period allowing all books used in 1985–86 to be used in 1986–87, pending a review to be completed in time for the 1987–88 academic year. Making no other changes to Hall's proposal, the board approved it by a unanimous vote.

One of the Mowat teachers who had helped establish its English program led the protest against the new board policy. Gloria Pipkin had chaired the English Department for four years and had been Mowat's Teacher of the Year in 1983. She also edited the *Florida English Journal* and was a former director of the Florida Council of Teachers of English and a former president of the Bay Language Arts Council. When classes resumed in the fall of 1986, she promptly submitted a request to teach *I Am the Cheese* to an advanced eighth-grade class. Creel consulted Hall, who sent him to the office of Collins's attorney. There he received a letter denying permission to use *I Am the Cheese* because it contains vulgar language and could encourage rebellion against parental authority. Creel sent the letter to Pipkin on Mowat stationery as his response to her request. She sent a revised rationale for *I Am the Cheese* to Hall, who replied that her principal's disapproval had ended the matter.

Despite Hall's letter, Pipkin asked to be listed on the agenda for the next school board meeting. When the meeting began, the chair tried to prevent her from speaking by reminding her that, as a Mowat employee, she was subject to Creel's authority. She was finally heard when the school board's attorney pointed out that she had to be allowed to speak because she was on the agenda. "Make no mistake about it," she asserted, "*I Am the Cheese* has been banned in the Bay County school system because the ideas it contains are offensive to a few: No ruse can obscure that fact" (*Panama City News Herald*, November 3, 1986). The board did not respond to her statement.

The Bay County textbook controversy became national news on January 4, 1987, when the *Washington Post*'s Sunday magazine ran a cover story, "A Chilling Case of Censorship," supporting the protesters. The story described threats and violence directed against some Mowat teachers and against a television reporter, Cindy Hill. According to the *Post*, action against Hill began immediately after she revealed that a petition Collins had presented to the school board had contained fewer than one-third the number of voter signatures claimed. Within fifteen minutes of the newscast, she began receiving telephone calls calling her a Communist, an atheist, and a daughter of Satan. One anonymous caller recited, "Roses are red / Violets are black / You'd look good / With a knife in your back" ("Chilling Case," p. 17). Within a few days, her apartment was set on fire and a fake bomb was taped inside her car engine. Collins, asked about these events, stated, "The thing in her car was just a joke. The fire didn't burn anything. It just smoked. That's a good way to get your apartment painted by the landlord. I'm thoroughly disgusted with these trite little people in this county" ("Chilling Case," p. 40). The Mowat teachers themselves suffered no physical violence, but they did receive verbal threats. Pipkin found a note in her school mailbox: "Woe to those who call evil good and good evil, who put darkness for light and light for darkness, who put bitter for sweet, for they have revoked the law of the lord. For this you all shall DIE. One by one, Hill, Hawks, Farrell, Pipkin" (Quoted in "Chilling Case," p. 10).

Approximately two months after the *Washington Post* article appeared, two Mowat teachers submitted a request to teach a nonfiction book, *Never Cry Wolf,* which describes the author's study of Arctic wolves. Creel and two county resource specialists had approved the request, and it was sent to Hall. He returned it with a memorandum asking Creel to reread the board policy and then reconsider his approval of *Never Cry Wolf.* Although Hall's action was not part of the review procedure, Creel promptly rejected the book. Hall later explained that *Never Cry Wolf* was unacceptable because of a single word that a dogsled driver shouted to a barking team: "FURCRISAKESTOPYOUGODAMNSONS-ABITCHES!" To the superintendent, one profanity was enough to damn a book.

The controversy focused at first on Mowat Junior High School, but teachers in the county's three senior high schools also had to submit rationales. Hall's academic background was in physical education and mathematics, so English teachers wondered what system he would use to decide which literature to recommend to the board. In the spring of 1987, he answered their question by adding a new step to the review procedure. Senior high school English teachers were required to classify each work of literature as Category I, II, or III. Category I was reserved for books containing "no vulgar, obscene, or sexually explicit material." Category II was for books containing "very limited vulgarity and no sexually explicit or obscene material." Category III books contained "quite a bit of vulgarity, or obscene and/or sexually explicit material" (Memorandum to School Board, May 6, 1987). When Hall received the lists, he accepted or rejected books by categories. His decisions were not the same for every school; for example, he accepted Categories I and II from Bay High School's report but only Category I from Mosley High School's report. As a result, some books that could be taught in one Bay County school were banned in another.

Cumulatively, Hall's decisions excluded a total of sixty-four classics from use in all or part of Bay County. Among the rejected books were Sophocles' *Oedipus Rex;* Chaucer's *Canterbury Tales;* Shakespeare's *Twelfth Night, The Merchant of Venice, King Lear,* and *Hamlet; The Autobiography of Benjamin Franklin;* Twain's *The Prince and the Pauper;* Dickens's *Great Expectations;* Crane's *The Red Badge of Courage;*

Brontë's *Wuthering Heights*; Hardy's *The Mayor of Casterbridge*; Fitzgerald's *The Great Gatsby*; Hemingway's *A Farewell to Arms* and *The Old Man and the Sea*; and Faulkner's *Intruder in the Dust*. Anticipating that his wholesale removal of literary classics would cause an uproar, Hall pointed out that parents who opposed his decisions could arrange for their own children to read the banned books in school on an independent study basis. Teachers were, however, forbidden to discuss the excluded material with more than one student at a time, even if thirty students' parents sent in requests for the same book.

Hall's action reversed the district's previous policy, in which books that were objectionable to some parents were taught as the norm, and their children were offered alternate readings. Under the new policy, it was the children of parents who approved of the banned books who would be segregated from the other students because of their parents' beliefs. Hall's policy coincided with a nationwide movement in which textbook activists who regard their own views as mainstream and those of public educators as objectionably humanistic protest that sending their children out of the classroom implies that their values are nonstandard. Rather, they contend, humanists' children should be the ones sent out of the classroom to do alternate assignments while the majority of the class works on material that, in the protesters' view, belongs in public schools.

Hall's exclusion of sixty-four classics led to a storm of public ridicule. An editorial cartoon in the local newspaper featured a shady character in an alley asking a Bay County student, "Pssst! Hey kid! Wanna buy a Category III?" In another cartoon, a student is asked, "Read any good books lately?" "Not really," the student replies; "I'm not allowed to" (*Panama City News Herald*, May 13, 1987). Letters to the *News Herald* editor were equally scathing. "It occurs to this writer," said one letter, "that perhaps we are committing a grave error in teaching our children to read. If we eliminate reading skills, we can eliminate access to *all* English literature which may contain a lot of vulgar language.... Let us exercise full control over what our children learn by promoting full illiteracy in Bay County schools.... Illiteracy is our most effective weapon against books" (May 14, 1987). Another letter writer was more succinct. "When," she asked, "is the next election?" (May 13, 1987).

On May 12, 1987, forty-four Bay County parents, teachers, and students filed suit against Hall, Creel, and the school board. PAW provided legal representation for the protesters. A student named Jennifer Farrell was listed first among the plaintiffs, and Hall was listed first among the defendants, so the case was named *Farrell v. Hall*. The school board called a meeting for the next day and arrived to find that the chairman of PAW and representatives of the television program *60 Minutes* were present. " 'You know you've got trouble,' a school spokesperson told a reporter, 'when Mike Wallace shows up at your door' " ("Burning Issues," *Bradenton Herald*, May 31, 1987). A *60 Minutes* producer conducted lengthy interviews with everyone involved in the case, but the show was never completed.

By the end of the meeting, which lasted for eight hours, the board had decided to hold another meeting to discuss proposed changes in the review policy. The next meeting resulted in a revised policy grandfathering any book used in 1986–87 and recommended by the school principal. Teachers would also be able to appeal the rejection of a book. The board contended that the revisions made *Farrell* moot, but the plaintiffs disagreed. From their perspective, the new policy did too little and came too late. *I Am the Cheese* and other young adult books were still banned at Mowat because Hall's prohibitions had prevented them from being used in 1986–87, so they could not be grandfathered under the new board policy. More significantly, the issue of the superintendent's control over the addition of new books to the curriculum had not been resolved to the satisfaction of his opponents.

The plaintiffs' complaint in *Farrell v. Hall* asked the court to restore *I Am the Cheese* and the other young adult books still excluded under the board's new policy. The complaint also attacked the policy itself, asserting that it produced a "chilling effect" on academic freedom by placing an unreasonable burden on teachers wishing to use materials other than state-approved textbooks. Any teacher keeping a classroom library, for example, would have to write rationales for approximately one hundred books. The new policy also allowed Hall to continue pressuring subordinates into rejecting books for reasons the plaintiffs considered unconstitutional. To them, the school board's review policy, even in its revised form, denied students their First Amendment rights to receive information and to be educated in accordance with the wishes of their parents. It also denied teachers their rights of free speech and academic freedom. Most importantly, the plaintiffs argued, Hall had violated the First Amendment by using his position as superintendent to exclude books solely because they violated his religious beliefs, and the new selection policy did nothing to prevent such behavior in the future.

Since school authorities have broad discretion in selecting instructional materials, Hall's motivation for banning certain books was essential to the plaintiffs' case. Even before the complaint was filed, local news reports had suggested that his actions were based on religion. In a newspaper interview, a school district spokesperson stated that "Leonard Hall is a devout fundamentalist. It is his opinion that the word 'goddamn,' in any book, one time, obliterates any literary value that book may have" ("Burning Issues"). The same news article states that Hall had been so uncompromising in his religious views as a state legislator "that his own party gerrymandered his district to force him out."

In an effort to prove Hall's religious motivation to the satisfaction of the court, the *Farrell* plaintiffs asked a faculty member at Florida State University to testify for them. John S. Simmons, a professor of English education and reading, had invited Hall to participate in a seminar on censorship. According to Simmons's affidavit, Hall began his presentation by saying "that he believed that he had been elected to the post of Superintendent in order to restore Christian values to the schools of Bay County" (August 5, 1986, pp. 1–2). Hall also, Simmons said, expressed a preference for limiting instruction to state-approved textbooks. In response to questions from seminar participants, he said that he would be open to the possibility of removing books on the basis of objections involving feminism, consumerism, environmentalism, racism, or other considerations. Simmons testified, "I then pointed out that, in principle, his approach could lead to a situation in which *no* books were available for classroom use because all contained ideas objectionable to one group or another. Mr. Hall stated that that was correct" (p. 2). As Simmons recalled the event, Hall appeared entirely untroubled by the prospect of excluding all novels, plays, and other literature except state-approved textbooks from elementary and secondary schools. Simmons's interpretation of Hall's willingness to restrict student reading was supported by a *Panama City News Herald* interview in which Hall warned that reading "is where you get ideas from. It puts ideas into their (students') heads" (June 11, 1987).

According to the plaintiffs, Hall's concern about the effects of student reading sometimes led him to reject books explicitly because of their ideas, as opposed to their language. He said publicly that he had removed *I Am the Cheese* because it presented a negative view of a United States government department, prompting a journalist to observe that the book "was banned because 'of its negative view of the federal government's witness-protection program.' Good grief! What will they protect Bay County children against next? The depressing knowledge of the size of the federal debt?" (*Jacksonville Journal,* July 1, 1987). The plaintiffs argued that Hall was violating the Constitution by removing books on the basis of his own religious or political beliefs. Their accusation also extended to books he banned solely for vulgar or obscene language because he refused to define what the words *vulgar* and *obscene* meant to him. His opponents contended that by keeping his standards for excluding books very vague, he was able to claim that he was removing them solely because of their language when he was in fact using language as an excuse to ban books whose ideas offended his religious beliefs. Pointing to Hall's overt religious statements and to his sweeping rejections of literary classics taught in Bay County for decades, the plaintiffs concluded that the school board had acted improperly in leaving him with so much authority over the selection and rejection of books.

Throughout the legal proceedings, the defendants continued to maintain that the revised selection policy answered most of the plaintiffs' complaints. Since *I Am the Cheese* could be resubmitted under the revised policy, they argued, complaints about its removal under the original policy were moot. The revised policy had not yet been tested, so any challenge to it was premature; and besides, courts should not interfere in educational matters. The plaintiffs replied vigorously that courts should indeed intervene when school boards violate the First Amendment. They also protested that the new policy, which provided no time limits, was allowing officials to exercise pocket vetos by doing nothing about teacher requests for months.

While the case was in progress, Pipkin again submitted a rationale for *I Am the Cheese*. This time, Creel and the county curriculum officials approved the book. Hall rejected it, and the board upheld his action by a vote of 4-1. The plaintiffs therefore asserted, "It is disingenuous at best for Defendant Hall to argue to this Court that the *I Am the Cheese* controversy is moot, or that the Defendants' minds are sufficiently open on this issue that it can or should be resubmitted to those minds" (Plaintiffs' Memorandum in Opposition to Defendant Hall's Motion to Dismiss, September 16, 1987, p. 22, n. 10).

Responding to voluminous paperwork from both sides, Judge Roger Vinson of the United States District Court for the Northern District of Florida issued an order upholding the plaintiffs in part and the defendants in part. In the teachers' favor, Vinson pointed out that Hall

> accepts as true . . . [that his] actions were motivated by his personal beliefs which form the basis for his conservative educational policy. Hall believes that his duty as superintendent is to restore Christian values to the Bay County school system. He thinks that one vulgarity in a work of literature is sufficient reason to keep the book from the Bay County school curriculum. Hall's opposition to *I Am the Cheese* arises solely from his personal opposition to the ideas expressed in

the book. He believes that it is improper to question the trustworthiness of the government. Thus, students should not be presented with such ideas. (Order, July 18, 1988, p. 10)

Vinson denied motions to dismiss the case and found that the school board's implementation of the revised policy continued most of the activities to which the plaintiffs had objected. He also ruled that federal courts have an obligation to intervene in educational matters when First Amendment issues are involved. On the other hand, he supported the defendants' position by sharply limiting the topics he would consider. Finding that removing books because of one vulgar word is within the school board's authority, he dismissed the parts of the plaintiffs' complaint relating to the banning of books on the basis of language.

Vinson took the middle ground in discussing the plaintiffs' accusation that the defendants had removed books because they disagreed with the ideas the books contained: "Local school officials may establish and implement the curriculum to transmit community values, a task which requires decisions based on the social and ethical values of the school officials.... On the other hand, the discretion of state and local school authorities must be exercised in a manner that comports with the first amendment. Local school officials may not suppress ideas simply because they disagree with those ideas so as to create a 'pall of orthodoxy' in the classroom" (pp. 30–31). At the end of his order, Vinson summarized his decisions. While denying the defendants' motions to dismiss the case entirely, he did dismiss all of the plaintiffs' claims except their assertion that Hall and the board had removed *I Am the Cheese* and other works in an effort to suppress ideas with which they disagreed. The review policy itself was, in the judgment of the court, acceptable because school boards have the right to choose books by whatever process they wish. If there is evidence that a board decision is made for illegal or arbitrary reasons, the *decision* can be challenged, but the *policy* is legal. Similarly, school boards have the right to regulate the content of school libraries, including classroom libraries, in any way they wish.

Both sides prepared documents responding to the judgment, but before the court had time to process the new arguments, the case changed radically. Hall had decided not to run for reelection, and on December 31, 1988, his term as superintendent of schools expired. As soon as he was out of office, he petitioned the court to dismiss the case against him, since he was no longer in a position to grant the relief the plaintiffs sought. His successor, Jack Simonson, asked for time to try to resolve the situation amicably. Vinson ruled that Simonson automatically re-placed Hall as a defendant and granted a sixty-day suspension.

The suspension lasted far beyond the original sixty days. After three years of settlement negotiations between the school board attorney and the PAW lawyers, a revised policy for approving new instructional materials was accepted by the school board after undergoing public review. Bay County teachers were pleased with the new policy, which sets time limits for each stage of the review process to prevent principals or school district personnel from keeping a book out of the schools by simply ignoring a teacher's request to use it. The revised policy also allows teachers to appeal negative decisions about adding new materials to the curriculum, and it spells out a procedure for handling challenges to materials that are already in the classroom. Finally, the new policy includes "sunshine" provisions to insure that all parents whose children use a particular book are aware of any complaint against it in time to support or oppose the complaint, and that parents and teachers know exactly what has or has not been approved for certain grade levels and why.

Since Superintendent Hall left office, several changes have taken place in the Bay County school district. The terms of two of the five board members have expired, and their successors favor less restrictive measures than those proposed by Hall. The remaining members include the one who consistently voted against Hall in 4–1 decisions, giving the board a potential 3–2 majority for a relatively liberal textbook selection policy. Mowat Junior High School, now Mowat Middle School, is under new leadership, and Creel is principal of a brand-new junior high school near the beach in Bay County. All eleven of the English teachers who were at Mowat during the controversy have resigned, and the department is no longer listed as a Center of Excellence by the National Council of Teachers of English.

The composition of the new school board is especially important because Vinson's order, like the decisions of other courts involved in textbook controversies, affirmed the board's almost unlimited power over curriculum. He was prepared to rule against inconsistent applications of policy or against specific decisions based on flagrant religious bias, but he dismissed all of the plaintiffs' complaints about the review policy itself. The policy was changed in a direction favorable to the *Farrell* plaintiffs because—and *only* because—the board agreed to it.

The crucial role that school boards play in deciding whether certain literary classics violate community moral standards was illustrated by case after case in the 1980s. In the Bay County dispute, the board countermanded Hall's exclusion of sixty-four classics in time to restore the books to the curriculum before classes resumed in September. Elsewhere in the country, however, literary classics have been taken out of the hands of students because school boards have decided that the books contain not only vulgarity, profanity, and sexuality, but also descriptions of situations that violate conventional moral values. Oedipus kills his father and marries his mother; Hamlet's uncle murders his brother in order to marry his brother's wife; and Gatsby hosts lavishly alcoholic parties. Public school personnel have traditionally assumed that allowing senior high school students to read *Oedipus Rex, Hamlet,* and *The Great Gatsby* does not violate reasonable standards of morality, but Hall was not alone in his conviction that no literary merit justifies the use of books that present immoral behavior. Throughout the 1980s, individuals and organizations across the country pitted their interpretation of community moral values against the importance of teaching the classics.

Controversies over the teaching of classic literature consistently involve the same two constitutional issues that the *Farrell* plaintiffs raised. First, is the stricter moral view unacceptably motivated by religious beliefs? Second, are charges of immorality merely excuses for removing books whose political or social ideas offend some people? John Steinbeck's novel *The Grapes of Wrath,* which was one of the most challenged books in American schools in the 1980s, was usually attacked for its use of profane language. It also presents capitalism in a negative light, and several groups of fundamentalist textbook activists have maintained that support for free enterprise is part of their religion. People who favor teaching *The Grapes of Wrath* contend that the profanity charge masks a desire to suppress socialistic ideas.

During the 1980s, the American Library Association reported challenges to a long list of books, including Sophocles' *Oedipus Rex*; Aristophanes' *Lysistrata*; Chaucer's *The Canterbury Tales*; Shakespeare's *Macbeth, Twelfth Night, The Merchant of Venice, Hamlet,* and *King Lear*; *The Autobiography of Benjamin Franklin*; Twain's *Huckleberry Finn*; Shelley's *Prometheus Unbound*; Hardy's *The Mayor of Casterbridge*; Steinbeck's *Of Mice and Men, The Grapes of Wrath, The Pearl,* and *East of Eden*; Miller's *Death of a Salesman* and *The Crucible*; O'Neill's *Long Day's Journey into Night, The Emperor Jones,* and *Desire Under the Elms*; Hemingway's *A Farewell to Arms* and *The Old Man and the Sea*; Williams's *The Glass Menagerie*; Fitzgerald's *The Great Gatsby*; and Faulkner's *As I Lay Dying* and *Intruder in the Dust.* Some protests succeeded, and school boards banned the challenged books. Others failed, and the books remained.

No matter which way a board ruled, the losing side almost always protested that the winners' religious views—humanistic or fundamentalist—were being given preferred status in the public schools. On the rare occasions when a school board's decision to ban a book included enough specific religious references to justify a First Amendment challenge, the task of the protesters' attorneys was not to prove that the excluded books were of great literary merit, or that the removal was opposed by a majority of the community, or that the books were not immoral. Since school boards have almost absolute authority to select instructional materials, those arguments would have been useless. What the protesters had to prove was that the banning of certain books had the motive or effect of promoting religion, because only on that basis would an establishment clause case have a chance of success.

One lawsuit in which parents challenged a school board's removal of classic literature began in Columbia County, Florida, in the spring of 1986. Unlike the controversy already in progress in neighboring Bay County, the Columbia County dispute involved state-approved literature anthologies. For approximately ten years, Columbia High School had offered a two-semester course called "Humanities to 1500." The only humanities book on the state-approved list was *The Humanities: Cultural Roots and Continuities;* Columbia High School was using Volume I for the first semester and Volume II for the second semester. The course was an elective for juniors and seniors, typically sixteen to eighteen years old. In addition to the optional status of the course as a whole, students in "Humanities to 1500" or their parents could request alternate readings if they found any of the assignments offensive.

During the 1985–86 academic year, the daughter of a fundamentalist minister, Reverend Fritz Fountain, took the humanities course. Fountain objected to two selections in Volume I of *Humanities*: "The Miller's Tale," by Chaucer, and *Lysistrata,* by Aristophanes. In *Lysistrata,* a fifth-century Greek drama, an Athenian woman persuades other women to deny sex to their husbands until the men promise to stop fighting wars. "The Miller's Tale," a fourteenth-century English *fabliau,* features a young wife who cuckolds her old husband. The students were not assigned to read either *Lysistrata* or "The Miller's Tale," although selections from *Lysistrata* were read aloud in class.

Fountain filled out a form requesting reconsideration of *Humanities,* Volume I. On the form, he mentioned not only vulgar language and sexual references but also "promotion of women's lib" (Request Form for Examination of School Media, no date). Just as Collins rejected both vulgar language and disrespect for government in *I Am the Cheese*, Fountain's request combined objections to sexuality with opposition to a liberal social movement. Both Collins and Fountain were also convinced that material they found objectionable did not belong in the hands of *any* high school student. Fountain therefore pursued his challenge to *The Humanities*, Volume I, even after his own daughter was no longer in the humanities class.

At the time Fountain handed in his request, the Columbia County School District had no policy for dealing with textbook protests. School officials promptly developed a proposal establishing such a policy. According to the proposal, an advisory committee would evaluate the challenged material and present a recommendation to the school board, which would make a final decision. Committee members would be required to read the material, but board members would not. The mother of a Columbia High School student pointed out that if the policy were adopted, people who had not read a book would have the authority to overrule people who had read it. The board's attorney argued that it might be more difficult to defend the board in a lawsuit if he had to prove that each member had read a book before voting on it. The board agreed with him and approved the policy by a vote of 4–1.

In compliance with the new policy, an advisory committee made up of Columbia County teachers read *Lysistrata* and "The Miller's Tale" and recommended retaining the textbook but not assigning either challenged work. The Columbia County Superintendent of Schools, Silas Pittman, disagreed. According to the school board minutes, Pittman stated "that he felt that any literature in which God's name is used in vain is not appropriate for use in the classroom" (April 22, 1986). He therefore recommended that the books be excluded altogether, or that the offending selections be cut out of them. The board voted unanimously to remove the books from the curriculum. All of the district's copies of *Humanities*, Volume I, were locked away in a closet, and Volume II was stretched over both semesters of the course.

The parents of some Columbia High School students protested that the narrow sectarian views of a few people, represented by Fountain, were affecting the education of all students in the school. The ACLU agreed to provide legal backing if the parents decided to go to court. Under threat of a lawsuit, the school board voted 4–1 to put one copy of *The Humanities*, Volume I, in the school library. Since the book was now available to Columbia High School students, the board members contended that they could not be accused of suppressing whatever ideas it contains. Despite the school board's move, ACLU attorneys brought suit against the board and Superintendent Pittman. The ACLU complaint, filed on November 24, 1986, stated that the removal of the books suppressed free speech and free thought while advancing religion through the public schools. Since a parent named Moyna Virgil was the plaintiff whose name was listed first, the case was called *Virgil v. School Board of Columbia County.*

The school authorities moved for dismissal, arguing that there was no case to answer. The challenged books were used for the first semester of the humanities course, and by the time they were locked up the first semester was long over. All the board members had done, they maintained, was to exercise their right to determine that *The Humanities, Volume I,* would not be used in future years. According to the defense, Pittman's remark about the Lord's name was irrelevant because the board's rejection of the books was based solely on age-inappropriate, sexually explicit scenes and language. The board contended that *Lysistrata* and "The Miller's Tale" reflect attitudes, such as humorous treatment of sex and tolerance of premarital sex, that most of Columbia County's population would find unacceptable. In the board members' view, they had not only the right, but the duty, to remove the books containing the offensive material.

The legal arguments in *Virgil* focused on a dispute about which Supreme Court precedent applied to the case. The ACLU contended that the relevant precedent was *Pico v. Board of Education* (1982), in which the Supreme Court had ruled that school boards do not have the right to remove books from high school libraries. The *Pico* decision emphasizes the fact that reading library books is a voluntary activity, and the ACLU argued that the same principle applied to *Virgil* because the challenged literary works were nonrequired readings in an elective course.

The defense argued that a more recent Supreme Court decision, *Hazelwood v. Kuhlmeier* (1988) was relevant to *Virgil*. In *Hazelwood* a high school principal objected to two stories in a school newspaper. One discussed teenage pregnancy; the other dealt with divorce. He forbade publication of the two pages on which those stories appeared, although the pages also contained other material. The Supreme Court's 5–3 ruling stated that the principal's removal of pages from the school newspaper did not violate the students' First Amendment rights as long as the action was "reasonably related to legitimate pedagogical concerns" (January 13, 1988, p. 12). The dissenting opinion argued that student speech can be limited if it interferes with education, but not if it is "merely incompatible" with the school's official stand on an issue.

According to the Columbia County School Board, the avoidance of sexually explicit material constituted a valid educational purpose for removing *The Humanities,* Volume I, from the curriculum. The ACLU replied that if the Supreme Court had intended *Hazelwood* to supersede *Pico,* the *Hazelwood* decision would have said so. Further, *Hazelwood* dealt with student writing, not with literary classics.

Virgil was heard by Judge Susan H. Black of the United States District Court for the Middle District of Florida. Black agreed with the defense that *Hazelwood* was the relevant Supreme Court precedent. According to her decision, "Although it did not specifically refer to textbooks, the Court [in *Hazelwood*] evidently sought to address a wide realm of 'curriculum' decisions, including those affecting textbooks" (Judgment in a Civil Case, January 29, 1988, p. 16, n. 4). Therefore, she ruled, as long as the school board had a valid educational purpose for removing *The Humanities,* Volume I, their decision did not violate the students' First Amendment rights. Her ruling was not without reservations; it was difficult, she observed, "to comprehend the harm which could conceivably be caused to a group of eleventh- and twelfth-grade students by exposure to Aristophanes and Chaucer" (p. 12). The removal of the entire textbook because of two selections was also, in her view, an unnecessarily restrictive response on the part of the school board. Nevertheless, the removal of the books was, in the language of the *Hazelwood* precedent, "reasonably related" to the legitimate goal of protecting Columbia High School students from material that the school board considered unsuitably vulgar and sexual. Accordingly, on January 29, 1988, Black granted the school board's motion to dismiss the ACLU complaint.

The ACLU appealed, arguing that *Hazelwood* does not apply to works of established literary merit and that the board's action was "rooted, indeed steeped, in philosophic valuing rather than pedagogical concern" (Appellants' Initial Brief, April 29, 1988, p. 25). According to the ACLU appeals brief, "Fear that adult or nearly adult students might choose voluntarily to acquaint themselves with Aristophanes or Chaucer must not be deemed legally reasonable grounds for suppression of works like 'Lysistrata' or 'The Miller's Tale.' . . . There must be some First Amendment recourse against the tyranny of board taste. Literary classics generally considered part and parcel of a liberal arts education cannot be constitutionally bannable because a board doesn't 'like' them" (p. 13).

The Humanities, Volume I, was on Florida's list of state-approved textbooks, motivating the Florida Department of Education to join other groups in filing an *amici curiae* brief upholding the ACLU position. Among the ACLU's other supporters were the American Association of University Professors, B'nai Brith, the Council of Chief State School Officers, the International Reading Association, the National Council of Teachers of English, PAW and the Union of American Hebrew Congregations. According to the *amici* brief, the court must "ascertain that a school board is not seeking to achieve the unconstitutional objective of suppressing a particular viewpoint or subject matter through the assertion of the possibly permissible ground of suppressing vulgar language" (Brief of *Amici Curiae* Supporting Reversal, April 29, 1988, p. 21).

The United States Court of Appeals for the Eleventh Circuit upheld both Black's decision and her reservations. "Of course," the Court of Appeals stated, "we do not endorse the Board's decision. Like the district court, we seriously question how young persons just below the age of majority can be harmed by these masterpieces of Western literature. However, having concluded that there is no constitutional violation, our role is not to second guess the wisdom of the Board's action" (Eleventh Circuit Court of Appeals Opinion, January 12, 1989, p. 13). The case did not go to the Supreme Court, which means that the Appeals Court ruling ended the dispute. *The Humanities*, Volume I, remains banned in Columbia County.

The outcome of *Virgil* was particularly disheartening to supporters of the ACLU position because the case included so many factors that should, in their view, have led to success. The textbook was on the state-approved list, the humanities course was an elective, *Lysistrata* and "The Miller's Tale" had never been assigned, the students in the course were close to adulthood, alternate readings were available, the challenged works are well-established literary classics, Fountain's protest included the ideas in the book as well as vulgarity and sexuality, and the superintendent of schools gave a religious reason for opposing the advisory committee's recommendation to retain the book. The defendants had only one argument and, as the case turned out, needed only one: no matter how little sense a school board decision seems to make, the board has the authority to determine curriculum unless protesters can prove the establishment of a religious or political orthodoxy.

Because the plaintiffs in *Virgil* lost a case that had seemed so strong, opponents of school board decisions in other parts of the country took the appeals court ruling as a warning. *Farrell*, for example, was still in progress when *Virgil* ended. According to Gloria Pipkin, the *Farrell* plaintiffs' decision to settle out of court was heavily influenced by the outcome of *Virgil*. In her words, she and the other plaintiffs were anxious "not to make any more bad law" (Telephone interview, April 9, 1991).

As the lawsuits discussed in this book indicate, the reluctance of judges to second-guess school boards does not favor any particular viewpoint. The courts upheld pro-humanist school board decisions in *Mozert* and *Smith* on the same basis as they upheld anti-humanist decisions in *Farrell* and *Virgil*. Obviously, the consistency of courts in leaving curricular decisions to school boards means that individuals who are concerned about the quality of education in their local schools have to emphasize not action in the courts but action at the polls. According to the American Library Association, challenges to textbooks and other instructional materials have skyrocketed since 1980. The increasing activism of both conservative and liberal protesters makes the composition of school boards more crucial than ever to the content of public education.

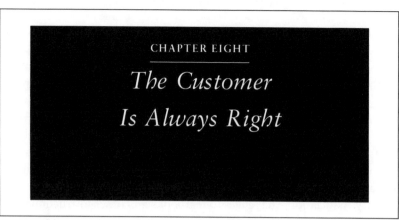

CHAPTER EIGHT

The Customer
Is Always Right

*When you're publishing a book, if there's something
that is controversial, it's better to take it out.*
—HOLT, RINEHART AND WINSTON REPRESENTATIVE

The impact of lawsuits on textbook content is indirect, since litigation is aimed at education authorities, not at publishers. At most, a judge might decide that a particular school board was within its rights in banning a book, but courts are not likely to dictate what publishers may or may not include in textbooks. The key to the influence of lawsuits on textbook content is not legal outcome, but self-censorship motivated by market forces. That is why Holt edited its Basic Reading Series to make it less "humanistic," even though the plaintiffs in *Mozert* lost their case. The same thing happened after *Smith,* in which the plaintiffs also lost, when publishers announced that their history and social studies books would include more about the positive contributions religion has made to world events, but little if anything about religious wars and persecutions. Conversely, even though proponents of evolution succeeded in having creationist laws declared unconstitutional in *McLean* and *Aguillard,* most textbooks omitted or masked discussions of evolution for several more years.

Clearly, the publicity and controversy surrounding a major lawsuit are more important than its outcome in affecting textbook content, and the primary reason lies in the textbook selection process in large states. Textbook publishing, like any for-profit business, is sensitive to customer demands—but in this particular industry the people who buy the product are not the ones who use it. Students do not select their own textbooks, and even teachers have only as much of a role as their school boards choose to give them. School boards, especially those controlling state-wide adoptions, are the customers whose choices control textbook sales.

When it comes to influence over textbook content, all fifty states are not created equal. In academic year 1990–91, Delaware had a total of 99,600 public school students in kindergarten through twelfth grade. In the same year, Texas had 174,300 public school students in just one *district*—Houston Consolidated—along with 124,100 in the Dallas Consolidated District. Overall, Texas has 1,066 school districts. Since publishers have no trouble counting, Texas has the opportunity to edit textbooks to suit itself, while smaller states like Delaware have one uncomplicated choice to make about each book: take it or leave it.

Apart from sheer size, another factor contributing to a state's influence over textbook content is its status as an "adoption" or "non-adoption" state. Twenty-seven states allow local school districts to purchase whatever textbooks they choose, without restriction. The other twenty-three, called adoption states, develop lists of state-approved books from which local districts can select. Most of the adoption states are in the South and West: Alabama, Arizona, Arkansas, California, Florida, Georgia, Hawaii, Idaho, Indiana, Kentucky, Louisiana, Mississippi, Nevada, New Mexico, North Carolina, Oklahoma, Oregon, South Carolina, Tennessee, Texas, Utah, Virginia, and West Virginia. Naturally, publishers vie with one another to produce books that will make the approved lists in states with the greatest purchasing power.

Texas and California are the two most lucrative textbook markets in the country. They are not by any means the only states to influence textbooks: in 1984–85, for example, Virginia took a well-publicized stand against censorship of literary classics, and other states routinely negotiate with publishers about textbook content. Nevertheless, according to representatives of the Association of American Publishers, California and Texas have more to say about textbook content than other states have.

Because of the amount of money involved, publishers submit textbooks to Texas and California for approval at an early stage of the publication process, which gives each state three options: accept a book, reject it, or accept it if the publisher agrees to make certain specified changes. Publishers sometimes produce special editions for these states, but more often the altered textbooks are sold nationwide. As a result, successful lobbyists in either of these states are likely to affect the education of students throughout the country.

The effects of the California and Texas adoptions on textbooks are both good and bad. On the positive side, both states correct numerous factual and typographical errors prior to publication. In 1991, for example, Texas officials caught several errors in American history books: Robert Kennedy and Martin Luther King were assassinated during the presidency of Lyndon Johnson, not Richard Nixon; George Bush was elected in 1988, not 1989; and the United States did not drop an atomic bomb on Korea. Depending on the year and the content area involved, each state has also made its own contributions to textbook content. Texas, for example, routinely demands up-to-date information on world events in history and geography books, discouraging publishers from putting new copyright dates on insufficiently updated material. Texas has also reversed its earlier anti-evolution stand and is now using its influence to promote the teaching of evolution in geology and biology books. California has, more than once, rejected all the books offered in a particular area when experts in the field raised too many questions about factual accuracy or clarity of presentation. The state has also earned praise for reversing its earlier trend toward trying to satisfy every demographic group's wishes about textbook representation, moving instead toward a more thoughtful synthesis of the ways in which various ethnic, religious, racial, and political groups co-exist not only in the United States, but in the world as a whole.

On the negative side, Texas and California contribute to sloppiness in textbooks by demanding that publishers meet state deadlines for submission. When Texas, in particular, invites publishers to submit books, the description of what should be in them is so detailed that publishers have to rush to get them ready on time. Both states also require publishers to develop charts showing how each textbook fits the state's curriculum guidelines, which adds to the cost of the books without benefiting any other state. The same is true of demands for sample copies and for sales representatives' time. Each state also has textbook laws and Board of Education regulations that steer publishers toward certain kinds of information and viewpoints. These rules, combined with the influence of protesters at public textbook hearings, give Texas and California a great deal to say about what goes into books used nationwide—and what stays out. Apart from the effects of specific California and Texas regulations, the process itself raises questions about connections between state politics and textbook content.

Requiring publishers to produce charts showing how each textbook correlates with the guidelines of California and Texas does more than just drive up costs; it also puts publishers on notice that their books had better conform as closely as possible to the curricula of those states. Since the two states have different content standards, publishers who want to get their books on both lists include at least a little information under each required heading. As selection committees are less likely to read whole books than to consult indexes or computer-generated lists of topics, publishers are motivated to repeat key words often enough to satisfy each state. Moreover, because textbooks have just so many pages, touching on a little of this and a little of that does not leave much space for in-depth coverage. The resulting fragmentation not only lowers the quality of books but also makes them boring to read because of the constant flitting from one topic to another.

Just as the topics covered in textbooks reflect a compromise between different sets of curriculum guidelines, the values expressed in the books represent an attempt to balance the competing demands of different groups. California has some conservative protesters and Texas some liberals, but on the whole Texas's influence on textbooks over the years has tended toward generally conservative values, and California's toward generally liberal values. Publishers aiming for the approved lists in both states have responded by producing books designed, as far as possible, not to offend anyone. In order to increase minority representation in textbooks, for example, publishers include Martin Luther King's "I Have a Dream" speech in high school literature anthologies—but only after removing references to racism in various Southern states, making the speech sound bland.

The overall impact of these compromises on textbook content is simpler to describe than to assess. Texas activists Mel and Norma Gabler, for example, point out that their lobbying has helped to eliminate Shirley Jackson's short story "The Lottery" from high school literature anthologies. The Gablers object to "The Lottery" because it implies a connection between religion and violence. There are many stories that equal or surpass "The Lottery" in literary merit, so from this perspective the omission of the Jackson story does not compromise the quality of American education. On the other hand, a pattern emerges when the Gablers' attack on "The Lottery" is considered alongside other demands for uncritically positive descriptions of religion, such as those made by the plaintiffs in *Mozert* and *Smith* and by the national organizations that backed them. Omitting "The Lottery" is not especially serious, but systematically suppressing the fact that religion can lead to violence not only falsifies history but also distorts contemporary world events involving religious militarism. It is rare that the omission of a particular story or piece of information is of world-shaking importance in itself, but the pattern of eliminating particular ideas wherever they occur is censorship in its most radical form.

Readers who thought that textbook content was determined solely by academic standards may be surprised to learn that decisions about what goes into books are heavily motivated by market considerations. Individual teachers could certainly counteract this influence, but there are three problems: awareness, time, and district rules.

The reluctance of publishers to say much about modifications they have made as a result of market pressures leaves two ways to get this information: travel to Texas and California to read through shelves and shelves of textbook adoption records or, for literary works, compare the original with the textbook version to see what has been omitted or changed. Such time-consuming and expensive procedures are, of course, beyond what a classroom teacher could possibly be expected to do; but without knowing what ideas are being systematically promoted or suppressed throughout whole series of books and from one discipline to another, it is difficult to evaluate or counteract the effects of Texas and California lobbyists on textbook content.

Even if teachers recognize where some of the gaps are, filling in with homemade lecture notes and other activities is not so easy as it may sound. Dedicated teachers do indeed take the time to produce their own materials and to prepare lessons that go beyond the information in the textbook, but the personal cost is high because time is such a scarce commodity for teachers. It is not uncommon for a public high school teacher to meet classes for twenty-five hours a week and supervise study halls or other activities for another five hours. Assuming a forty-hour work week, even a teacher with the unusually light load of 120 students would have only five minutes per student per week to grade homework, essays, and tests. Few teachers can get by with so little grading time, and they still have to prepare classes, keep records, attend meetings, and confer with parents. Considering the realities of a typical teacher's schedule, it is not surprising that even experienced teachers welcome the detailed manuals, handouts, tests, activity sheets, and other supplementary materials that accompany today's textbooks. Some districts also discourage teachers from going beyond what is in state-approved or district-approved textbooks—and, as the outcome of *Farrell* suggests, they are within their rights to do so. These districts may be trying to maintain uniformity of instruction, or they may fear parental protests about teacher-made materials not submitted for district approval. For all of these reasons, textbooks and their accompanying instructional aids are crucial to American education. If special interest groups can affect the content of textbooks sold nationwide, they can, in a very real sense, touch the vast majority of American elementary and secondary school students.

The process of developing lists of approved textbooks in California and Texas includes public hearings in which all residents, including representatives of advocacy groups, can express their views. The details of the procedure vary, but final decisions are made by state boards of education on the recommendation of textbook committees. The board members, who are either elected officials or political appointees, are open to lobbying by activist groups. Each state also has laws giving broad guidelines for instructional content, and education officials routinely check textbooks for compliance.

California's textbook law, adopted in 1976, features "social content standards" relating to cultural diversity, consumer and environmental issues, and economics. Some of its provisions are controversial, not only because of what they actually say, but also because of the ways education officials and publishers interpret them. The law reads:

When adopting instructional materials for use in the schools, governing boards shall include only instructional materials which, in their determination, accurately portray the cultural and racial diversity of our society, including:

a) The contributions of both men and women in all types of roles, including professional, vocational, and executive roles.

b) The role and contributions of American Indians, American Negroes, Mexican Americans, Asian Americans, European Americans, and members of other ethnic and cultural groups to the total development of California and the United States.

c) The role and contributions of the entrepreneur and labor in the total development of California and the United States.

When adopting instructional materials for use in the schools, governing boards shall include only instructional materials which accurately portray, whenever appropriate:

a) Man's [later changed to Humanity's] place in ecological systems and the necessity for the protection of our environment.

b) The effects on the human system of the use of tobacco, alcohol, narcotics and restricted dangerous drugs as defined in Section 11032 of the Health and Safety Code, and other dangerous substances. When adopting instructional materials for use in the schools, governing boards shall require such materials as they deem necessary and proper to encourage thrift, fire prevention and the humane treatment of animals and people....

No instructional materials shall be adopted by any governing board for use in the schools which, in its determination, contain:

a) Any matter reflecting adversely upon persons because of their race, color, creed, national origin, ancestry, sex, handicap *[added later]*, or occupation.

b) Any sectarian or denominational doctrine or propaganda contrary to law. (Quoted in State of California Curriculum Framework and Textbook Development Unit, Standards for Evaluation of Instructional Materials with Respect to Social Content, 1986, p. 7; headings and section numbers have been omitted)

According to a handbook distributed by the California Department of Education, the law means that textbooks should include males, females, and a variety of racial, ethnic, religious, and age groups in an equitable way. Stereotyping with regard to occupations, achievements, mental and physical activities, and parenting roles is unacceptable. Textbooks should also present nonjudgmental descriptions of different occupations and socioeconomic backgrounds and should discuss not only the root culture of various ethnic groups but also their role in America.

California's emphasis on diversity places it squarely in the middle of the nationwide controversy over removing traditional educational material to make room for information about different groups. The social content guidelines also touch on free speech by stating or implying the viewpoint that textbooks are to adopt toward certain issues. It is hard to see, for example, how a psychology book could be accepted in California if it discussed eugenic theories of intelligence without stating that they are wrong. The key question is whether California is balancing textbooks or biasing them, and the answer depends at least in part on the extent to which the material California is requiring for social reasons is also educationally sound.

In order to evaluate California's influence on textbooks, it is necessary to consider how the adoption process works and exactly what changes publishers are required to make. Each year, reviewers appointed by the Board of Education examine the textbooks submitted for inclusion on the California list. If a book is judged to be out of compliance with the social content guidelines, its publisher has three choices: suggest revisions, appeal the ruling, or withdraw the book from consideration. On rare occasions, publishers choose the third option to avoid making extensive changes. More often, publishers begin by appealing; if that fails, they propose changes addressing whatever guidelines they have not met. Roughly a third of all appeals are granted, usually for one of two reasons: the publisher satisfies the appeals panel that the book does in fact comply with the standards; or the panel finds that a "special purpose" justifies failure to comply. If, say, a literary classic demeans women or minorities by today's standards, California will accept the book with the provision, "Discussion material should be included in the teacher's edition indicating that, although a particular attitude toward women or a minority group was prevalent during a certain period in history, that attitude has changed or is in the process of change" (p. 1).

Publishers who do not appeal or whose appeals fail are required to propose changes to bring their textbooks into compliance with the social content standards. One of the most common reasons for altering text-books is to add more minorities, women, or disabled people. A few modifications involve written text; for example, one publisher added a learning-disabled child to a story in an elementary school reader. Such changes are usually made in readers or in history or social studies text-books, since books on other subjects are less likely to address social issues. All textbooks, however, include pictures, and California requires publishers to use pictures that show different racial, ethnic, and age groups; males and females in nontraditional roles; and people using eyeglasses, hearing aids, wheelchairs, and crutches.

Sometimes, books that include minorities, women, elderly people, and disabled individuals still fall foul of the rules because their presentation of these groups is judged to be stereotyped. Books are routinely cited for such violations as showing men and women only in traditional roles, Canadian Indians only as construction workers, Asian men only as hou-seboys, elderly people doing nothing but sitting in rockers, and African Americans eating nothing but fried chicken and sweet potato pie. The social content guidelines, as they are written, would permit depictions of people in stereotyped situations so long as they were also shown in other roles; but in practice publishers respond to California citations by removing all of the stereotypes.

Stereotyping, especially if it presents a negative image of a particular group, can become a self-fulfilling prophecy as new generations of students are taught to relegate themselves and others to very limited traditional roles. On the other hand, to the extent that a stereotype is an accurate reflection of an aspect of ethnicity, or a stage in the development of a particular group, the books are the poorer for the loss. Publishers could approach the problem by providing explanations of the stereotypes or by showing people of that group in other roles, but generally they do not. This treatment of stereotypes, combined with other examples discussed later in the chapter, suggests that a publisher's response to state textbook regulations can go beyond the regulations themselves, exaggerating the state's influence in ways that its own education officials might not endorse.

Apart from the social content review that is automatically conducted by the Department of Education, the California adoption process includes public hearings at which any citizen may make a presentation as an individual or on behalf of a group. Especially when history and social studies books are being considered, representatives of various nationalities and religions crowd public meetings to call for expanded or modified treatment of their particular groups. Most of their comments address stereotyping, negativity, and inaccuracy. If the Board of Education agrees with the protesters, publishers are required to make changes accordingly if they want to sell their books in California; if the board does not agree, the books remain as they were.

When the most recent adoption of history books took place in 1990, African Americans, atheists, Chinese Americans, Eastern Europeans, feminists, Hispanics, homosexuals, Jews, Muslims, and Native Americans made presentations to the board about the proposed textbooks. The comments made by representatives of Jewish groups, together with the board's responses, provide a good example of how the dynamics of California textbook adoptions work. Speakers at a public hearing objected to a New Testament quotation about a "new covenant" and to one book's implication that Christianity had replaced Judaism, whereas in fact Judaism continues to flourish. They also maintained that the books portrayed Judaism in an exaggeratedly legalistic way and contained errors about Jewish holidays. Finally, they did not think that Gentile authors could adequately prepare text about Judaism. The State Board of Education agreed with their contention that Judaism was presented almost entirely in terms of legalistic distinctions and required the publishers to broaden their approach. The board also agreed that textbooks should include correct descriptions of Jewish holidays and that they should not suggest what the protesters called "replacement theology." On the other hand, the board refused to require publishers to remove the statement that Jesus had called for a "new covenant" as long as the expression was defined as something an historic figure had said, not as something all students have to believe. The board also agreed with the publishers that historians do not have to belong to a particular religious or ethnic group in order to write about it. Similar interactions took place between the board and other protesting groups, each of which got some, but not all, of what it wanted.

Some effects of the California process, such as the wholesale and un-critical elimination of stereotypes, are open to question. Other effects, such as the correction of factual errors about Judaism, contribute to the quality of American education. But even if the only result of California's intervention were to produce more balanced and accurate textbooks than would otherwise have been on the market, the process itself would still raise questions. Readers who agree with the changes California requires may be thankful for the buying power that makes them possible, but suppose California citizens persuaded the board to require changes that you did *not* agree with? The textbook changes discussed in the remainder of this book are intended not only to give an idea of how California and Texas affect textbook content but also to invite consideration of the market-based textbook development process that dominates American education.

Although cultural diversity plays a large role in California textbook adop-tions, it is not the only topic covered by the state's social content guide-lines. Other citations for noncompliance involve environmental issues and unsafe practices. One textbook, for example, was cited for discussing several major engineering projects without mentioning possible effects on the environment. Another book was not accepted until the publisher had supplemented a section on whale hunting with information about the near-extinction of whales. To comply with California safety stan-dards, a publisher removed a slingshot and broken glass from a picture, added adults to pictures of children using knives or fire, and removed a picture of a boat whose passengers had no life jackets.

California educational policy also discourages the portrayal of foods of low nutritive value. The "California junk food rule," enacted in the 1970s because of lobbying by health food groups, is one of the most controversial parts of the social content standards. California education officials, stung by endless questions and occasional ridicule, deny that they are trying to eliminate junk food from textbooks; as they see it, the regulation is intended simply to downplay such foods. A few years ago, for example, California accepted a book showing a recipe for candy after the publisher had agreed to change an accompanying illustration to highlight powdered milk and peanut butter while blurring powdered sugar and corn syrup.

The power of the California adoption process is obvious from the textbook changes that come out of it, but its effect is even greater than it appears because of decisions publishers themselves make in an effort to avoid unfavorable reviews. The treatment of Patricia Zettner's short story "A Perfect Day for Ice Cream" is a good example. The story originally appeared in *Seventeen* magazine, and two textbook publishers arranged to reprint it in junior high school literature anthologies. Because of California's junk food rule, the publishers deleted references to chili burgers, pizza, and ice cream, and changed the title to "A Perfect Day." They also removed the expression "kamikaze ball," an argument between siblings, and a reference to Gloria Steinem. When Zettner asked for an explanation of the changes, she was told that they had been made in anticipation of California complaints about junk food and ethnic stereotyping and Texas protests about family conflict and feminism. "A Perfect Day for Ice Cream" had never been anthologized before, so no one in either state had raised any objections to it. The publishers were self-censoring their own material to avoid tangling with review committees and textbook protesters in powerful states. The public rarely learns about pre-submission changes made by the publishers themselves, and that ignorance makes it very difficult to assess the real impact of the state adoption process on textbook content.

The "spillover" power of the large adoption states sometimes allows textbook activists to bypass the official textbook adoption process altogether. In one such situation, a Fresno group called Interested Monitoring Persons Against Contemporary Textbooks (IMPACT) angered school officials by going directly to Holt, Rinehart and Winston with complaints about the 1980 Basic Reading Series. The readers, an earlier edition of the series challenged in *Mozert,* included three pictures that IMPACT considered obscene. A member of the group explained that she had used "high-powered magnifying glasses" to search for "subliminal" messages not readily visible to the naked eye ("Fresno Group," *Los Angeles Times,* September 9, 1982). In one picture, a little girl was wearing a "transparent skirt" which allegedly showed the shape of her legs. A second picture showed a female runner who was, according to IMPACT, endowed with a penis. The third illustration featured a boy standing in a doorway; the protesters maintained that his genitals were outlined. IMPACT persuaded a new member of the California Board of Education to speak to a Holt representative, and although the board as a whole had not been consulted, the company changed the pictures. As the representative explained, "When you're publishing a book, if there's something that is controversial, it's better to take it out" ("Fresno Group").

If we look only at modifications made in public during the adoption process in California, the addition of minorities, women, the aged, and the disabled does not seem to fragment books or interfere significantly with academic freedom. Few changes are made to written words; most compliance issues are handled by diversifying pictures that were already in the books. People may have different ideas about whether such diversification is necessary, but it would be difficult to argue that it undermines educational values. In fact, including different kinds of people in textbooks tends toward promoting tolerance for diversity among all students, as well as a positive self-image among children who fall into previously ignored categories.

Other implications of self-censorship by publishers are difficult for anyone outside the publishing industry to explore. The changes that show on the surface seem minor and confined mostly to pictures, but there is no way of measuring how much influence California's diversity guidelines have on the early stages of selecting textbook material. Are stories accepted or rejected because of the demographic groups they feature? How heavily do social concerns influence what goes into history and social studies books? What information is being left out to make room for other material? Until these questions can be answered, there is no way to assess either the extent to which California influences textbook content or the effect of that influence on educational quality. Diversifying textbooks could improve education in many ways, but it could also lead to shallowness, fragmentation, and the omission of important literary works or historic events because they reflect badly on a particular group. In any case, two things are clear: first, textbook content is not determined solely on the basis of academic or educational considerations, but is heavily influenced by market forces; second, the effects of state regulations go beyond what appears on the surface of public textbook reviews.

Earlier chapters of this book mentioned Far Right organizations, such as the Eagle Forum and Citizens for Excellence in Education, which lobby for textbook changes without participating directly in lawsuits or in the textbook adoption process. In *Battle of the Books*, Lee Burress describes organizations operating in a similar way from the left. One of these, the Council on Interracial Books for Children (CIBC), has gone so far in trying to eliminate racism and sexism from children's literature that it is open to the charge of censorship. The organization lobbies school officials, librarians, and publishers to remove books containing *any* material that CIBC considers biased against women or minorities. As Burress notes, "It should also be remembered that a characteristic of censorship is its tendency to judge a publication by a single episode, use of language or another single aspect of the work, instead of considering a publication 'as a whole' before judgments can be made about it.... A judgment about a work based solely on whether it contains racist or sexist language or episodes does seem to fit the pattern that censors have frequently used" *(Battle of the Books* [Metuchen, N.J.: Scarecrow Press, 1989], p. 117).

The behind-the-scenes influence of organizations like CIBC could certainly magnify the effect of California's social content guidelines to the point where historical data and literary works are excluded solely because they include racist or sexist elements. Eliminating racism and sexism from our culture is a worthy goal in itself, but omitting or expurgating all mention of past attitudes falsifies history, waters down literature, and does nothing to guarantee future improvements.

The power of left-wing censors is best illustrated by the treatment of *Huckleberry Finn,* which has become one of the most frequently challenged works taught in secondary schools. Fundamentalists occasionally oppose the novel's portrayal of religion and its glorification of moral independence, but most of its opponents attack its racist language, particularly the word *nigger.*

Huckleberry Finn, which is strongly anti-slavery, is set in the pre–Civil War South. Its characters include slaveowners who are shown as ignorant, hypocritical, and narrow-minded. Realistically, what should students think such people would say? "Invite the African Americans to come in from the fields"? This kind of material needs careful handling in the classroom to explain its historical and social context, but it is an important part of the American literary tradition and truthfully describes a significant period of American history. Deleting the slaveowners' racist comments would, ironically, make slavery look more benign than it actually was. Excluding *Huckleberry Finn* and similar books altogether, thereby pretending that what happened did not happen, would undermine the contemporary civil rights movement by reducing awareness of past events that led to it. In more general terms, obscuring the fact that racism, sexism, and other forms of prejudice have occurred in world history and in the American past or suggesting by omission that they are not powerful forces today censors education just as much as anything the Far Right could do.

Early in each year's adoption process, sample copies of textbooks proposed for use in California are made available to the public in centers throughout the state. Any citizen may review the books, fill out an "Instructional Materials Review Report for Use by General Public" form, and submit it to the Department of Education. In general, Californians who advocate environmentalism, nutrition education, globalism, and the inclusion of women and minorities in textbooks do not have to make personal efforts to have those topics incorporated into state-approved books; the Department of Education takes care of that for them. Opponents of those viewpoints have to be active if they want their beliefs considered at all, so they account for most of the public comment sheets on file at the Department of Education. (All Instructional Materials Review Report forms are undated, and most are anonymous.)

The remarks on the comment sheets sound very much like the testimony in *Mozert, Smith,* and other lawsuits discussed in this book. Some protesters target statements that, in their view, suggest disrespect for parents: "She [Mother] said in a very cold voice," "Glad Pop wasn't home," "Dad made me," "She pulled away from her mother and stood out of reach." Other remarks oppose global education, particularly with regard to Communist countries. In response to a textbook statement that "Moscow, the capital of the Soviet Union, is in the western part of the country," one protester wrote, "Our children need to learn more about America, not the Soviet Union!!!!!!" Another writer asked whether a reference to the Moscow Zoo could "possibly be a way to get children so used to hearing about Russia that they think they won't be surprised when communism takes over, over here? (or so the Russians *think*)." References to the Holocaust provoked similar comments: "I feel that these kinds of stories do not do any good and only tends [sic] to cause racial problems. Our children need to learn more about our founding fathers and our American heritage." Another protester responded to the Holocaust material by asking, "Why does'nt [sic] anyone ever mention the slaughter of Christians? That also happened, but is never mentioned. Wonder why?????????" The same writer went on to object to teaching acronyms for one-world or liberal organizations, such as UNICEF, NATO, and NOW. California protesters also challenge material about non-Christian religions and myths on the grounds that children might think either that "false" religions are acceptable or that Bible stories are myths.

In some years, almost all of the public comment sheets relate to evolution. One protester objected to the word *prehistoric* and the names of prehistoric periods on the grounds that those words imply evolution. The same writer also challenged the statement that the word *paleontology* comes from Greek words meaning "the study of ancient being" because the definition implies that such a study exists. Other commentators objected to a fable about a crow acting like a human and to a story explaining why animals in zoos need privacy. Both selections were labeled evolutionary for suggesting that animals have feelings and rights comparable to those of humans.

The creation/evolution controversy reached the California state courts in 1981, when the Creationist-Science Research Center joined other plaintiffs in a lawsuit about an educational policy requiring that "dogmatism be changed to conditional statements where speculation is offered as explanation for origins and that science emphasizes 'how' and not 'ultimate cause' for origins" (State Board of Education Action Establishing the Charge to the Consulting Committee, quoted in *Segraves v. California,* Findings of Fact and Conclusions of Law, June 12, 1981, p. 2). The plaintiffs in *Segraves v. California* argued that teachers in California schools had violated both the policy and the plaintiffs' religious rights by teaching evolution as fact. The court ruled that the policy was acceptable in itself but should be more effectively disseminated to science teachers.

The *Segraves* ruling was followed by a blizzard of protests about the teaching of evolution, all citing the "anti-dogmatism" policy. In 1983, protesters led by the Segraves family objected to world history books that included timelines going back to prehistoric periods. Two years later, activists invoked the "anti-dogmatism" rule against such statements as, "It is estimated that it took 6 billion years for the earth to solidify and cool enough to form the first rocks" and "However, dinosaurs have never been observed; therefore, our knowledge of what they looked like is inferential" (Letter from the Creation-Science Research Center to the California Board of Education, September 12, 1985). The protesters also responded negatively to attempts to qualify descriptions of evolution by preceding them with "Scientists believe" or "Scientists think." To the protesters, anti-dogmatism did not mean qualifying statements with words like *estimated, inferential, believe,* and *think;* it meant nothing less than the presentation of creationism as a rebuttal to evolution wherever it appears in textbooks.

During the 1985 adoption of science books, creationists associated evolution with a general decline in the moral and academic quality of

American students. "The more evolution theory is presented and the less creation theory is presented," one protester wrote, "the less respect is given not only to Deity but society in general and to our students [sic] attitudes toward what is good and wholesome. Let us quit cramming evolution and get on with reading, writing and arithmetic so that we can again graduate winners" (Letter to the California State Board of Education, September 12, 1985).

California scientists attended that year's public hearings in record numbers to argue that the protesters did not understand the scientific process, particularly the meaning of the word *theory*. A scientific theory, they said, is not just any unproven idea; it is an hypothesis which has withstood empirical testing and is subject to further testing. Evolution has withstood so many tests that virtually the entire scientific community accepts it. Creationism, on the other hand, is a religious belief that is not subject to testing. Giving equal weight to evolutionist and creationist views in science textbooks would, therefore, be misleading.

After a series of contentious public meetings, the California Board of Education reached a compromise; it adopted textbooks that satisfied nobody. To creationists, the new books were filled with implications that evolution is an accepted fact. Scientists, on the other hand, expressed dismay because the books covered evolution very lightly and tentatively, often isolating it in a separate chapter instead of using it as an organizing principle of biology.

In 1989, California tried to put an end to the anti-dogmatism wars by revising the policy itself to support evolution while prohibiting creationist dogma. The new statement, entitled "State Board of Education Policy Statement on the Teaching of Natural Science," mandates, "Nothing in science or any other field of knowledge shall be taught dogmatically. A dogma is a system of beliefs that is not subject to scientific test and refutation." Teachers may have occasion to discuss "divine creation, ultimate purposes, or ultimate causes" in history or English classes, but not in science. If asked to teach "content that does not meet the criteria of scientific fact, hypothesis, and theory as these terms are used in natural science and defined in this policy," science teachers should refer students to family or clergy. "Neither the California nor the U.S. Constitution requires, in order to accommodate the religious views of those who object to certain material or activities that are presented in science classes, that time be given in the curriculum to those particular religious views."

Later the same year, California adopted a textbook guideline requiring that evolution be taught as the only scientific theory of human origins. The policy, which was prepared over several months by a panel of experts, was designed to distinguish between the established scientific status of evolution and the nonscientific meaning of the word *theory*. Accordingly, the guideline states that although evolution is technically known as a theory, it engenders no more *scientific* controversy than the theories of gravity or electricity; the evidence against it is religious, not scientific.

At the last minute, in a move that the California state superintendent of schools described as a "political concession" to fundamentalists, education authorities deleted the statement, "There is no scientific dispute that evolution has occurred and continues to occur; this is why evolution is regarded as scientific fact." One of the scientists involved in preparing the document expressed dismay that "the State Department of Education backed down and that a framework, a solid framework that was in its third draft and had been written by an eminently qualified panel, was adulterated at the last minute in response to fundamentalist pressures. As a result, the recent proceedings can only encourage publishers to continue their long-established practices of waffling, obfuscating and evading any legitimate, straightforward presentation of the subject of organic evolution and the history of life" (American Library Association, *Newsletter on Intellectual Freedom,* January 1990, p. 29). Michael Hudson, Western Director of PAW, agreed: "I think they could have put the Scopes trial to rest here once and for all but they left the door opened, unfortunately, so the battle continues" (p. 28).

Creationists cheered the eleventh-hour deletion, which confirmed their own continuing political clout. As the director of the National Center for Science Education conceded, "I think it is clear that the religious right is still a force in education and that we cannot write off these people" (p. 29). All the same, the omission of that particular sentence was a symbolic rather than a substantive victory. The policy still retains all the reasoning that led up to the deleted sentence, so, as the superintendent of schools affirmed, "it is very clear in the document that evolution will be taught and creationism will not" (p. 29).

California's anti-creationist stand will affect science textbooks that previously included creationism as a balance to evolution. Combined with the new Texas pro-evolution policy discussed in chapter 9, California's guidelines will also help to embolden publishers to discuss evolution more explicitly and pervasively. On the other hand, the reason American textbooks approached the 1990s without discussing evolution in the way the scientific community had long advocated is that the scientific community does not decide how science is taught in elementary and secondary schools. It was only when, and because, evolution became practical politics that the changes occurred.

California is a major force in determining textbook content. It is so powerful that publishers not only make changes required by state education officials but also try to anticipate what protesters are likely to target. As the IMPACT incident indicates, publishers will even alter books outside of the regular adoption process to avoid controversy. Changes made during the adoption process itself may therefore be no more than the tip of the iceberg in comparison with in-house, self-generated decisions based on what publishers *think* will sell in California. The state adoption process also means that elected or politically appointed officials of unknown educational credentials can overrule scientists about what goes into science books, historians about the content of history books, and literary experts about the selection of literary works.

Market

Force

*I do not patronize poor, ill educated, or disenfranchised people by exempting
them from the same critical examination I feel free to direct toward the rest of
society, however much I might champion the same minority or
disadvantaged group in the forums of that society.*
—JAMES MOFFETT

California and Texas textbook adoptions share the same configuration:
submission of books proposed for use in the state, public hearings, recommendations by textbook committees, publishers' agreements to make
required changes, compliance reviews by education officials, final selections by state boards of education. There are, however, two significant
differences in the way the two states handle textbook adoptions. First,
Texas's approved list goes from kindergarten through Grade 12, while
California's covers only kindergarten through Grade 8. Books for grades
9 through 12 must meet the California social content standards and
conform to the state's model curriculum guidelines, but local districts
are free to select their own books within those parameters; there is no
state-level adoption of high school textbooks. The Texas adoptions therefore cover a greater variety of textbooks and deal with higher-level and
more complex material than California's state selection process does.
Second, California tells publishers where their books fail to meet state
standards and then waits for them to propose revisions. Texas is much
more directive; it is normal practice for publishers to be told that their
books will not receive Texas approval unless state education officials are
allowed to rewrite whole paragraphs.

In textbook laws, as in adoption procedures, the two states are similar in some ways and different in others. Texas's textbook law, like California's, requires, "Illustrations and written materials shall avoid bias toward any particular group or individual and should present a wide range of goal choices. Particular care should be taken in the treatment of ethnic groups, roles of men and women, and the dignity of workers, and respect for the work ethic." Further, Texas law mandates, "The book shall present examples of men and women participating in a variety of roles and activities and shall further present the economic, political, social, and cultural contributions of both men and women, past and present. ...Traditional and contemporary roles of men, women, boys, and girls shall be included" (Texas Administrative Code and Statutory Citations, Title 19, Part II, Instructional Resources, Chapter 81, Subchapter D, 1972, amended 1986). Texas's reference to *the work ethic* where California uses the more general term *entrepreneurs and labor,* and the Texas law's less specific recommendations about the treatment of minorities and women, give it a somewhat more conservative flavor than its California counterpart. Nevertheless, it quite clearly includes a version of social content standards.

The difference between California and Texas in educational law is, primarily, one of emphasis. Where California highlights environmentalism and cultural diversity, Texas stresses patriotism and authority. "Textbook content shall promote citizenship and understanding of the essentials and benefits of the free enterprise system, emphasize patriotism and respect for recognized authority, and promote respect for individual rights." Textbooks shall not "include selections or works which encourage or condone civil disorder, social strife, or disregard of the law," nor shall they "contain material which serves to undermine authority" or "which would cause embarrassing situations or interference in the learning atmosphere of the classroom." Finally, textbooks approved for use in Texas "shall not encourage life styles deviating from generally accepted standards of society." The Texas law's endorsement of free enterprise and traditional lifestyles and its prohibition of lawlessness and rebellion are regularly cited by textbook activists to support their efforts to remove material which, in their view, promotes socialism, immorality, or disobedience.

Texas's textbook adoption records go back to the 1920s, but its current system began in 1961, when Mel and Norma Gabler first became involved in textbook selection. According to *Textbooks on Trial,* a book written by James Hefley and distributed by the Gablers, their activism began when their son, a high school junior, showed them his history textbook.

The Gablers, strong advocates of states' rights, were appalled to find that the book emphasized the power of the federal government and said little about the authority of individual states. They also found, to their dismay, that the nationalistic approach they remembered from their own school days had been replaced by a more international perspective.

When the Gablers learned that the Texas Society of Daughters of the American Revolution (TSDAR) and other groups had been lobbying against the new textbooks with little success, they threw themselves into the task. Their perseverance, dedication, and sheer hard work are impressive, even to people who believe that their impact on textbooks has damaged American education. Every year for three decades they have prepared lengthy textbook reviews, called bills of particulars, urging the Board of Education to reject "liberal" textbooks and to require massive changes in the books that are adopted.

Over the years, the Gablers, using the organizational name Educational Research Analysts, have been successful in influencing the Texas Board of Education to eliminate material they consider unpatriotic, socialistic, communistic, humanistic, anti-religious, anti-creationist, anti-authoritarian, and anti-family. They also distribute textbook reviews and other materials nationwide. The Hawkins County protesters quoted extensively from the Gablers' handbook on humanism and from their review of the Holt readers, and the Gablers were among the expert witnesses in *Mozert.*

Coincidentally, just as the Hawkins County controversy was starting, the Gablers and other Texas textbook protesters hit two major obstacles, one right after the other. Under the original rules, public textbook hearings in Texas were open only to participants who wanted to speak against the proposed books; people who supported them were excluded. As a result, opponents of contemporary textbooks had a monopoly on public input into selection decisions. The Gablers, CEE members, and TSDAR representatives dominated the hearings, although feminists, atheists, and civil rights advocates occasionally testified against books they considered patriarchal, religious, or stereotyped. Michael Hudson, Western director of PAW, led the fight to open the hearings to people who wanted to defend books proposed for use in Texas. In 1983, he won. For the first time, protesters faced direct opposition as textbook advocates refuted their educational viewpoint and some of their statements of fact.

In the summer of 1984, a year after textbook defenders were first allowed to speak, the Gablers and their allies received another blow when Ross Perot, a well-known Texas billionaire, succeeded in having the elected Board of Education replaced by an appointed board for five years.

The change seems to have been motivated at least as much by school sports scandals as by textbook selection issues, but it was crucial because the elected members had been more vulnerable to pressure than the appointed board proved to be. Nevertheless, the Gablers were far from beaten. They won fewer victories under the appointed board, but they did not always lose.

The responsibility for selecting Texas textbooks is shared by the state Board of Education and a textbook selection committee. Every summer the committee, which is made up of teachers from all parts of the state, reviews the textbooks proposed for use in Texas. Committee members solicit advice from experts in the fields being considered, hear public testimony and publishers' replies, and decide which books to recommend for the state-approved list. The following November, the Board of Education votes on the textbook committee's recommendations. The board can reject any book, regardless of the committee's opinion, but it cannot accept books that the committee does not recommend.

In the interval between the textbook committee's work and the board vote, staff members at the Texas Education Agency (TEA) prepare a document entitled "Report of the Commissioner of Education Concerning Recommended Changes and Corrections in Textbooks." (Over the years, this report has had several titles, including "Changes Requested of Publishers" and "Textbook Adoption Changes and Corrections Requested of Publishers.") The report enumerates, alphabetically by publisher, the changes that must be made in each textbook before it receives final Texas approval. Required changes, which are based on recommendations made by the textbook committee and by education officials, usually focus on topics covered in written and oral public testimony. Although the document is called "Report of the Commissioner," its contents are cleared with the Board of Education and implemented under board authority. Once in a while, the board itself votes to require additional changes. Education officials negotiate with publishers ahead of time, so on the rare occasions when a publisher removes a book from consideration to avoid extensive changes, the action happens before the final board vote is taken. After making the necessary modifications, publishers submit the corrected textbooks to the TEA for a compliance check. Only then is a book finally approved for use in Texas.

The design of the adoption process allows activists to try to influence two separate decisions: whether to approve a book at all, and whether to require certain changes in it. The Gablers and their allies have often claimed victory when the textbook selection committee or the Board of Education has turned down a book that they had criticized. An examination of textbook adoption records since 1961 supports the Gablers' overall contention that they and their associates have had considerable influence on textbook selection, but proving that their activities were responsible for the failure of a specific book is not always easy.

The Gablers, the TSDAR, and other right-wing protesters submit long bills of particulars against most—if not all—of the books submitted in any category, and they sometimes repeat certain objections word for word in their comments on several different books. Even when they do focus their criticism on one or two books that they find inordinately offensive and the books are not approved, there is no way of assessing what effect that decision has on the education of students outside of Texas. In the short term, rejected books are less affected by the adoption process than those that are accepted because the Board of Education cannot require changes in a book that is not going to be sold in Texas. In the long term, the rejection of a book might result in future editions that are more acceptable to the Texas protesters, but this is at best only educated speculation. No one outside the publishing company knows what is changed in-house and why, and it is understandable that the publisher is not going to give out that information. Any specific book that is rejected is, except for possible self-censorship by the publisher, unaffected by the Texas adoption. This chapter will therefore concentrate on changes ordered by the Texas Board of Education and made in books that are, for the most part, used by students throughout the country.

Texas's annual list of required changes is usually about 150 pages long, although the 1989 document ran a whopping 382 pages. Some of the changes are nothing more than corrections of mechanical or typographical errors, but others involve removing whole sections of text or replacing the publisher's version with material written by Texas education authorities. Publishers occasionally produce Texas editions, but in most instances changes made to accommodate Texas appear in books sold nationwide.

Some of the changes required by Texas are straightforward replacements of one piece of material with another. That is how one of the few selections in the Holt Basic Reading Series that was *not* challenged in *Mozert* found its way into the book. Originally, the 1980 edition of the series—which was very similar to the 1983 version at issue in *Mozert*—included a section called "Man, Animal, and Written Words." It contained the lines,

Early man was ill to look upon
Hairy, with clawed hands and flung-down head
He groped for remnants after lions fed.
Prey of all things, man slept in trees at first.

The Gablers protested the "evolutionary tone" of the work, and the board ordered Holt to replace this selection with "Post Early for Space," by Peter J. Henniker-Heaton. Accordingly, "Post Early for Space," a poem about the glories of the American space program, took its place in the Holt series. More recently, the appointed board ordered the publisher of a 1988 environmental science book to delete the statement, "Continued economic growth can be devastating" and say instead "that continued economic growth can become devastating without concern for its environmental impact in an urban setting" (Minutes of the State Board of Education, November 10–11, 1988, p. 10). This change reflects a long-standing Texas tendency to qualify statements opposing any aspect of capitalism. Depending on the context in which the statement occurs, the specification of urban settings could also minimize, by omission, environmental concerns about unpopulated areas.

In both of the examples given in the preceding paragraph, the deleted material is spelled out, so it is possible to see what was removed. Unfortunately, most changes required by Texas are not so clearly stated. More often, the Report of the Commissioner includes only the material that the board wants *in* the book, without specifying what is being taken out. One of the phrases used repeatedly in the commissioner's annual reports says, "Delete and substitute more appropriate activity or questions." But delete what? And what does "appropriate" mean? Similarly, a 1989 home economics book was altered: "Delete chart and replace with information similar to publisher's rebuttal to a petitioner regarding this chart" (p. 117), whatever that means. Also in 1989, the board required a publisher to delete a total of five paragraphs, three illustrations, and two charts from five pages of a home economics book, representing a significant modification to the text. The changes were listed only by page, without explanation—for example, "P. 122: Left column: Delete second and third paragraphs" (p. 114). Without a copy of the pre-publication text, there is no way of knowing what all that was about. The lack of explanatory material about required changes also produces some startling effects: one publisher was ordered, without explanation, to change Scotland to France, and another was given the drastic directive to eliminate overpopulation.

Tracing Texas-made changes ranges from difficult to impossible because textbooks submitted for consideration by the Texas Board of Education are usually pre-publication copies. Once the modifications are made, there is often no record outside the publishing company itself to show what the book originally said. Edward Jenkinson summarized what is likely to happen when a researcher tries to get information on censorship from publishers: "Several [textbook publishers] wrote to me that they had experienced no censorship problems; a few of them were the subjects of bitter bills of particulars in Texas, for example, and had lost thousands of dollars in sales. Apparently those publishers did not want to admit to censorship pressures in fear of losing more sales. Other publishers indicated that the censors would whitewash all textbooks if they could" (*Censors in the Classroom* [Carbondale, Ill.: Southern Illinois University Press, 1979, p. 162). The research for my own book ran into exactly the same obstacles; and even publishers who acknowledged the general problem were understandably reluctant to provide specific examples of material they themselves had deleted from their books in response to economic pressure.

Since the early 1980s, more and more of the modifications required by Texas have been handwritten in the margins of textbooks that are then returned to the publishers, leaving no clue as to what has been done to them. Each year's Report of the Commissioner is peppered with the notation, "Make all corrections submitted in the hand-corrected copies." This comment almost always appears at the end of the list of changes required in a particular book, with no indication of where or what the additional alterations are. Some of the hidden modifications must be more than just typographical corrections because from time to time a Report of the Commissioner carries a note telling a publisher *not* to delete a paragraph marked for removal in the hand-corrected copy. Unless Texas education authorities change their minds and order a publisher not to omit something after all, the increasing use of hand-corrected copies leaves absolutely no trace of whether anything has been taken out, let alone what material has been affected. For that reason, it is hard to assess the significance of the unusually short 1991 report, which contains only sixty-eight pages. Almost every page includes the notation, "Make all corrections submitted in the hand-corrected copies"; indeed, that sentence appears on some pages two or three times. One of two things has been reduced: either the number of changes Texas is making, or the visibility of those changes to anyone other than state education officials and textbook publishers.

An earlier section of this chapter mentioned that elected boards serving before 1984 were vulnerable to public pressure. That statement should not be interpreted to mean that elected boards gave the protesters everything they wanted. At no time have the Gablers or any other activists come close to getting even half of what they requested, and many statements are simply ignored. A fundamentalist minister, for example, maintained that it is impossible to believe in both evolution and women's liberation because evolution reduces humans to animals and removes moral absolutes, so the male has no reason not to use his superior strength to dominate the female. Another protester, observing that Hispanics have both the lowest suicide rate and the highest dropout rate in the country, concluded that missing as many years of public education as possible prevents suicide. The same protester objected to the statement that the Church of England had split off from the Roman Catholic Church because, she said, the Anglican Church was already established in England before the Romans, led by Julius Caesar, invaded.

Since the board has never responded to statements like these, they may seem harmless. They are, however, costly not only to the TEA but also to textbook publishers, who pass the expense along to their customers. After protesters file their petitions, the TEA has to make copies of them for all the publishers and for other individuals and organizations that have requested them. This runs into thousands of pages of photocopying and mailing. Publishers then have the option of replying to the public comments. Because the Texas adoption is so important, and it is hard to tell what the board might endorse, publishers almost always answer every complaint.

In 1988, a TSDAR representative wrote about ninety pages against the literature books proposed for use that year. Her submission was much shorter than the Gablers', who have been known to prepare documents of that length on a single book. Among her targets were works by Ambrose Bierce, William Cullen Bryant, James Fenimore Cooper, Stephen Crane, Countee Cullen, e. e. cummings, Emily Dickinson, Robert Frost, Graham Greene, Nathaniel Hawthorne, O. Henry, Randall Jarrell, Herman Melville, Grace Paley, Edgar Allan Poe, John Crowe Ransom, Adrienne Rich, William Shakespeare, John Steinbeck, Jonathan Swift, Walt Whitman, and Richard Wright.

A few examples will serve to give the gist of the TSDAR comments. Jonathan Swift's eighteenth-century satire "A Modest Proposal" will incite Texas youth to eat people. John Hersey's "Hiroshima" should be balanced by an account of the bombing of the *Arizona.* Poems by African

Americans about racism are Communist propaganda reflecting dishonor on the United States. Students should not be asked to compare Emily Dickinson's poetry with more modern work because her poems were not published until 1950, so she could not have influenced modern writers. Poe's "The Tell-Tale Heart" is a bad example of career education, and "The Cask of Amontillado" describes an unconventional way to treat friends. Poe's works should not be used at all because he was a cocaine addict. *Romeo and Juliet* promotes teenage suicide. The *Diary of Anne Frank* is unacceptable because it is sad. All of the 1988 literature anthologies are part of a leftist movement to sabotage the United States through poetry and other literature, and the unacceptable authors listed above should be replaced by Eleanor H. Porter (author of *Pollyanna*) and Booth Tarkington.

Responses to 1988 protests of the type summarized above ran from forty to sixty-eight pages per publisher. In response to the TSDAR, publishers said, for example, that it is not clear whether Poe was a cocaine addict; and even if he was, his stories are classics. Fiction written by self-proclaimed Communists does not necessarily promote Communism, and some of the writers the protester accuses of being Communists may not have been. And so on, point by point. In 1991, the same protester caused a publisher to take the time to explain, in writing, why an American history textbook cannot use the expression "chickened out" to describe President Kennedy's conduct of the Bay of Pigs invasion. Publishers seldom have reason to answer public comments in California unless education officials endorse them, but the design of the Texas process allows a single citizen, regardless of educational background or motivation, to tie up hours of staff time in each of the participating publishing companies.

One reason why the Texas Board of Education has never granted more than a fraction of the activists' requests is that those requests are so extensive. Given such a large base, the complaints that *have* found their way into the annual Report of the Commissioner have had a significant impact on textbooks. In their heyday, protesters could affect half to two-thirds of the books proposed for use in Texas—and, in most cases, sold nationwide.

The best way to get an idea of what happened to textbooks before an appointed board took office is to look at the number and variety of modifications made in a single year under a pre–1984 elected board. The 1983 adoption seems a logical one to focus on because books submitted that year, carrying 1983 or 1984 copyright dates, may still be in use in some classrooms. More importantly, new editions of an elementary or secondary school textbook are often very similar to older editions. Text-books are usually updated every five or six years, so most of the 1983 versions have been revised only once since then. Changes made in that adoption almost certainly remain in books with newer dates.

In 1983, Texas was considering world history books, which begin by describing fossil records of pre-human periods. In accordance with the creationist belief that the Earth is only a few thousand years old, the board ordered publishers to make several changes omitting or blurring the fact that fossil records go back millions of years. Any reference to an older Earth was framed as a statement of some people's opinion, without reference to scientific evidence. Apart from creationism, the world history books raised four other areas of contention involving religion as such. One book said, "The Hebrews developed a religion based on a belief in one God." "This is not a factual statement," the Gablers protested. "The Hebrews did not contrive their religion. God revealed Himself and His laws to the Hebrews" (Bill of Particulars, 1983, p. 5). The board told the publisher, "Rewrite to read 'The Hebrew's [sic] religion was based on a belief in one God'" (1983 Textbook Adoption Changes and Corrections Requested of Publishers, p. 27). The Gablers also contended that another book's favorable portrayal of Renaissance humanism advanced the religion of secular humanism, and the board ordered the publisher, "Change sentence to read 'Many Renaissance humanists were also devout Christians'" (p. 94).

Since Martin Luther is a Protestant religious figure, the Gablers were concerned about an unsympathetic portrayal of his response to the Peasants' Revolt. The controversial passage stated, "But Luther did not back the peasants in their revolt. He thought that a prince or lord had the right to decide the religious affairs of the people on his land. He told the princes to crush the revolt, and they did." According to the Gablers, "Other accounts say that Luther did not back the peasants in their revolt because of the violence and bloodshed" (p. 6). The Board of Education agreed. "Delete," the board said, "and substitute, 'He was opposed to the violence and bloodshed and thought the peasants should obey the princes or lords'" (p. 28).*

The 1983 changes summarized so far represent three levels of signif-

*The Gablers' 1983 defense of Luther was not their first; ten years earlier, they had attacked an essay comparing Luther with Martin Luther King. "These two men should not be put in the same category. Martin Luther was a religiously-dedicated, nonviolent man" (Bill of Particulars, August 10, 1973, p. 21). King, they asserted, was a Communist who advocated violence and disrespect for authority. The publisher voluntarily removed the essay.

icance, and all Texas textbook alterations can be classified the same way. On the first level, it is true that the Hebrews believe in one God and that many Renaissance humanists were devout Christians; the only issues such modifications raise are the way they are made and the reasons for them. On the second level, saying that "some people think" the earth is more than a few thousand years old implies a degree of doubt that does not exist and fails to discriminate between scientific opinion and religious faith. On the third level, rewriting the passage about Martin Luther to include language suggested by the Gablers introduces factual error into the history book. Early in the Peasants' Revolt, Luther advised the peasants—not the princes—to refrain from bloodshed, not because he was squeamish about violence in itself, but because he believed in the peasants' obligation to obey their lords. Although he encouraged the princes to consider the people's complaints, he lost sympathy with the peasants as soon as they moved beyond prayer and petition to force. At that point, he urged the princes to smite the peasants hip and thigh—not that they needed much urging. In a treatise entitled "Against the Robbing and Murdering Hordes of Peasants" (1525), he wrote:

> If [a prince] can punish and does not—even though the punishment consist in the taking of life and the shedding of blood—then he is guilty of all the murder and all the evil which [the peasants] commit, because, by wilful neglect of the divine command, he permits them to practice their wickedness, though he can prevent it, and is in duty bound to do so. Here, then, there is no time for sleeping; no place for patience or mercy. It is the time of the sword, not the day of peace. . . . Stab, smite, slay, whoever can. If you die in doing it, well for you! A more blessed death can never be yours, for you die in obeying the divine Word and commandment in Romans xiii, and in loving service of your neighbor, whom you are rescuing from the bonds of hell and of the devil. (*Works of Martin Luther*, vol. 4 [Philadelphia: Holman, 1931], pp. 251–53)

Through the medium of the Texas adoption process, Mel Gabler, with less than a year of college, and Norma Gabler, with a high school diploma, succeeded in superseding the work of professional historians and giving students a falsely pacifistic image of Luther. Since 1961, they have repeatedly intervened to present religious figures and events in a wholly favorable light by twentieth-century standards, divorcing them entirely from violence—regardless of the facts. When, at the conclusion of *Smith*, publishers announced that they would change their history books to include more about the contributions of religion but would not touch its negative side, they were acting on the basis of years of experience with this type of protest.

The changes brought about by the Gablers and other protesters in 1983 were not confined to religious matters. Their written reports on all of the world history books included the argument that because of Texas's pro-free enterprise educational law, socialism and Communism must be portrayed negatively and capitalism must be extolled. The Board of Education's list of changes told the publisher of that book, "Delete entire section [on socialism] and substitute a discussion of Adam Smith and capitalism" and "Delete 'What were the benefits of the Cooperative System?' and substitute 'What are the Essential Ideas of Capitalism?' " (p. 29). Board responses to other 1983 books included, "Delete and substitute 'Why do many people argue against government programs such as aid to education and public housing?' " (p. 18); "Add 'Have a class discussion on why the economic prosperity of Germany and other European nations depended upon the stability of American capitalism' " (p. 105); "Add teacher note: 'Have a class discussion on why the Marshall Plan is an example of American capitalism that affected the economic development of Western Europe after World War II' " (p. 106).

Texas's 1983 pro-capitalist changes are hard to evaluate without seeing copies of the pre-publication books in their entirety. If the books originally gave only the negative side of capitalism and the positive side of socialism, as the Gablers alleged, then Texas's changes produced more balanced texts. If the books were relatively balanced to begin with, then the modifications contributed to turning them into capitalist propaganda.

The Gablers' strong opposition to socialism has often led them to attack favorable presentations of federal social programs and government regulation of business. One of their targets in the 1983 adoption was Franklin Roosevelt's New Deal, an administration which, in their eyes, promoted economically disastrous policies. One sentence they considered misleading was, "These [New Deal] programs and policies were generally successful in restoring the prosperity of many Americans." The board told the publisher, "Change to read " 'In spite of this, by the time the United States entered World War II, most of the nation was still suffering from the Great Depression' " (p. 58). Obviously, historians disagree about the economic significance of the New Deal, but expert opinions have nothing to do with the way this history book was changed. Its emphasis was reversed, not because of a measured consideration of relevant data, but because of political pressure on elected officials.

Besides objecting to favorable treatment of Roosevelt's administration in the text itself, the Gablers wanted to omit the New Deal from a timeline of important events in American history. The publisher protested that the inclusion of the New Deal was not an endorsement of it, but an acknowledgment of its significance in American history. The board over-ruled the publisher and ordered, "Timeline, 1932 date: Delete 'New Deal program begins' " (59). Instead of redoing the timeline, the publisher simply whited out the New Deal, leaving a gap like a missing tooth just above Pearl Harbor.

Even if a sharp-eyed history teacher noticed the extra space in the timeline, it is unlikely that the teacher would say, "Aha! I know what happened here. The Gablers, working through the Texas Board of Ed-ucation, had the New Deal removed because they consider it unacceptably socialistic." If teachers *did* realize that, and even better, if they tied the timeline omission to the way the New Deal is presented in the text, they could balance the Gablers' influence by bringing in information of their own—if they had time, and if their districts permitted teacher-made ma-terials. More likely, though, a teacher would blame the extra space on the publisher's computer graphics, and therein lies both the power of textbook activists and the reason for *What Johnny Shouldn't Read*. No matter how good a teacher is, there is just so much time to study a textbook to try to figure out what is *not* there. Textbook protesters are entirely within their rights in lobbying elected or appointed officials to produce textbooks to their specifications, but they are more likely to be successful if the mass of people who would oppose them are only mar-ginally aware of what they are doing.

Texas's emphasis on capitalism is tied to opposition to Communism, and protesters often complain that textbooks are "soft" on the Soviet Union. The world history books proposed for adoption in 1983 drew anti-Communist fire from the Gablers and others for presenting favorable accounts of the Soviet Union's success with Sputnik. The board did not remove references to Sputnik, but it did require publishers to give prec-edence to the United States space program. "Add 3 to read 'The space era began in 1957 with the launching of the Soviet satellite *Sputnik*. Using reference materials in your library, prepare a report on why the United States has emerged as the world leader in space exploration. Based on your research, what are some reasons for the success of the United States space program?' " (p. 45). "Add teacher note: 'Have class discussion on ways the United States has advanced beyond Russia in the space race since Russia started the space era with the launching of *Sputnik*' " (p. 106).

Apart from their coverage of Sputnik, 1983 world history books contained several passages that protesters persuaded the board to change or delete on the grounds that they were pro-Communist. One such change was, "Add sentence to the end of paragraph to read 'To this day, the Soviet Union uses covert means to spread Communist aims' " (p. 18). Without specifying what material was being altered, the board also ordered, "Change the last three sentences to read 'As in all dictatorships, the people of Communist China had little freedom. During the period from 1949 to 1952, the government seized farmland from landlords against their will. In the process, it is estimated that up to several million landlords were killed' " (p. 18). Finally, in keeping with the Gablers' views on the acceptability of nuclear weapons, the board instructed a publisher to end a section on nuclear war with the sentence, "Other people believe that a nuclear freeze will only benefit the Soviet Union and hurt the United States and its allies" (p. 19).

Coverage of some non-Communist countries was also affected by Texas protesters. The Gablers, for example, objected to criticism of the Shah of Iran, who, they argued, was pro-American and therefore better than the Ayatollah who succeeded him. Without spelling out what material was being dropped, the board said, "Change to read 'The Shah made concessions but they came too late. The militants who seized American hostages were protesting the admission of the Shah into the United States for medical treatment' " (p. 47). The reign of the Shah, like the administration of Franklin Roosevelt, is open to a variety of interpretations. Once again, however, expert opinion had nothing to do with the way this material got into textbooks.

It would be misleading to suggest that the 1983 board complied with all of the protesters' requests. In opposing the United Nations, for example, the Gablers wanted books to say that the organization is heavily subsidized by the United States but dominated by Third World countries, and this viewpoint was not reflected in the Report of the Commissioner at all. In other areas, the board agreed to require some, but not all, of the changes the Gablers had requested. With regard to creationism, for example, the board watered down statements about the age of the earth but ignored challenges to social and linguistic evolution. The following quotations from one of the Gablers' 1983 petitions gives an idea of the kind of reasoning the board rejected:

> This discussion of early cultures presents as fact only the evolutionary assumption that human society slowly evolved from the simple (i.e. nomadic life) to the complex (i.e. community life). Evolutionary conjecture is no more empirically verifiable when extended to human

prehistory than when it is applied to human origins. An alternative theory of origins, no less scientific than evolution, and held by many citizens, maintains that human cultures organized highly integrated social structures quickly and simultaneously. That is, agricultural and urban systems sprang up in the second generation of human life on earth. Why is such a valid theory censored from this text? (pp. 3–4)

Similarly, the Gablers objected to accounts of the development of language: "This evolutionary presumption is not empirically verifiable. Some of the most primitive languages are among the most complex in existence. There is no factual basis for assuming that people developed spoken languages—only evolutionary speculation" (1983 Bill of Particulars, p. 4).

In addition to ignoring some of the Gablers' views, the 1983 elected board required a few changes that corresponded to requests from liberal groups. Following protests about history books describing men's daily lives but not women's, the board told one publisher, "Add 'Women moved from rural areas to the cities, earned wages for their labor, and entered new professions' " (p. 46). Another publisher was told, "Change 'businessmen uses' to 'business uses' " (p. 28), and was ordered to substitute "people" for "men" in several passages.

The 1983 board also responded favorably, though not extensively, to requests for coverage of African achievements. The publisher of a high school history book was told,

Change to read "The Cushites were not the only people who used iron for making tools and weapons. A group of people who lived in the West African Kingdom of Ghana (GAH-nuh) also knew how to make iron weapons and tools. By the 700s A.D., Ghana, which was then located northwest of where the nation of Ghana is today, had become an important Kingdom. Other African peoples near Ghana did not have such excellent tools and weapons. The use of iron helped Ghana to conquer other peoples and to become a powerful nation." (p. 15)

While requiring additional information about Africa, the board ignored requests for better coverage of African Americans. The tendency to try to placate minority groups by discussing their root culture while downplaying their significance in America eventually led California to make a rule forbidding this practice.

Although the 1983 board agreed to a few changes concerning women and minorities, it ignored far more liberal viewpoints than it endorsed. Hudson made a plea, largely ignored, against the exclusion of valuable information and creative thinking because of what he described as the narrow views of petitioners opposed to public education on principle. Elizabeth Judge, Director of a Texas-based liberal organization called Broader Perspectives, called for much greater representation of women and minorities than the board required. Madalyn Murry O'Hair, President of American Atheists, spoke as heatedly against the Texas protesters as they speak against atheists. Using language strong enough to be intentionally offensive, she protested against requirements "which are imposed on the publishers for material acceptable to the educationally backward State of Texas" (Hearing Before the Commissioner of Education and the State Textbook Committee, August 1, 1983, p. 71). She also objected to "the Christianization of world history" (p. 71) and to the use of "ruses and outright deceit to avoid the unreasonable and unscientific State of Texas demand that the science of Evolution be treated as mere theory" (p. 72). She concluded, "Each textbook, realistically, should be required to carry an introductory statement that religious fundamentalists are intruding into the public school system with demands to make our nation's schools a forum for religious dogma" (p. 73). Not surprisingly, the board did nothing that she recommended; indeed, the changes it required about prehistory, Jewish history, Renaissance humanism, and Martin Luther directly contradicted her arguments.

Even this brief look at the 1983 adoption, which generated thousands of pages of written and oral testimony, shows that the Gablers' views were endorsed over those of any other group. They did not get everything they wanted, but they did succeed in having nationally marketed textbooks altered in accordance with their ideas about secular as well as religious issues.

When the appointed board took office in 1984, the Gablers' opponents looked forward to witnessing their total and resounding defeat. That is not exactly what happened. Especially in its early years, the new board continued to require some textbook changes corresponding to the demands of the Gablers and their allies. The proportion of such modifications was lower, but they still existed.

Communism is one topic that has generally drawn fire from Texas boards of education, elected or appointed. The appointed board was less likely than its predecessors to require specific textbook changes regarding Communism, but, in 1985, it enacted a procedural change that the Gablers had wanted for years. The new policy required publishers submitting books to Texas to "footnote known factual political affiliations of those people who are quoted directly in the textbook" (Report of the State Board of Education Committee of the Whole, November 7, 1985). The change represented a partial response to long-standing opposition to teaching the literary works or public accomplishments of self-proclaimed or alleged Communists, such as Sherwood Anderson, James Baldwin, Ralph Bunche, Stokely Carmichael, Charlie Chaplin, Countee Cullen, e. e. cummings, W. E. B. DuBois, Lillian Hellman, Langston Hughes, Jesse Jackson, Martin Luther King, Jack London, Archibald MacLeish, Malcolm X, Arthur Miller, Pablo Picasso, John Steinbeck, and Richard Wright. According to Texas protesters, all of them are or were Communists—whether they themselves said so or not.

When publishers pointed out that textbook material by or about these controversial people had nothing to do with Communism, the protesters replied that that made things worse. Innocent children were being deceived into respecting the accomplishments of Communists without being given the opportunity to know them for what they were. Over and over, protesters demanded that the party memberships of people mentioned in textbooks be stated. The 1987 policy was limited to persons directly quoted in books and to verifiable political affiliations, so it did not give the protesters all they wanted. Nevertheless, the board action appeared to endorse the general idea that the political views of writers and public figures are relevant to whatever they write or say.

Texas law requires that free enterprise be presented in a favorable light, and the appointed board continued its predecessors' defense of capitalist economics. In 1987, the board told a publisher, "Rewrite to state, 'Supply-side economics includes economic policies that concentrate on creating jobs and increasing supply' " (p. 14); "Delete period and add 'or could lead to the creation of new industries and jobs thereby increasing the demand for workers' " (p. 14). The favorable tone toward supply-side economics is clear, but it would be interesting to see what the book originally said. Like so many of Texas's modifications, these cannot be evaluated without knowing whether they create a balance or upset one.

Communism and capitalism were not the only topics on which the appointed board, like its elected predecessors, backed the Gablers' position. In 1985, the board ordered the publisher of a history book to include material not only mentioning support for traditional sex roles but specifically describing Phyllis Schlafly's activity in this area. A separate requirement reminded the publisher to include Schlafly in the index.

Two years later, the publisher of a social studies book was told to rewrite paragraphs on South Africa to say in a neutral way that blacks do not like being ruled by the white minority, and that the South African government has begun reforms. The book should, the board said, feature black leaders who work against apartheid in a peaceful way. The sense of the required changes is clear: apartheid can be discussed, but its violent aspects should be downplayed and governmental concessions should be emphasized. The changes do not go as far as some protesters would have liked, but they do respond to that year's written petitions and public testimony.

Texas educational law says that textbooks must not "include selections or works which encourage or condone civil disorder, social strife, or disregard of the law." Books are also required to "present positive aspects of the United States and its heritage." Texas protesters often refer to these provisions in opposing references to social injustice, particularly in the United States. To them, discussing American racism or the civil rights movement puts the United States in a bad light and promotes racial hatred. They also oppose accounts of injustices committed by Christians against non-Christians or by non-Communist governments (especially pro-American ones) against their own citizens. Some protesters either deny that events like the Holocaust ever occurred or call for textbooks saying that most victimizing is done by non-Christians and Communists. The common thread running through all complaints of this type is the assumption that acknowledging evil deeds on the part of *any* Christians or capitalists is a way of discrediting Christianity and capitalism overall.

Although the appointed board continued to endorse some of the Gablers' positions, it totally rejected this one. From the beginning, the new board required textbooks to include candid, if brief, acknowledgements of injustices committed against various minority groups. Required changes included, "Add 'To the Indians, Custer was known as "Squaw Killer, a man who killed just for glory" ' " (Report of the Commissioner of Education Concerning Recommended Changes and Corrections in Textbooks, 1985, p. 72). "Rewrite to read 'New Era business people took little interest in the masses of Latin Americans. Many countries became ruled by military dictators who exploited and impoverished their own culture' " (p. 73). Texas education authorities also instructed the publisher to add, " 'Without moral codes and governmental safeguards, this kind of catastrophe [the Holocaust] might occur in any place, at any time' " (p. 74).

The board did not require many changes involving human rights, but the fact that it addressed the topic at all represents a significant change in Texas's influence on textbooks. The state still places less emphasis on social justice issues than California does in its 1988 Model Curriculum for Human Rights and Genocide, but the two states appear to be converging more than they did five years ago. The convergence is also apparent in Texas's post–1984 treatment of minorities and women.

African Americans are disproportionately represented in complaints by Texas protesters about the presence of self-acknowledged or alleged Communists in textbooks; in fact, it is not unusual for every African American included in a literature series or a history book to appear on such a list. Protesters sometimes quote self-identified African American Communists, such as Langston Hughes and Richard Wright, and then imply that the other African Americans mentioned in the same sentence must be Communists, too. Innuendo plays a large role in identifying Communists; protesters suggest that anyone who criticizes the economic and social arrangements of the United States, past or present, must be a Communist, which covers most contemporary African American writers and public figures. They also imply that civil rights activity is a way of keeping the United States government off balance and promoting welfare and other social programs, thus preparing the country for Communism.

Another strategy for connecting African Americans with Communism is to state, without citing evidence, that various civil rights organizations are Communist fronts. This tactic is not confined to civil rights; one protester objected to a history book on the grounds that its author belonged to a subversive organization: the American Association of University Professors.

In 1961, a protester who regarded a particular history book as unacceptably liberal pointed out that its author was a member of the Southern Conference Educational Fund. The protester maintained that the fund was a Communist front organization and that, in calling a meeting to propose a Civil Rights Commission, the Fund "recruited left-wing niggers from throughout the South, and they turned it [the meeting] into a sounding board for the agitation of racial equality" (Texas State Textbook Committee Hearing, September 14, 1961, p. 42). Since then, overtly racist epithets have been rare in the Texas adoption process, but the overall association of civil rights with Communism persists.

Several African American writers and civil rights leaders did belong to the Communist Party or at least dabble in Communism at some point in their lives. Some Texas protesters, disclaiming racism, regularly petition the board to remove these persons from textbooks on the grounds that they are subversives. When literary works are involved, publishers repeatedly point out that the poems and stories reprinted in their anthologies have nothing to do with Communism. As far as the protesters are concerned, the publishers' reply misses the point for two reasons. First, omitting overtly Communistic material is a way of deceiving the students about who the writer really is. Second, the fact that someone was or may have been a Communist outweighs any other consideration. When one publisher defended Langston Hughes by listing all the awards he had won, a protester denied that that had anything to do with literary merit; it just showed the degeneracy of the people who give the awards.

The appointment of a new Board of Education did not change the nature of the protesters' allegations. In 1985, a TSDAR representative objected to the inclusion of Hughes, Wright, and other African American writers in literature books on the grounds that they were Communists. "Black is not necessarily beautiful all the time," she testified. Shortly afterward, she got into a debate with a textbook committee member over the meaning of Hughes's poem "Rivers." Her interpretation was that the poem showed how blacks are spreading out all over the world. "I mean, that's his impact as you read it. Or at least it should be when you see his big black picture next to it" (Transcript of Proceedings Before the Commissioner of Education and the State Textbook Committee, 1985, p. 82). Like other Texas protesters, she also objected to material describing Jim Crow laws, lynchings, denials of voting rights, segregated education, or anything else suggesting that African Americans have ever suffered injustices. Raking all that up, she argued, would simply give students a bad impression of the United States and foster racial hatred.

Three years later, in 1988, a different TSDAR representative called for the elimination of African American writers from a communications textbook considered that year, "not because of race or color; but because of their unpatriotic activities" (Hearing Before the Commissioner of Education and the State Textbook Committee, July 1988, p. 81). She wanted books featuring African Americans who accept American society as it presently exists and focus on ways in which African Americans can fit in better. Martin Luther King and Jesse Jackson should be excluded from textbooks because, she asserted, the Louisiana Joint Legislative Committee on Un-American Activities had said that King had Communist connections, an assertion that also taints Jackson by association. Over the years, other protesters have expressed the same viewpoint: if African Americans are going to be in textbooks, then publishers should choose law-abiding individuals like Booker T. Washington and George Washington Carver, not Malcolm X and Martin Luther King.

The distinction that some Texas protesters make between racism and anti-Communism is not always obvious to other people. The 1985 TSDAR comment about Hughes's "big black picture," for example, does not seem to relate to his political views. Apart from that, it is hard to see the fairness in dismissing as Communistic even peaceful attempts to open polls, schools, colleges, and job opportunities to minorities, particularly African Americans. The subset of Texas protesters that routinely addresses this issue would, if it could, exclude from textbooks not only responses to past injustices, but also all record of the injustices themselves.

As far as it is possible to tell from the annual Report of the Commissioner, pre–1984 boards of education do not seem to have endorsed requests to exclude African Americans from textbooks. In fact, on at least two occasions an elected board required the addition of a minority person to a textbook illustration. The appointed board followed suit. In 1989 the board told a publisher, "More photographs are needed portraying minorities, especially Orientals and Hispanics, in adult and professional roles. Photographs should represent a better balance of youth from all ethnic groups (including Black, Hispanic, and Oriental). Achieve a more balanced distribution of photographs depicting minorities throughout the book."

The Texas Board of Education has never come close to placing the emphasis on minority representation and stereotyping that its California counterpart does, and despite occasional references to Asians, Hispanics, and Native Americans, Texas tends to concentrate on African Americans. All the same, the appointed board has called for more frequent and favorable depictions of minorities in the face of strong opposition from one segment of the Texas public. Elected boards required a few minor changes for "social content" reasons, but the appointed board made minority representation a higher priority.

Texas's convergence with California in requiring more, and more favorable, portrayals of minorities virtually guarantees publisher compliance. The positive effect of this use of market force is obvious: excluding material by and about minorities from textbooks is a reprehensible practice, and arguments to the effect that it should continue because minority material is not "traditional" are circular at best. On the other hand, advocates of more favorable minority representation are overstating the case when they deny that they could possibly be censors because they are interested in including, not excluding, material. When they get into the question of how to represent minorities, they *are* raising the possibility of excluding certain factual material because of the effect it might have.

Decisions about how to portray groups that have suffered serious prejudice depend on no less an issue than the purpose of education itself. If the primary business of American schools is to bring about social justice through attitude formation, then textbooks should show previously abused minorities in an entirely favorable light in order to overcome negative stereotypes that linger in the present. If, however, the unvarnished truth takes precedence, then no group of human beings can be shown without warts. Even if it is true that social justice requires, for the present, only positive portrayals of minorities that have been treated with gross injustice in the past and are still struggling to reach parity, there is no justification for doing something and then denying its significance. If textbooks include only favorable material about any group, that is as much a biased presentation—whatever its motive—as saying only positive things about capitalism or religion.

The portrayal of women in textbooks has always been a sticky issue in Texas adoptions, and the board's response to it has undergone the same changes that have characterized its treatment of minority issues. In 1972, a protester objected to a state policy that required "emphasizing the historical significance and impact of peoples of various religious, national, racial, and ethnic backgrounds" (quoted in State Textbook Committee Hearing, September 21–22, 1972, p. 6) without reference to women. The reason the protester opposed the policy was that a publisher had recently used it to justify history books dealing almost exclusively with men. The 1972 commissioner of education told the protester, "We'll accept responsibility for the fact you don't have more women in the book if you want to blame it on us" (p. 7). The following year, however, a publisher was required to add "one or more black females" to a chapter, and to change "the occupation of the father" to "the occupation of the parents." Such changes were few and far between; the next one did not appear until ten years later, when the 1983 board required three additional references to women in a history book.

Even without much impetus from Texas, textbooks gradually included more women, and more women in nontraditional roles, because of California's 1976 social content standards. The Gablers disagreed with the new emphasis on women working outside the home. In 1980, they challenged a psychology book for saying that women do not have to have children. "This is women's liberation propaganda," they wrote (Bill of Particulars, 1980, p. 14). Eight years later, Norma Gabler continued to assert that most representations of women should show them in traditional roles. She estimated that about 50 percent of all mothers work, and that at least 75 percent of them consider motherhood more important than a career. Adding the women who do not go out to work to those who work but give priority to motherhood, Gabler concluded that 88 percent of all women should be classified primarily as wives and mothers. So, she said, 88 percent of the women portrayed in textbooks should be shown in domestic roles. Another protester objected to a psychology book because although it stated that some people are happy with traditional roles, it also said that some women do not want to be full-time wives and mothers.

On the other side of the argument, individual protesters and representatives of women's groups, such as the National Organization for Women and the American Association of University Women, have appeared at Texas textbook hearings every year to question the shortage of women in literature, science, and history books. A 1972 protester, for example, objected to a sentence about Susan B. Anthony. The sentence, as she quoted it, read, "Her work is dealt with in another section on women's roles on pages 409 through 410, which traces the long history of the American woman's fight both for her own rights and those of others." "Well," the protester said, "if there is such a long history, how come it only got two pages?" (State Textbook Committee Hearing, September 21–22, 1972, p. 92). In 1983, Elizabeth Judge, of Broader Perspectives, raised a similar point. "The question," she said, "is not, 'Why should a little-known person of accomplishment be included?' Rather, the question is, 'Why is such an accomplished person so little known?'" (Hearing Before the Commissioner of Education and the State Textbook Committee, August 2, 1983, p. 47). That year's elected Board of Education did require a few changes in wording to acknowledge women, but it voted down a motion by one of its own members to change a history book's presentation of Magna Carta. The motion would have required the publisher to add to the discussion of "the rights of free men" a sentence saying that later movements had acknowledged similar rights for women.

In 1986, Texas required the publisher of a 1986 book on United States government to explain why women have tended to cluster in lower-paying jobs, but overall the appointed board did not make women's issues a priority. Beginning in 1989, however, a new elected board did. The publisher of a home economics book was required to replace a statement about older sisters taking care of younger children with a reference to older siblings of both sexes. Another publisher was told, "Both males and females are being depicted in very traditional roles (sister helps make bedspread, brother has lumber on hand, brother helps put up bookshelves). Adjust" (Report of the Commissioner of Education Concerning Recommended Changes and Corrections in Textbooks, 1989, p. 319). The 1989 board also mandated changes from *girls* to *young women* and from *unwed* to *single*. In the 1990 adoption, the publisher of a business book was required to show pictures of a female executive, a female construction worker, and a male child-care worker. The 1989 and 1990 requirements represent more action on women's issues than Texas had ever seen. Before 1989, it was not unusual for a single change to be followed by years of inactivity.

Norma Gabler's mathematical argument suggests that she would settle for seeing 88 percent of women shown in domestic roles, but in practice she and other protesters routinely attack *any* portrayal of women in nontraditional situations. On the other side, some protesters attack *every* traditional presentation of women on the grounds that those roles are so ingrained in American culture that textbooks should decondition children by associating women with leadership roles, construction work, sports, and other activities that have tended to be dominated by men.

From the traditionalist viewpoint, the issue is simple: God created women to be helpmates to men and mothers of children, so there is no reason to promote any other role. To nontraditionalists, the problem is more complicated. It is true that one reason many women still cluster in traditional situations is the lack of role models and grass-roots social acceptance of change. On the other hand, if women have choices, then it is illogical and unfair to downgrade the choice of being full-time wives and mothers by omitting it from textbooks as if women who select that option should be ashamed of themselves.

Texas has given significantly less attention to women's issues than it has to Communism, capitalism, religion, evolution, and, more recently, race relations—perhaps because, by the time it began to focus on this area at all, California-mandated alterations had already brought the representation of women at least as far as Texas would have gone. The few changes Texas does require have, since 1989, favored nontraditionalists exclusively. The difficulty with evaluating these changes without being able to see the pre-publication text is the same with women's issues as with other topics: without knowing how a book originally handled men's and women's accomplishments overall, it is impossible to tell whether particular alterations balance or unbalance it.

A recent change in Texas textbook politics is the most dramatic turnaround in the history of the adoption process. For years, Texas led the nation in rejecting evolution, requiring textbooks that mentioned the subject to put a disclaimer on the title page—similar to a surgeon general's warning—saying that the theory of evolution has not been proven. A 1974 Texas rule requiring that evolution be presented in "a manner not detrimental to other theories of origin" helped to make textbooks produced in the 1970s and 1980s less thorough in their coverage of evolution than 1960s books had been.

Around the time of *McLean* and *Aguillard,* when national creationist organizations were strongly advocating "balanced treatment" of creationism and evolution, the Texas Board of Education passed a rule mandating equal coverage of both theories. The policy was withdrawn when the state attorney general, citing *McLean,* said that it was unconstitutional.

In addition to establishing anti-evolution policies, Texas boards of education required changes that eliminated or masked the role of gradual development in history, psychology, and sociology as well as in science. In 1973, the Gablers attacked a sociology book for saying that humans are "social animals." According to the Gablers, "This is the degrading viewpoint of the Humanistic religion. SCIENTIFICALLY man's flesh is vastly different than any other flesh providing strong evidence that man was created apart from animals." The Board of Education told the publisher, "Substitute the word 'beings' for 'animals' " (Bills of Particulars Filed in Protest of Certain Textbooks Being Considered for Adoption in 1973 and Publishers' Answers to the Bills of Particulars, p. 91). In 1980, the board required the publisher of a psychology book to change the word *evolution,* used in a generic way to mean gradual progress, to *development.* The publisher was also told to change a passage on the human brain to omit references to evolution over time and to its development from nonhuman species.

Some members of the elected Board of Education proposed a pro-evolution policy early in 1984. Following an explosion of public comment on both sides, the measure failed. All the same, during the 1985 adoption of life science books, the newly appointed board came down on the side of evolutionists by requiring a publisher to add paragraphs saying that monkeys, gorillas, and mice have similar blood chemistries, and that the similarities among these placental animals suggest a common ancestry. The publisher was also instructed to discuss DNA analysis, the fossil record, and embryo similarities as evidence of evolution. These changes do not explicitly address human origins, but they represent the first acknowledgement by a Texas Board of Education that evolution exists at all.

In 1988, the appointed board adopted a policy requiring geology books to include material on evolution. As a result of the board's action, a state that had been one of the nation's strongest opponents of evolution became the first state to mandate its inclusion. Even the appointed board, however, tread warily around the subject of human origins. Because the new policy covered geology, not biology, books, it affected debates about the age of the earth without necessarily saying that humans evolved from another species. The board also bowed to public lobbying by making a last-minute addition to the policy to include other scientific theories, "if any," which left the door open for continued arguments about the scientific validity of creationism.

Shortly after passing the evolution policy, the appointed board completed its term. It was succeeded by a new elected board that took office on January 1, 1989. Despite fears of a return to Gabler-dominated textbook adoptions, the new board proved to be even less swayed by their testimony than its predecessor had been.

Although the pro-evolution policy put in place by the appointed board related to geology books, its reference to other scientific theories added suspense to the 1990 biology adoption. Creationists and evolutionists alike waited to see how the notion of alternate theories would affect the teaching of human origins. The board received over a thousand telephone calls urging the rejection of biology books teaching evolution, but, as Michael Hudson reported in a jubilant memo to PAW headquarters, "the Texas Board—in sharp contrast to past practice—refused to be swayed" (November 14, 1990). The board not only adopted books teaching evolution but also required a publisher to

> Delete the section on scientific creationism, and substitute information such as the following: "SCIENTISTS' CONSENSUS REGARDING EVOLUTION: There are virtually no differences of opinion among biologists, and indeed nearly all scientists on the following major points regarding evolution: (1) the earth is about 4.5 billion years old. There is no scientific evidence to support the hypothesis that the earth is only a few thousands year old [sic]; (2) organisms have inhabited the earth for the greater part of that time; and (3) all living things, including human beings, have evolved from earlier, simpler living things. There is no scientific evidence that indicates that every species of organism was created separately. The antiquity of the earth and the role that the process of evolution played in the production of all organisms, living and extinct, is accepted by virtually all scientists." (Report of the Commissioner of Education Concerning Recommended Changes and Corrections in Textbooks, 1990, p. 74)

The Gablers accused the board of censoring creationism and of presenting evolution as fact when it is nothing more than the religious belief of a small number of people. Their view was supported by an article in a CEE newsletter arguing that the Texas Board of Education had violated its own policy by adopting books that did not present alternatives to evolution. "The bigoted publishers (bigotry is defined as intolerantly holding to an opinion) of the thirteen biology books defied the state board by ignoring these requirements [for alternate theories]. The state textbook committee and TEA failed in their responsibility to hold the publishers to the pre-set specifications" (CEE, "News from Around the World," no date, p. 1).

Hudson offered a different interpretation of the board's action. To him, the rejection of creationism meant, not that a valid scientific theory was being omitted, but that there are no valid scientific theories other than evolution to explain the development of species. He and other anti-creationist protesters saw the board's action as liberating textbook publishers to distinguish science from religion, after years of subjection to creationist lobbying.

The evolutionists' sense of total victory lasted for only a year. In 1991, the board issued a call for new life science books for junior high schools. An anti-evolutionist board member wanted to require the books to present evidence against natural selection, which, she argued, is only a theory. Opponents protested that once again the scientific use of the word *theory* was being misunderstood. They, like the California scientists, asserted that natural selection is as accepted as any scientific notion can be, and that the evidence against it is religious, not scientific. Besides, they argued, targeting natural selection for special treatment suggests that it is somehow less established than other scientific theories, such as gravity. Nevertheless, the board finally decided to require evidence for and against evolution. A headline in the next Eagle Forum newsletter proclaimed, "Creationists Claim Victory in Texas Education Vote." Evolutionists also asserted that they had made some important gains, but, as Hudson observed, the door has yet to close on creationism in the science classroom.

The results of the 1991 adoption of life science books were mixed. Creationists raised the usual objections to teaching evolution, arguing that defining people as animals would remove all moral and social restraints. One protester urged the rejection of a particular textbook on the grounds that evolution "is supportive of the sexual revolution, because animals may copulate freely without the condemnation of God or men. As a teenager, eager to spread venereal disease and illegitimate children across the landscape, what could be sweeter? their behavior seems almost scientifically endorsed, doesn't it?" (Transcript of Proceedings: Joint Hearing before the Commissioner of Education and the State

Textbook Secondary Science Committee, July 8, 1991, p. 49). Nevertheless, the publishers' lack of concern was evident in the unusual brevity of their replies to the protesters' written comments. The publisher whose book was attacked for promoting teenage promiscuity wrote a single paragraph responding to the combined remarks of six protesters, and the textbook committee endorsed that publisher's book on the first ballot. The Board of Education also accepted the book and, as far as it is possible to tell from the Report of the Commissioner, required only one significant alteration: "Change 'things have a common ancestor' to 'thing may have a common ancestor' " (p. 15). Without knowing the context of the altered sentence—what thing or things have or may have had a common ancestor?—it is impossible to assess the importance of the change. There is, however, little likelihood that the modification will satisfy either side of the evolution/creation debate. Scientists will assert that this type of waffling is no more necessary or appropriate in discussing evolution than in discussing gravity or electricity, and creationists will continue to maintain that a legitimate scientific theory of human origins is being censored.

In the last few years, boards of education in California and Texas have tried hard to distinguish between scientific evidence and religious belief in science instruction. Without denying the possibility that further testing could refute at least some aspects of today's understanding of evolution, both states have rejected the idea that the teaching of human origins in science classes should be affected by anyone's religious beliefs. All the same, recent Texas and California policies on evolution have been watered down by last-minute changes made, not because of scientific arguments, but because of creationist clout. As one California scientist pointed out in dismay, the opinion of a panel of experts chosen for their prominence in their fields can be overruled in a moment by authorities acting under political pressure.

Both Texas and California have undoubtedly made some good decisions over the years, and their market power insures that publishers will comply. From the standpoint of censorship, however, the vulnerability of boards of education to political pressure raises serious questions about the way in which final decisions are made about instructional material. No matter how much specialized knowledge textbook authors have, they are routinely second-guessed by officials with absolutely no background in the field. It was not long ago that the New Deal was taken off a timeline of important American events, not because historians believe it was unimportant, but because its policies conflicted with the religio-political stand of influential Texas protesters. In 1991, publishers' replies to creationist protesters were based entirely on the books' conformity to

Texas's pro-evolution requirements; scientific accuracy as such was not even mentioned. As long as the present system of determining textbook content remains in place, no matter how its power is being used at any particular moment, the potential for censorship at the behest of a politically influential minority still exists. In that sense, improvements only serve to blunt awareness of the underlying issue.

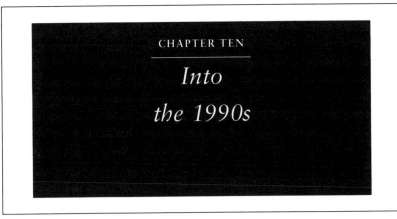

CHAPTER TEN

Into
the 1990s

Parents who want their children to grow up free to read, free to think, and free to make the critical decisions that will affect their lives must become involved. They dare not leave the business of the schools to the censors who have already become involved and who are attempting to make some drastic changes in the schools. Parents who believe in the Constitution and the Bill of Rights must begin reading and responding to bills affecting the schools that are introduced in their state legislatures and in Congress. Parents concerned about the rights of their children must be willing to protect those rights.
—EDWARD JENKINSON

Textbook protests are by no means an isolated issue in the 1990s. Within the first year of the decade, similar controversies erupted over homoerotic exhibits funded by the National Endowment for the Arts, unflattering portrayals of pioneers in a Smithsonian display, abortion counseling in federally funded clinics, and non-Western perspectives in Columbus quincentennial programs. The nation appears to be going through a crisis in freedom of speech: some conservatives object to the use of federal funds to support anything offensive to their particular religious or social views, while some feminists and minority group members object to language they perceive as violating their civil rights.

Within this overall climate of First Amendment activism, the Eagle Forum, Concerned Women for America, and Citizens for Excellence in Education continue to encourage school protests against ideas and approaches they find offensive. The January 1990 issue of the CWA magazine, for example, contains a list of "what can really be expected from today's education" (*Concerned Women*, p. 18). The list is a good illustration of the way in which problems most people would acknowledge—teenage pregnancy, sexual activity, violence, lack of discipline, drugs, illiteracy, high dropout rates, poor mathematics skills, poor knowledge of geography—are combined with CWA's own issues: evolution, sex education, death education, values clarification, globalism, environmentalism, fear of nuclear war, positive depictions of the Soviet Union, and New Age religion in place of Christianity. Similarly, the August 1991 issue of the *Phyllis Schlafly Report* continues the Eagle Forum's drive to promote hostility between parents and the public schools with headlines proclaiming, "NEA Disrespect for Home and Parents," "How the Teachers Union Checkmates Parents," and "Schools Launch Offensive Against Parents." The issue also promotes an Eagle Forum flier entitled "Does Your School Encourage Children to Do Drugs?"

The CWA reference to New Age religion reflects one of the most important movements in 1990s textbook activism. Trying to define New Age religion is like trying to define secular humanism: both are nebulous terms used to justify the accusation that public education is teaching a religion other than Christianity, both involve words that are used differently by different people, and both function as umbrella headings for a varied assortment of ideas. New Age thought is described by at least some of its adherents as a religion, so in this sense its First Amendment status is clearer than secular humanism's. Beyond that, *clarity* is not the first word that leaps to mind in identifying New Age beliefs.

J. Gordon Melton, an authority on comparative religions who testified for the *Mozert* defendants, has compiled a *New Age Almanac*. The first two sentences of the introduction read, "An attempt to understand the New Age Movement easily can be frustrated by the movement's diversity. The New Age Movement has no single leader, no central organization, no firm agenda, and no group of official spokespersons" (p. ix). Melton later explains that "New Agers have either experienced or are diligently seeking a profound personal transformation from an old, unacceptable life to a new, exciting future.... Having experienced a personal transformation, New Agers project the possibility of the transformation not of just a number of additional individuals, but of the culture and of humanity itself.... Healing projected into the larger social context has become a movement to heal the earth, the ideological foundation for the movement's support of peace and ecological activism" (p. 3). Among the topics covered in the *New Age Almanac* are astrology, channeling, communes, cosmic awareness, dreams, holistic health, hypnosis and self-hypnosis, meditation, parapsychology, past-life therapy, reincarnation, Tarot, theosophistry, UFOs, vegetarianism, and yoga.

Some New Age ideas, such as belief in astrology and paranormal phenomena, have been greeted with skepticism by large portions of the general public. Other concepts, such as the need for environmentalism and international understanding, enjoy much wider acceptance. Organizations like CEE, CWA, and the Eagle Forum, however, do not distinguish among the different elements of the New Age movement. To them, the New Age is in the process of replacing secular humanism as the single entity that embodies all the ideas with which they disagree. The vagueness and comprehensiveness of the New Age movement, coupled with its advocacy of Eastern religious practices, environmentalism, globalism, the occult, and personal growth from within, make it possible for ultraconservative textbook protesters to emphasize and expand on those aspects of New Age ideology that overlap the earlier secular humanist agenda.

The textbook protesters' assertion that New Age beliefs are very different from their own faith is unassailable, but their application of the term *New Age* to public school instruction is broad enough to raise serious questions. In 1990 and 1991, the Michigan Model for Comprehensive School Health Education came under fire from protesters supported by the Eagle Forum and other national groups. They maintained that teaching problem-solving techniques, holistic health principles, and decision-making skills undermined authority and the American family structure while promoting New Age religion. Some of them also alleged that having students do breathing exercises in health class could lead to New Age mind control. In one Michigan district, protesters argued against lessons on fire safety and traffic rules on the grounds that those lessons were tainted by association with the rest of the Michigan Model. The district terminated the entire program. Other districts opted to keep the program despite the protests, prompting national groups to threaten First Amendment lawsuits.

Other accusations that public schools are teaching New Age religion involve the concept of self-improvement. An article in the *Phyllis Schlafly Report* for July 1990 argues that New Age techniques are being used to teach self-esteem, although according to the report it is highly questionable whether schools should use any method of promoting that quality. Further, "Since there is no academic discipline called self-esteem, and there are no guidelines or standards, writers of self-esteem curricula reach out for any ideas they can find. To the dismay of many parents, some public school courses involve techniques and practices commonly associated with the New Age ideology, and that makes these courses a vio-lation of the First Amendment rights of schoolchildren and their parents." Among the challenged practices are "visualization, relaxation, and affir-mations" (p. 3).

The textbook protesters' use of the New Age movement, like their use of secular humanism, is open to the criticism that they want to take ideas that merely happen to coincide with a particular belief system out of the schools on constitutional grounds. The fact that New Agers believe in environmentalism, for example, is enough to convince some protesters that teaching high school students about global warming violates the First Amendment. Similarly, fairy tales and ghost stories that antedate the New Age movement by centuries are called unconstitutional because they involve supernatural beings, and the occult is part of New Age ideology. Overall, references to New Age beliefs serve to bring into the 1990s the same battles that have been fought, and are still being fought in a few places, under the name of secular humanism. The emphasis has shifted somewhat—for example, New Age challenges focus relatively more on the occult and relatively less on evolution—but no idea that was opposed in *Mozert* and *Smith* for promoting secular humanism is entirely absent from today's controversies involving New Age religion.

In addition to long-standing groups like CEE, CWA, and the Eagle Forum, new national organizations are entering the fight against what they de-scribe as New Age religion in the public schools. Donald Wildmon's Mississippi-based American Family Association (AFA), which alleged in 1988 that the cartoon character Mighty Mouse was secretly inhaling cocaine when he smelled flowers, is beginning to become active in text-book disputes. Another newcomer is Focus on the Family, an organization based in California and headed by psychologist James Dobson, a former member of the Meese Commission on Pornography whose books ad-vocating corporal punishment were challenged in a Minnesota school district. The primary target of both AFA and Focus on the Family is *Impressions,* a reading series published by Holt, Rinehart and Winston, whose 1983 Basic Reading Series was at issue in *Mozert.* (Because Holt recently became a subsidiary of the publishing firm Harcourt Brace Jov-anovich, some sources identify *Impressions* as a Harcourt publication. Holt's elementary school textbooks, however, still appear under the old name.)

All six of the 1991 issues of the American Library Association's *News-letter on Intellectual Freedom* contained accounts of protests against *Impressions.* People for the American Way counted forty-five separate challenges to the series in 1990–91, giving it the dubious distinction of being by far the most controversial instructional material in use that year. The primary objection leveled against the books, which are intended for children in the first through sixth grades, is that they include stories about witches and ghosts. According to opponents of the series, public schools that use it are teaching New Age religion. The fact that Holt, Rinehart and Winston is based in Canada has also led to the allegation that the series fosters Canadian rather than American heritage. An earlier version was criticized for its "Canadianisms," which have since been removed from United States editions.

A newspaper account of a dispute in Boise, Idaho, stated that twenty-two of the 822 selections in *Impressions* deal with ghosts, goblins, and witches. Opponents of the series, however, find far more satanic references: CEE cited a "scholarly study" showing that 52 percent of the Holt stories deal with the occult, and a parent in Lakewood, New York, gave the same figure during an anti-*Impressions* campaign there. The reason the count is so high is that the protesters interpret certain words and pictures idiosyncratically. In their view, six-pointed stars, regardless of context, are evidence of devil worship; eight-pointed stars, such as those appearing in pictures of Aztec calendars, represent days on which children were sacrificed; and pictures of the rainbow promote New Age religion and therefore acceptance of the occult.

According to a news story about an event in Box Elder, South Dakota, parents chanted "blood and gore" and yelled obscenities to protest the use of *Impressions*. Betty Bowers, a principal in the Douglas School District near Rapid City, was disconcerted by someone who said, "Get me the hearts of the superintendent and principal." "That is the one that really upset us because that's pretty gross," Bowers told a reporter. School officials and parents who opposed the protesters also observed that the protesters' language was as violent and morbid as anything they were challenging in the books. After a meeting in which the school board voted 4–1 to continue using *Impressions*, a teacher "was grabbed by a parent and told 'the prince of darkness will get you'" (*Sioux Falls Argus Leader,* November 27, December 13, 1990; quoted in *Newsletter,* March 1991, p. 48).

In Lakewood, New York, parents objected to a third-grade Holt story, "Witch Goes Shopping," because it mentions witchcraft and because the teachers' manual suggests asking children to discuss spells and to make up chants based on the witch's shopping list. The leader of the protesting parents told a newspaper reporter, "We believe there is a desensitizing effect here. Pretty soon, casting and chanting spells will seem so commonplace to kids that, when they're confronted with the advances of satanic groups on a darker level, it will seem more acceptable. There's no shock value that would deter them." Another parent disagreed. "They make it sound like the whole series has an overriding theme dealing with chants and spells, but they can't substantiate that. To me, it's totally harmless... I think if they get this cut, it sets a precedent. It starts to give those people a control over the curriculum" (*Buffalo News,* March 10, 1991; quoted in *Newsletter,* May 1991, pp. 76–77).

The AFA, CEE, CWA, Eagle Forum, and Focus on the Family have made the *Impressions* series the target of newsletters and other mailings. Throughout the country, school officials and protesters alike report that the controversy is being fueled by the publications of these organizations rather than by spontaneous local responses to the books themselves. The leader of an anti-*Impressions* movement in Fairbanks, Alaska, stated that his dissatisfaction with the series began after his wife had heard in a Bible study meeting that the books are dangerous. Fairbanks school officials said that everyone who telephoned them about the Holt books quoted an article in the *Citizen,* a publication of Focus on the Family.

During a debate over including *Impressions* on Georgia's state-approved list, some of the protesters had not read the books but used the *Citizen* to identify offensive material contained in them. The Georgia Board of Education subsequently voted 13–8 against approving the series. A board member acknowledged that the board's discussion had dealt almost exclusively with the handful of stories targeted by the protesters, ignoring the rest of the series. To the opponents of *Impressions,* this focus is fully justified. Believing that the books threaten traditional Christian values, a California protester told a reporter, "We must send these books back and send a message back to the publisher that a little of this stuff is too much" (*Grass Valley* [California] *Union,* March 11, 1991; quoted in *Newsletter,* July 1991, p. 107).

School officials and parents who oppose the protesters maintain that the Holt books are neutral on religion and that it is the protesters who seek to bring sectarian religious beliefs into the selection of instructional materials for public schools. A review committee member in Lakewood, New York, expressed the prevailing opinion that the series "allows the students to read about the beliefs of many groups without promotion or instruction of one particular way of life" (*Buffalo News,* March 10, 1991; quoted in *Newsletter,* July 1991, p. 132). A New Mexico parent expressed similar ideas shortly after the Board of Education had voted to include *Impressions* on the state-approved list. She told a reporter that the protesters' loud insistence that school authorities are trampling on the rights of parents belied the fact that the majority of parents see nothing wrong with the series.

It has become standard practice for unsuccessful protesters to vow to take legal action, and lawsuits have in fact been filed in two situations involving *Impressions*. In Willard, Ohio, the AFA filed suit on the grounds that the series advances the religion of Wicca or witchcraft. Parents involved in the Ohio suit also alleged that the books teach excessive regard for animals and that a picture showing two women and a child dancing promotes homosexuality. PAW agreed to fund the defense, but the suit was dropped. The AFA later filed a similar suit, *Brown v. Woodland Joint Unified School District,* on behalf of a couple in Woodland, California, after an attempt to remove the series through the district's re-review process failed.

After listing more than forty objectionable selections and activities, the complaint in *Brown* states, "The purchase and use of these portions of the *Impressions* curriculum has a real and substantial effect of affiliating the School District with the Witchcraft and/or Neo-Pagan religions. . . . Parents [the Browns] are practicing Christians. Their Christian faith is predicated on the belief that their own salvation and that of their children is possible only through unqualified faith in Jesus Christ and the observance of his teachings as set forth in the Bible. The Bible prohibits Christians from involvement in witchcraft, sorcery, or pagan rites" (Second Amended Complaint, n.d., pp. 10–11). Although New Age religion figures prominently in anti-*Impressions* controversies throughout the country, it has not been mentioned so far in connection with this lawsuit. The complaint concludes by requesting the court to prohibit the school district from purchasing or using any portion of the Holt readers found to violate the United States Constitution or the California Constitution.

On May 6, 1991, PAW attorneys filed a petition on behalf of the "Woodland Parents," eleven supporters of the Holt series who wanted to join the case as defendant-intervenors. Ten of the petitioners are parents of Woodland elementary school children, most of whom are using *Impressions*. Two of the Woodland Parents are teachers using the series in their classes. Having the same stake in Woodland elementary education as the Browns, the petitioners praised *Impressions* for its variety of ideas, high interest level, and positive effect on the children's reading skills. In anticipation of joining the case, the petitioners prepared an answer to the Browns' complaint, stating that the removal of *Impressions* from the district would "violate the First Amendment rights of the Woodland Parents and their children by tailoring public school curriculum to satisfy plaintiffs' religious beliefs, and by depriving the children of the Woodland Parents of their right to receive information and to have access to the dissemination and discussion of ideas (The Woodland Parents' Answer in Intervention to First Amended Complaint, April 5, 1991, p. 5). Their petition to intervene was accepted, and the suit is now pending in the United States Court for the Eastern District of California. The plaintiffs and the defendant-intervenors have filed cross-motions for summary judgment, each side asserting that its own position is clear as a matter of law and requires no further litigation. The defendant-intervenors maintain that the readers do not promote or inhibit religion, and that the school district handled the Browns' complaint appropriately. The plaintiffs contend that, because their challenge to *Impressions* is religious, the school authorities became unconstitutionally entangled with religion as soon as they attempted to evaluate it. In the unlikely event that the courts accept this argument, school officials faced with any religiously based protest would have no alternative but to yield without question, since any attempt to weigh the merits of the complaint would be unconstitutional.

Naturally, the AFA named the school district, not parents who support the *Impressions* series, as defendants in the lawsuit. On that basis, *Brown*, as it was originally configured, was a good example of the image promoted by national organizations like the Eagle Forum: Christian parents trying to compel hostile authorities to acknowledge parental rights over the education of their children. The involvement of the Woodland Parents changed the question from "When do school officials have the right to overrule parents?" to "When does one set of parents have the right to force the removal of textbooks that other parents support?" Since the Browns are requesting removal of the series rather than alternate assignments for their own children, they will have to prove not only that their children should not read stories that do not conform to their religious beliefs but that no public school child should read them.

The question of parental involvement in public education is a difficult one: parents have the right to oversee their children's upbringing, but, as the defendants in *Mozert* indicated, public schools cannot function with each parent exercising firsthand control of his or her child's instruction. The system of having public education overseen by school boards that are either elected themselves or appointed by elected officials does give parents, along with other taxpayers, some power over school governance; but the present arrangement, in the view of its opponents, offers too little opportunity for parental input. People who are intent on effecting particular changes in the schools chafe at the indirectness of merely voting, along with thousands of other citizens, for school board members. They also complain that lay boards are unduly deferential to the opinions of education professionals. Ironically, other critics express concern about the power of elected or appointed boards for exactly the opposite reason, that it makes education the only profession to be controlled so completely by people who may, and often do, have no training in it. Moreover, putting final decisions into the hands of elected or appointed officials who are thereby vulnerable to pressure from special interest groups politicizes education itself, as the textbook adoption process in California and Texas illustrates.

The reasoning behind giving final authority to boards of education that are either elected or appointed by elected officials is entirely consistent with the representative system of government that is used to decide other issues, from income tax to highway construction. Economists advise legislators on tax matters, but they do not make final decisions. Engineers give their opinions, but roads are built where elected officials decide they should be. It would be naive to think that decisions about taxes and highways are entirely independent of political considerations, and, judging from letters to the editor and other public forums, Americans in general do not think so.

Where education is concerned, the situation is a little different. In an informal survey conducted as part of the research for this book, the vast majority of participants thought that textbook content is determined either by experts in each field, or by teachers and school administrators, or by the two combined. One reason for my writing the book is to inform parents and other concerned citizens of the kinds of changes that occur in textbooks for reasons that have nothing to do with experts or educators. Evolution was not featured in textbooks when scientists concluded that it is on a par with the theories of electricity and gravity; it was omitted or masked until California and Texas state politics permitted its emergence.

Market forces—exemplified by the California and Texas textbook adoptions—put teeth into federal lawsuits and lead to the selection of textbook material for political rather than instructional reasons. So what do we do about it? The question is logical but not easy. Federal courts consistently uphold the principle that boards of education have the final word on instructional matters unless they do something blatantly unconstitutional, and trying to undo that system could easily cause more problems than it solves.

Given the authority of school boards in general, the Texas and California state boards have a perfect right to tell publishers what they would like textbooks to include, and publishers are entitled to try to produce books that will sell in large markets. Besides, recent changes in both states show that if they themselves take a firm stand against special interest groups and insist on books that reflect the best knowledge in the field, past weaknesses in textbooks can be rectified within the present system—without, of course, eliminating the risk of the pendulum swinging back the other way at some point. Other large adoption states or coalitions of smaller states could also bring their own influence to bear on publishers if they took strong stands on particular issues, but there is no reason to believe that special interest groups in those states could not have the same effect that they have had in California and Texas.

Possible solutions to these problems are likely to go in one of two directions: toward centralization or away from it. One centralized approach might be a national curriculum that would drive textbook content. Even if the tremendous practical problems of establishing such a curriculum were overcome, however, the lobbying of special interest groups could well be even more intense at the national level than at the state level. There may be reasons for a national curriculum that do not fall within the scope of this book, but where potential censorship of politically volatile ideas is concerned, federalization does not leap out as the best hope for the future.

An example of a decentralized approach is self-publishing by local school districts and private schools. Some publishers are already offering to tailor textbooks to the requirements of districts that are in a position to purchase some minimum number of the customized books, but that service is quite expensive. There is, however, no reason why school districts have to be tied to textbooks produced by large companies. Trial and error, creativity, and university-school partnerships could result in excellent educational materials produced by combinations of teachers and specialists in various fields.

Locally produced materials would not have to be developed for every topic covered in textbooks—at least, not if the goal is to address censorship issues. Pressure groups target a wide range of topics, but they are actually effective in a much smaller number of areas, such as religion, portrayals of various demographic groups, junk food, capitalism, Communism, and evolution. Districts that are particularly concerned about how any or all of these issues are handled could consider releasing a few high-quality teachers from some of their present duties to give them time to collaborate with specialists, perhaps from a nearby university or research institute, to produce materials that could be used throughout the district or state to supplement textbooks.

The feasibility of this approach depends on four factors: the amount of flexibility each state gives local districts, the district's willingness to release teachers from classroom duties, the quality of the people available to work on such projects, and the funds to reproduce and distribute the finished product. If projects are poorly done, the results could be disastrous. There could also be a lot of duplicated effort as teams in different districts or states work on the same problems. On the other hand, this approach would allow a few representative teachers to do what each teacher, individually, could not be expected to do in terms of reviewing textbooks and preparing supplementary materials. Preparing instructional materials could also stimulate greater professionalism among teachers and increase the involvement of content area specialists with the school system. In the best of all possible scenarios, some of the approaches generated by such teams might even filter into nationally marketed textbooks. Besides, knowing that it is not the only game in town is likely to inspire better performance on the part of any business.

Schools can go a long way toward offsetting the effects of censorship, but they cannot do the whole job. Just as censorship problems arise from the public and not from the schools themselves, any real solution to those problems requires active community participation. When I give talks on textbook censorship, members of the audience often ask, "How do we stop pressure groups that affect textbook content?" Stop them from doing what? From filing lawsuits if they do not like what their children are learning in school? From lobbying elected officials and campaigning for candidates whose views reflect their own? Who decides when other people are so "crazy" that they deserve to be disenfranchised? It is true that conservative, moderate, and liberal parents who disapprove of censorship have the right to a decent education for their children, but that is not the same as being entitled to such an education without effort. Parents in school districts that have experienced no local textbook activism may assume that they can sit back and relax, but, as this book illustrates, textbook censorship affects students in all American schools, public and private alike. Until large numbers of parents and other taxpayers who disapprove of censorship become active, why should the status quo change?

Sources

Chapter Two: Power Struggle

Bernard Weiss et al., eds., Holt, Rinehart and Winston Basic Reading Series, Grades 1–8.

Rules, Regulations, and Minimum Standards for the Governance of Public Schools in the State of Tennessee, October 1, 1982.

Ken Crowder, "Hawkins Textbook 'Telepathy' Reference Opposed," *Kingsport* [Tennessee] *Times-News,* September 2, 1983.

Betty Kauffman, "6th Grade Reader Called Subliminally Anti-Christ," *Norristown* [Tennessee] *Citizen-Tribune,* September 2, 1983.

Hawkins County Board of Education Minutes, September 8, October 1, 13, November 10, December 8, 1983.

Ken Crowder, "Hawkins Refuses to Ban Textbook," *Kingsport* [Tennessee] *Times-News,* September 9, 1983.

Robert B. Mozert, Jr., "Stamp Out Humanism," *Times-News,* October 6, 1983.

Letter from the National Rifle Association to Vicki Frost, October 11, 1983.

Notes written by Jean Price, October 13, 18, 20; November 19, 21, 22, 23, 25, 1983.

Letter from Jennie Wilson to the Hawkins County Board of Education, October 14, 1983.

Betty Kauffman, "Children Removed from Church Hill School," *Citizen-Tribune,* October 19, 1983.

David Brooks, "Hawkins, Text-Firm Officials Huddle on Reading Books," *Times-News*, October 26, 1983.

Memorandum from Superintendent Bill Snodgrass to Hawkins County School Principals, November 11, 1983.

David Brooks, "Showdown Possible Over Hawkins Textbooks," *Times-News*, November 13, 1983.

David Brooks, "Hawkins Text Dispute Reaches 'Impasse,' " *Times-News*, November 15, 1983.

David Brooks, "Hawkins Text Fight Heats Up," *Times-News*, November 16, 1983.

Beth McLeod, "Suspensions Follow Refusal to Use Texts," *Johnson City* [Tennessee] *Press-Chronicle*, November 16, 1983.

Two letters from Vicki Frost to Jean Price, November 23, 1983.

Mardee Roberts, "Mother Arrested for Trespass in Hawkins Textbook Protest," *Knoxville Journal*, November 24, 1983.

Letters to the Editor, *Times-News*, November 25, 1983.

Mozert v. Hawkins County Public Schools, Complaint for Preliminary and Permanent Injunctive Relief and for Damages for Violation of Federal Civil Rights, December 2, 1983.

David Brooks, "Anti-COBS Groups to Battle 'Extremists,' " *Times-News*, December 6, 1983.

Mozert, Affidavit of G. Reece Gibson, December 7, 1983.

Mozert, Affidavit of Robert L. McElrath, December 7, 1983.

Letter from Governor Lamar Alexander to Vicki Frost, December 8, 1983.

"COBS Suit Names School Board, Four School Principals," *Rogersville* [Tennessee] *Review*, December 8, 1983.

"Emotions Fly High at PTA Meeting," *Rogersville Review*, December 8, 1983.

Mozert, Affidavit of Gay Grabeel, December 8, 1983.

Mozert, Affidavit of James W. Salley, December 8, 1983.

Mozert, Memorandum in Support of Motion for Preliminary Injunction, December 8, 1983.

Mozert, Motion to Dismiss, December 8, 1983.

Letters to the Editor, *Times-News*, December 9, 1983.

Mozert, Affidavit of Bill Snodgrass, December 9, 1983.

Mozert, Memorandum Brief in Support of Defendants' Objections to Plaintiffs' Motion for Preliminary Injunction and Defendants' Motion to Dismiss, December 9, 1983.

Mardee Roberts, "Court to Reinstate Suspended Students," *Knoxville Journal*, December 10, 1983.

Betty Kauffman, "Hull Rules for Hawkins School, Wants Evidence of 'Humanism,' " *Citizen-Tribune*, December 11, 1983.

Mardee Roberts, "Church Hill Book Battle Heats Up," *Knoxville Journal*, December 12, 1983.

Mozert, First Amended Complaint, December 16, 1983.

Mozert, Response to Motion to Dismiss, December 19, 1983.

Letter from Vicki and Roger Frost to the National Rifle Association, n.d. (internal evidence suggests December 1983).

Notes by a Church Hill Middle School administrator (James Salley?) regarding student suspensions, n.d. (internal evidence suggests December 1983).

David Bollier, *The Witch Hunt Against Secular Humanism* (Washington, D.C.: PAW, 1983).

Mozert, Supplemental Affidavit of Bill Snodgrass, January 3, 1984.

Mozert, Order, January 10, 1983 (unless otherwise stipulated, all orders, judgments, memorandum opinions, and decisions are those of the United States District Court in Greeneville, Tennessee).

Mozert, Response to Court Orders of January 10, 30, 1984.

Mozert, Answer of the Defendants, Jean Price and James Salley, January 11, 1984.

Mozert, Memorandum in Support of Motion for Protective Order, January 13, 1984.

Mozert, Motion to Dismiss and in the Alternative Motion for Summary Judgment, January 13, 1984.

Mozert, Motion for Protective Order, January 13, 1984.

Mozert, Supplemental Brief in Support of Defendants' Motion to Dismiss and in the Alternative Motion for Summary Judgment, January 13, 1984.

Mozert, Alternative Motion to Dismiss and for Summary Judgment, January 16, 1984.

Open Letter from Beverly LaHaye, January 16, 1984.

Mozert, Response to Motion for Protective Order, January 30, 1984.

"Parents on Trial," Concerned Women for America newsletter, February, 1984.

Roberta Hantgan interviews with COBS members on behalf of Citizens for Constitutional Concerns, February 3, 1984.

Mozert, Memorandum and Order, February 15, 1984.

Mozert, Memorandum and Order, February 24, 1984.

David Brooks, "Hawkins Text Suit Now Religious Question," *Times-News,* February 25, 1984.

Betty Kauffman, "Judge Dismisses Most of Textbook Suit," *Citizen- Tribune,* February 26, 1984.

Mozert, Memorandum Regarding Stories on Issue of Salvation, March 12, 1984.

Mozert, Memorandum and Order, March 15, 1984.

David Brooks, "Hawkins Textbook Decision Appealed by Religious Group," *Times-News,* April 11, 1984.

Open Letter from Beverly LaHaye, April 20, 1984.

Mozert, Appellants' Opening Brief, July 12, 1984.

Mozert, Brief for Appellees, August 1, 1984.

Mozert, Brief for the Appellees, Jean Price and James Salley, August 17, 1984.

Mozert, Appellants' Reply Brief, September 14, 1984.

Open letter from Beverly LaHaye, November 5, 1984.

Frost v. Snodgrass, First Amended Complaint, November 21, 1984.

Mike Bradley, "Hawkins Woman Sues School Board," *Times-News,* November 24, 1984.

Frost, Answer (Snodgrass), December 28, 1984.

Frost, Answer (Ashbrook), December 31, 1984.

Ron Schaming, "False Arrest Suit Against Hawkins Schools Under Way," *Greeneville Sun,* January 22, 1985.

Frost, Second Amended Complaint, February 1, 1985.

Frost, Report and Recommendation, March 19, 1985.

Mike Dye, "Hawkins Book Suit Appeal Hinges on Constitutional Rights Questions," *Times-News,* April 6, 1985.

Mozert, Motion for Leave of Court to File Supplemental Brief, April 10, 1985.

Mozert, Supplemental Brief, April 10, 1985.

Mozert, Sixth Circuit Court of Appeals Opinion, June 18, 1985.

Mike Dye, "February Trial Likely in Hawkins 'COBS' Case," *Times-News,* July 14, 1985.

Mozert, Pretrial Order, July 22, 1985.

Mozert, Order, August 6, 1985.

Open letter from Beverly LaHaye, August 6, 1985.

Mozert, Answer to the First Amended Complaint of the Plaintiffs, September 3, 1985.

Frost, Pre-Trial Discovery Deposition of Judge Kendall Tate Lawson, December 17, 1985.

Citizens Organized for Better Schools, Statement of Purpose, n.d.

Citizens Advocating Right to Education, Statement of Purpose, n.d.

Chapter Three: A Clash of Symbols

Bernard Weiss et al., eds., Holt, Rinehart and Winston Basic Reading Series, Grades 1–8.

Phyllis Schlafly Report, August 1983.

Mozert, Pre-Trial Discovery Deposition of G. Reece Gibson, December 18, 1985.

Mozert, Pre-Trial Discovery Deposition of Billy Broten Snodgrass, December 18, 1985.

Mozert, Pre-Trial Discovery Deposition of Jean Price, December 19, 1985.

Mozert, Pre-Trial Discovery Deposition of Charles Berkley Bell, Jr., December 27, 1985.

Mozert, Pre-Trial Discovery Deposition of Philip Boyd, December 27, 1985.

Mozert, Pre-Trial Discovery Deposition of Michael Farris, December 27, 1985.

Mozert, Pre-Trial Discovery Deposition of James Salley, December 27, 1985.

Mozert, Pre-Trial Discovery Deposition of Camille Dillard, January 13, 1986.

Mozert, Deposition of Bernard Weiss, January 25, 1986.

Mozert, Pre-Trial Discovery Deposition of Bob Mozert, January 27, 1986.

Mozert, Pre-Trial Discovery Deposition of Alice Mozert, January 28, 1986.

Mozert, Pre-Trial Discovery Deposition of Travis Mozert, January 28, 1986.

Mozert, Pre-Trial Discovery Deposition of Rachel Baker, January 28–29, 1986.

Mozert, Motion for Protective Order, January 29, 1986.

Mozert, Pre-Trial Discovery Deposition of James F. Baker, January 29, 1986.

Mozert, Pre-Trial Discovery Deposition of Jimmy D. Eaton, January 29–30, 1986.

Mozert, Pre-Trial Discovery Deposition of James Bradley Eaton, January 30, 1986.

Mozert, Pre-Trial Discovery Deposition of Virginia Sue Eaton, January 30, 1986.

Mozert, Pre-Trial Discovery Deposition of Sandra Couch, January 30–31, 1986.

Mozert, Pre-Trial Discovery Deposition of Billy Couch, February 2, 1986.

Mozert, Pre-Trial Discovery Deposition of Janet Whitaker, February 2, 1986.

Mozert, Pre-Trial Discovery Deposition of Angie Meade, February 3, 1986.

Mozert, Pre-Trial Discovery Deposition of Christine Meade, February 3, 1986.

Mozert, Pre-Trial Discovery Deposition of Ernest Whitaker, February 3, 1986.

Mozert, Pre-Trial Discovery Deposition of Steve Whitaker, February 3, 1986.

Mike Dye, "Frost's Attorneys Accused of Improper Acts in Case," *Times-News,* February 6, 1986.

Mike Dye, "Magistrate Orders Frost Case Subpoenas Returned," *Times-News,* February 9, 1986.

Kathy Bean, "Judge Ponders Conduct of Frost's Attorneys," *Rogersville Review,* February 13, 1986.

Mozert, Pre-Trial Discovery Deposition of Marty Frost, February 25, 1986.

Mozert, Pre-Trial Discovery Deposition of Rebecca Frost, February 25, 1986.

Mozert, Pre-Trial Discovery Deposition of Sarah Frost, February 25, 1986.

Mozert, Pre-Trial Discovery Deposition of Jennie Wilson, February 26–27, 1986.

Mozert, Affidavit of Michael Farris, February 28, 1986.

Mozert, Plaintiffs' "Memorandum of Law Regarding Subpoena Issued to Obtain Telephone Records of Milligan, Coleman, Fletcher, Gaby, Kilday and Woods," February 28, 1986.

Mozert, Pre-Trial Discovery Deposition of Larry Anderson, March 3, 1986.

Mozert, Pre-Trial Discovery Deposition of Joe Goad, March 3, 1986.

Mozert, Pre-Trial Discovery Deposition of Gary Bradley, March 4, 1986.

Mozert, Defendants' Reply to Plaintiffs' "Memorandum of Law Regarding Subpoena Issued to Obtain Telephone Records of Milligan, Coleman, Fletcher, Gaby, Kilday and Woods" and "Memorandum Re: Sanctions," March 6, 1986.

Mozert, Deposition of Barbara Theobald, March 11, 1986.

Mozert, Deposition of Thomas Murphy, March 12, 1986.

"See Jim and Pat Cook. Jim Cooks First," *New York Times,* March 13, 1986.

Mozert, Pre-Trial Discovery Deposition of Vicki Frost, March 19- 20, 1986.

Mozert, Appeal from Memorandum and Order of Magistrate Filed March 11, 1986, March 20, 1986.

Mozert, Pre-Trial Discovery Deposition of Judy Bethard, March 26, 1986.

Phyllis Schlafly Report, March 1986.

Mozert, Defendants' Reply to Plaintiffs' Appeal from Memorandum and Order of Magistrate Filed March 11, 1986, April 1, 1986.

Mozert, Continuation of Pre-Trial Deposition of Vicki Frost, April 2–3, 1986.

Mozert, Deposition of Mel Gabler, April 9, 1986.

Mozert, Deposition of Norma Gabler, April 9, 1986.

Mozert, Brief in Support of Appeal of Magistrate's Ruling Re: Sanctions, April 10, 1986.

Mozert, Affidavit of Michael Farris, April 11, 1986.

Mozert, Affidavit of Jane Doe, April 14, 1986.

Mozert, Pre-Trial Discovery Deposition of Brenda Marshall, April 15, 1986.

Mozert, Resumption of Pre-Trial Discovery Deposition of Vicki Frost, April 15–16, 1986.

Mozert, Pre-Trial Discovery Deposition of Gina Marshall, April 16, 1986.

Mozert, Pre-Trial Discovery Deposition of Lofton Marshall, Jr., April 16, 1986.

Mozert, Defendants' Reply to Michael P. Farris's Appeal from Memorandum and Order of Magistrate Filed March 11, 1986, April 17, 1986.

Mozert, Pre-Trial Discovery Deposition of Gary Garhardt, April 22, 1986.

Mozert, Pre-Trial Discovery Deposition of Conléy Bailey, April 23, 1986.

Motion to Be Joined to the Case as a Plaintiff (Citizens for God and Country), April 29, 1986.

Mozert, Deposition of John Gordon Melton, April 30, 1986.

Phyllis Schlafly Report, April 1986.

Paul Vitz, "An Evaluation of the Bias Against Biblical Protestantism in the Holt Basic Reading Series, Grades 1–8," typescript draft, May 7, 1986.

Mozert, Deposition of Paul C. Vitz, May 8, 1986.

Mozert, Deposition of Jerry Horner, May 9, 1986.

Mozert, Deposition of James Fields, May 14, 1986.

Mozert, Pre-Trial Discovery Deposition of Roger Frost, May 14, 1986.

Mozert, Order, May 23, 1986.

Mozert, Pre-Trial Discovery Deposition of W. Wayne Allen, May 26, 1986.

"Judge Denies Appeals in Vicki Frost Case," *Rogersville Review,* May 29, 1986.

Letter from Anne Neamon to Judge Thomas Hull, May 29, 1986.

Frost, Brief of Appellant/Oral Argument Requested, May 30, 1986.

Mozert, Trial Transcript, July 14–23, 1986.

Chapter Four: Judgment Day

Mozert, Defendants' Pretrial Brief, July 3, 1986.

Mozert, Plaintiffs' Trial Brief, July 3, 1986.

Letter from Anne Neamon to Judge Thomas Hull, July 5, 1986.

Letter from Thomas Wright to Anne Neamon, July 8, 1986.

Mozert, Telephone Deposition of Mel Gabler, July 8, 1986.

Mike Dye, "D.C. Firms to Handle Brunt of Book Case," *Times-News,* July 10, 1986.

Mozert, Trial Transcript, July 14–23, 1986.

Keith B. Richburg, "Battle of Beliefs Is Fought Again in Tennessee: 'Scopes II'

Case Underscores Change in Church- State Debate," *Washington Post*, July 14, 1986.

Mozert, Plaintiffs' Summary of Arguments, July 14, 1986.

Anne Perry, "Mother Fears Books Lead to Feminism," *Johnson City Press,* July 15, 1986.

Amy McRary, "Textbooks Harmed Son, Court Told," *Philadelphia Inquirer,* July 18, 1986.

John Schidlovsky, "Tennessee Trial—A Textbook Case for Fundamentalists," *Baltimore Sun,* July 18, 1986.

"Intolerant Zealots Threaten Our Schools," *USA Today,* July 23, 1986.

Ray Waddle, "No Live Monkeys, Just the First Amendment," *USA Today,* July 23, 1986.

Tottie Ellis, "Books Still Threaten Our Public Education," *USA Today,* August 11, 1986.

Michael Farris, "Fundamentalists Often Targets of Bigotry," *USA Today,* August 11, 1986.

Edwin M. Yoder, "Textbooks on Trial in Tennessee," *U.S. News and World Report,* August 11, 1986.

Russell Baker, "Bearing a Burden," *Sunday Observer,* August 12, 1986.

Mozert, Memorandum of Authorities Re: Establishment Clause and State Funding of Religious Education, August 21, 1986.

Mozert, Plaintiffs' Proposed Findings of Fact and Conclusions of Law, August 21, 1986.

Mozert, Memorandum Opinion, October 24, 1986.

Curtis J. Sitomer, "Tennessee Textbook Ruling Fuels Religion-in- Schools Controversy," *Christian Science Monitor,* October 27, 1986.

James J. Kilpatrick, "Puree of Textbook," *Washington Post,* October 30, 1986.

Richard Cohen, "Propagating Ignorance," *Washington Post,* October 31, 1986.

Beverly LaHaye, "This Great Decision Will Help Our Kids," *USA Today,* October 31, 1986.

Murry Nelson, "'Sincerity Test' Threatens Education," *USA Today,* October 31, 1986.

"When Learning Has To Be Homogenized," *Anchorage Daily News,* October 31, 1986.

John Dart, "Victors in Textbook Trial Look to Alabama Case for Another Triumph," *Los Angeles Times,* November 1, 1986.

George F. Will, "Tailored Textbooks," *Washington Post,* November 9, 1986.

Ellen Goodman, "Denying Diversity," *Washington Post,* November 11, 1986.

"Anne Frank Center to Appeal Tennessee Book Decision," *Jewish World,* November 12, 1986.

Curtis Sitomer, "Learning Religious Tolerance: The Constitution and the Bible Need Not Be at Odds," *Christian Science Monitor,* November 13, 1986.

C. Glennon Rowell, "Allowing Parents to 'Screen' Textbooks Would Lead to Anarchy in the Schools," *Chronicle of Higher Education,* November 26, 1986.

Mozert, Judgment in a Civil Case, December 18, 1986.

Robert Parks, "District Judge Backs Free Exercise Rights of Fundamentalists," *Legal Times,* January 5, 1987.

Mozert, Brief of *Amici Curiae* State of Ohio, Superintendent of Public Instruction; State of Arkansas; California State Board of Education; and State of Oregon, in Support of Defendants-Appellants and Intervening Defendant-Appellant, January 23, 1987.

Mozert, Brief of Intervening Defendant-Appellant, January 23, 1987.

Mozert, Brief for the National Education Association as Amicus Curiae in Support of Appellants, January 23, 1987.

Mozert, Brief of *Amici Curiae* American Association of School Administrators, American Association of Colleges for Teacher Education, American Association of University Professors, Americans for Religious Liberty, Association of American Publishers, Inc., California State Superintendent of Public Instruction Bill Honig, Council of Chief State School Officers, International Reading Association, Maryland State Board of Education, National Association of Elementary School Principals, National Association of State Boards of Education, National Congress of Parents and Teachers, National Council for the Social Studies, National School Boards Association, New York Committee for Public Education and Religious Liberty, New York State Education Department, Tennessee Organization of School Superintendents, Tennessee School Boards Association, Wyoming State Department of Education, January 26, 1987.

Mozert, Brief of the American Jewish Committee; the Union of American Hebrew Congregations; the Members of the Faculty of the New York Theological Seminary; Rabbi Balfour Brickner; and the Right Reverend Paul Moore, Jr. as *Amici Curiae* in Support of Defendant-Appellants, January 27, 1987.

Mozert, Brief of Appellants Hawkins County Public Schools, January 28, 1987.

Mike Simpson, "Sects Education in the Schools," NEA *Today,* January/February 1987.

Mozert, Brief of the Christian Legal Society and National Association of Evangelicals as *Amici Curiae* in Support of Appellees, March 2, 1987.

Mozert, Brief of Appellees, March 4, 1987.

Mozert, Brief for the Catholic League for Religious and Civil Rights, Amicus Curiae, in Support of Appellees, March 4, 1987.

Mozert, Reply Brief of Appellant Hawkins County Public Schools, March 23, 1987.

Mozert, Brief of National Council of Churches of Christ in the U.S.A. as Amicus Curiae, May 28, 1987.

Mozert, Sixth Circuit Court of Appeals Opinion, August 24, 1987; Kennedy, concurring; Boggs, concurring.

"Good Parents and Good Witches," *New York Times,* August 26, 1987.

Beverly LaHaye, "These Judges Have Set a Dangerous Precedent," *USA Today*, August 28, 1987.

"These Court Rulings Can Save Our Schools," *USA Today*, August 28, 1987.

Richard Lacayo, "Going Back to the Books: Fundamentalists Lose Two Court Battles Against 'Godless' Texts," *Time*, September 7, 1987.

Madalynne Reuter, "Fundamentalists Lose Two Textbook Cases in Federal Appeals Courts," *Publishers Weekly*, September 11, 1987.

Mozert, Petition for a Writ of Certiorari to the United States Court of Appeals for the Sixth Circuit, December 31, 1987.

Keith Waldman, "Appealing to a Higher Law: Conservative Christian Legal Action Groups Bring Suit to Challenge Public School Curricula and Reading Materials," *Rutgers Law Journal*, Winter 1987.

Mozert, Brief of Respondents Hawkins County Public Schools in Opposition, January 29, 1988.

Sue Welch, "Questions and Answers about Home Schooling," *Concerned Women*, September 1989.

Barbara Gailey, "Minimizing Mom's Frustrations in Home Schooling," *Concerned Women*, September 1989.

Chapter Five: This Message Will Repeat Itself

Paul Kurtz, "Humanist Manifesto II," *Humanist*, September/October, 1973.

Stephen Arons and Charles Lawrence III, "The Manipulation of Consciousness: A First Amendment Critique of Schooling," *Harvard Civil Rights–Civil Liberties Law Review*, 1980.

F. Tayton Dencer, "The Establishment Clause, Secondary Religious Effects, and Humanistic Education," *Yale Law Journal*, May 1982.

Jaffree v. Board of School Commissioners of Mobile County, Judgment, January 14, 1983 (unless otherwise stipulated, all judgments, orders, memorandum opinions, and decisions in *Jaffree* and *Smith* are those of the United States District Court in Mobile, Alabama).

Jaffree, Eleventh Circuit Court of Appeals Opinion, May 12, 1983.

Open letter from Beverly LaHaye, August 17, 1983.

Request from Anne Neamon to allow Citizens for God and Country to participate in *Smith*, March 12, 1985.

Jaffree, Order, August 15, 1985.

Smith v. Board of School Commissioners of Mobile County, Memorandum of Law of Plaintiffs Smith, with Appendices, October 10, 1985.

D. G. L., "Note: The Myth of Religious Neutrality by Separation in Education," *Virginia Law Review*, 1985.

"Mobile Signs Humanism Decree," *Decatur Daily*, February 27, 1986.

PAW memoranda, March 5, April 2, October 21, 1986; March 9, 1987.

James J. Kilpatrick, "Religion? It Never Happened," *Washington Post*, March 11, 1986.

Paul Vitz, "Too Many Texts Ignore Religion," *USA Today*, August 11, 1986.

Smith, Defendant-Intervenors' Pre-Trial Brief, October 5, 1986.

Smith, Pretrial Order, October 6, 1986.

Smith, Trial Transcript, October 6–22, 1986.

Charles Krauthammer, "Secular Humanism on Trial," *Washington Post*, October 10, 1986.

Ezra Bowen, "A Courtroom Clash over Textbooks: Evangelicals Attack Secular Humanism in Alabama Schools," *Time*, October 27, 1986.

Request by Anne Neamon to participate in *Smith*, October 27, 1986.

Kenneth Woodward with Katherine Taylor, "Secular Humanism in the Dock: Are Public Schools Teaching a False Religion?" *Newsweek*, October 27, 1986.

Smith, Proposed Findings of Fact and Conclusions of Law Submitted on Behalf of the Alabama State Board of Education and State Superintendent of Education, December 5, 1986.

Smith, Defendant-Intervenors' Proposed Findings of Fact and Conclusions of Law, December 8, 1986.

Smith, Brief of Plaintiffs Smith in Response to Defendant- Intervenors' Proposed Findings of Fact and Conclusions of Law, January 12, 1987.

Smith, Findings of Fact and Conclusions of Law, March 4, 1987.

Smith, Judgment, March 4, 1987.

Robin Toner, "Schoolbooks Ruled Biased on Religion," *New York Times*, March 5, 1987.

"U.S. Judge Bans 32 Textbooks," *San Francisco Chronicle*, March 5, 1987.

William Raspberry, "Judge Hand...," *Washington Post*, March 7, 1987.

Thomas Boyer, "Robertson Praises Ban on Textbooks," *Virginia Pilot*, March 8, 1987.

Smith, Amended Judgment, March 9, 1987.

Smith, Order, March 9, 1987.

James J. Kilpatrick, "Is 'Secular Humanism' a Religion?" *Philadelphia Inquirer*, March 13, 1987.

Smith, Order, March 17, 1987.

Smith, Order, March 19, 1987.

Lincoln Caplan, "A Good Ol' Boy Sitting on the Federal Bench," *Los Angeles Times*, March 29, 1987.

Smith, Memorandum of Points and Authorities in Support of Defendant-Intervenors' Motion to Suspend Injunction During Pendency of Appeal, March 1987.

Francis Wilkinson, "Judge Hand's Holy War," *American Lawyer*, May 1987.

Walt Harrington, "What's Wrong with America?" *Washington Post Magazine*, July 26, 1987.

Smith, Eleventh Circuit Court of Appeals Opinion, August 26, 1987.

Chapter Six: A Monkey's Uncle

Charles Darwin, *The Origin of Species* (New York: Collier, 1909).

Leslie Henri Allen, ed. and comp., *Bryan and Darrow at Dayton: The Record and Documents of the "Bible-Evolution Trial"* (New York: A. Lee, 1925).

L. Sprague de Camp, *The Great Monkey Trial* (New York: Doubleday, 1968.)

Arthur and Lila Weinberg, *Clarence Darrow: A Sentimental Rebel* (New York: Putnam, 1980).

American Library Association, *Newsletter on Intellectual Freedom,* July 1981.

McLean v. Arkansas Board of Education, United States District Court Decision, January 5, 1982.

Keith v. Louisiana Department of Education, United States District Court Decision, December 20, 1982.

Aguillard v. Treen, Supreme Court of Louisiana Ruling, October 17, 1983.

Aguillard v. Treen, United States District Court Decision, January 10, 1985.

Aguillard v. Edwards, Fifth Circuit Court of Appeals Opinion, July 8, 1985.

United States Law Week, "Schools and Colleges—Church and State," June 16, 1987.

Wayne V. McIntosh, "Litigating Scientific Creationism, Or 'Scopes' II, III, . . . ," *Law and Policy,* July 1985.

Karen O'Connor and Gregg Ivers, "Creationism, Evolution and the Courts," PS: *Political Science and Politics,* Winter 1988.

Marsha Nye Adler, "The Politics of Censorship," PS: *Political Science and Politics,* Winter 1988.

Chapter Seven: Theme and Variations

FARRELL V. HALL

Review of Robert Cormier, *I Am the Cheese, Booklist,* May, 1977.

Review of Cormier, *Cheese, School Library Journal,* May 15, 1977.

Review of Cormier, *Cheese, New York Times,* November 13, 1977.

George A. Woods, "Books of the Times," *New York Times,* December 9, 1977.

Review of Cormier, *Cheese, Newsweek,* December 19, 1977.

"Best Books for Young Adults, 1977," *Booklist,* 1977.

Merri Rosenberg, "Teen-Agers Face Evil," *New York Times,* May 5, 1985.

Letter from Leonard Hall to Marion Collins, November 14, 1985.

Letter from Marion Collins to Leonard Hall, January 29, 1986.

Letter from Marion Collins to Joel Creel, February 3, 1986.

Request for Reconsideration of Instructional Materials forms on Cormier, *Cheese* and Susan Beth Pfeffer, *About David,* filled out by Claudia Shumaker, April 22, 1986.

Open letter from Charles Collins, May 22, 1986.

Janice L. Lucas, "Book Ban Issue: Parents' Rights vs. Censorship," *Panama City* [Florida] *News Herald,* June 1, 1986.

Open letter from Ann Richards, July 18, 1986.

Farrell, Affidavit of John S. Simmons, August 5, 1986.

Letter from Gloria Pipkin to Hall, August 12, 1986.

ReLeah Cossett Hawks, "The Year They Came to Arrest the Books (with Apologies to Nat Hentoff), *Florida English Journal,* Fall 1986.

Letter from Pipkin to Creel, September 2, 1986 (with rationale for *Cheese*).

Letter from Creel to Pipkin, September 11, 1986.

Letter from Pipkin to Hall, September 28, 1986.

Letter from Hall to Pipkin, October 3, 1986.

Letter from Pipkin to Hall, October 22, 1986.

Statement by Pipkin to the Bay County School Board, November 12, 1986.

Janice L. Lucas, "Teacher Vows Fight: Plea for Board to Reinstate Novel Falls on Deaf Ears," *Panama City News Herald,* November 13, 1986.

Peter Carlson, "A Chilling Case of Censorship," *Washington Post Magazine,* January 4, 1987.

Memorandum from Hall to School Board, May 6, 1987.

Jennifer Linn, "Lawsuit Filed Against Hall, School Board," *Panama City News Herald,* May 13, 1987.

Jennifer Linn, "Library Takes Stand on Censorship: Books Banned by Hall for Classrooms Displayed Prominently," *Panama City News Herald,* May 13, 1987.

Editorial cartoons, *Panama City News Herald,* May 13, 1987.

Jennifer Linn, "School Board Lifts Hall's Ban on 64 Books," *Panama City News Herald,* May 14, 1987.

"22-Cent Forum: Readers Write to the Editor," *Panama City News Herald,* May 13, 14; June 10, 1987.

"Retreat in Florida on School Board Ban: Board in a Panhandle County Wants Out of the Dispute over 'Vulgar' Readings," *The New York Times,* May 15, 1987.

Dave von Drehle, "Burning Issues," *Bradenton* [Florida] *Herald,* May 31, 1987.

Jennifer Linn, "Mowat Principal Joel Creel Tries To Bail Out," *Panama City News Herald,* June 3, 1987.

Farrell, Memorandum of Law in Support of Defendant Creel's Motion To Dismiss, June 3, 1987.

Jennifer Linn, "School Board Makes Textbooks a Priority," *Panama City News Herald,* June 11, 1987.

Farrell, Plaintiffs' Memorandum in Opposition to Defendant Creel's Motion To Dismiss," June 15, 1987.

Farrell, Motion for Withdrawal of Defendant Creel's Motion to Dismiss, June 25, 1987.

School Board Policy on Curriculum, Rule 3.15, effective June 29, 1987.

"Just a Little Bit of Censorship," *Jacksonville* [Florida] *Journal,* July 1, 1987.

Farrell, Memorandum of Law in Support of Defendant, Hall's, Motion to Dismiss, July 2, 1987.

Farrell, Memorandum of Law in Support of Defendants School Board and Creel's Motion to Dismiss for Lack of Subject Matter Jurisdiction, July 2, 1987.

Farrell, Motion to Dismiss for Failure to State a Claim upon Which Relief Can Be Granted, July 2, 1987.

Farrell, Motion to Dismiss for Lack of Jurisdiction over the Subject Matter, July 2, 1987.

Jennifer Linn, "Working It Out: School Board Tackles New Review Policy Guidelines," *Panama City News Herald,* July 27, 1987.

Jennifer Linn, "School Board Adopts Book Review Plan," *Panama City News Herald,* July 28, 1987.

Farrell, Plaintiffs' Memorandum in Opposition to Defendants' Motion to Dismiss, July 29, 1987.

Farrell, First Amended Complaint, July 1987.

Nat Hentoff, "Why Teach Us to Read and Then Say We Can't?" *Washington Post,* September 3, 1987.

"School Chief Bans Book a Second Time; Appeal Is Scheduled," *Gainesville* [Florida] *Sun,* September 3, 1987.

Farrell, Plaintiffs' Memorandum in Opposition to Defendant Hall's Motion to Dismiss, September 10, 1987.

Jennifer Linn, "Board Bans 'I Am the Cheese': Novel Banished from Bay Schools by Vote of 4–1," *Panama City News Herald,* September 10, 1987.

"Battling," NEA *Today,* October 1987.

Farrell, Order, July 18, 1988 (unless otherwise stipulated, all orders, memorandum opinions, judgments, and decisions are those of the United States District Court in Panama City, Florida).

"Judge Upholds Policy Allowing Panama City to Pull Books Off Shelves," *St. Petersburg Times,* July 22, 1988.

Farrell, Second Amended Complaint, August 1988.

Farrell, Motion to Dismiss the Plaintiffs' Complaint and Motion for the Imposition of Sanctions, September 5, 1988.

Farrell, Memorandum of Law in Support of Defendants' Motion to Strike Plaintiffs' Second Amended Compliant and Motion for Imposition of Sanctions, September 15, 1988.

Farrell, Motion to Strike Plaintiffs' Second Amended Complaint and Motion for Imposition of Sanctions, September 15, 1988.

Farrell, Memorandum in Opposition to Defendant Hall's Motion to Dismiss and for Sanctions, October 5, 1988.

Farrell, Memorandum in Opposition to Defendants School Board and Creel's Motion to Strike and for Sanctions, October 13, 1988.

Farrell, Order, December 20, 1988.

Farrell, Motion to Dismiss, January 31, 1989.

Farrell, Memorandum in Response to Defendant Hall's Motion to Dismiss, February 11, 1989.

Farrell, Order, February 21, 1989.

Telephone interviews with Gloria Pipkin, April 9, 1991, and plaintiffs' attorney Pamela Dru Sutton, May 4, 1990; July 12, November 17, 1991; February 15, 1992.

VIRGIL V. SCHOOL BOARD OF COLUMBIA COUNTY

Request Form for Examination of School Media opposing *The Humanities,* Volume I, filled out by Fritz M. Fountain, n.d. (internal evidence suggests early 1986).

School Board of Columbia County Minutes, April 8, 1986.

Virgil, Stipulation as to Facts, April 22, 1986.

Virgil, Affidavit of Silas Pittman, June 15, 1987.

Virgil, Stipulation Concerning Board Reasons, June 22, 1987.

Virgil, Judgment in a Civil Case, January 29, 1988 (unless otherwise stipulated, all judgments, orders, memorandum opinions, and decisions are those of the United States District Court in Jacksonville, Florida).

Virgil, Brief of People for the American Way as *Amicus Curiae* in Support of Appellants, April 20, 1988 (draft).

Virgil, Appellants' Initial Brief, April 29, 1988.

Virgil, Brief of *Amici Curiae* Supporting Reversal: People for the American Way, State of California Department of Education, State of Florida Department of Education, State of Maryland Department of Education, State of Wyoming Department of Education, American Association of University Women, American Association of University Professors, Americans for Religious Liberty, Association for Supervision and Curriculum Development, B'nai Brith, Council of Chief State School Officers, Freedom to Read Foundation, Humanists of Florida, International Reading Association, National Coalition for Public Education and Religious Liberty, National Council of Teachers of English, Union of American Hebrew Congregations, Unitarian Universalist Association, April 29, 1988.

Gray Thomas, "State Joins Bid to Halt Book Ban," *Florida Times-Union,* May 5, 1988.

Virgil, Appellees' Answer Brief, June 8, 1988.

Virgil, Appellants' Reply Brief, August 30, 1988.

Virgil, Joinder in Brief of Amici Curiae Supporting Reversal: Florida Education Association United, American Federation of Teachers, AFL/CIO, September 8, 1988.

Virgil, Brief of the Florida State University Law Review as Amicus Curiae in Support of Appellants, n.d.

Virgil, Eleventh Circuit Court of Appeals Opinion, January 12, 1989.

Chapter Eight: The Customer Is Always Right

Report of Actions Taken by the State Board of Education, January 6–8, 1976: Views of Human Origins.

Letter from Kenji Kalohelani to California Board of Education, March 2, 1981; reply, March 4, 1981.

Letter from N. Markofer to California Board of Education, March 7, 1981; reply March 20, 1981.

Segraves v. State of California, Findings of Fact and Conclusions of Law, June 12, 1981.

Letter from California State Board of Education to Holt, Rinehart Winston, November 23, 1981.

Letter from California State Board of Education to Citizens for Scientific Creation, May 13, 1982.

Instructional Materials Compilation Form for Citations of Noncompliance, May 1982.

Report of the Findings of the First Level Appeals Panel of the Legal Compliance Committee of the State Board of Education, June 1982.

William Trombley, "Some Officials Now Question Textbook Bill," *Los Angeles Times,* July 15, 1982.

Report of the Findings of the Second Level Appeals Panel of the Legal Compliance Committee of the State Board of Education, July 1982.

William Trombley, "Fresno Group Gets Textbooks Changed," *Los Angeles Times,* September 9, 1982.

"The Textbook Snoops," *Sacramento Bee,* Sepember 16, 1982.

William Trombley, "State School Board Asks Brown to Veto Book Bill," *Los Angeles Times,* n.d.

Letter from Open Court Publishing Company to California Board of Education, November 2, 1982; reply December 27, 1982; reply January 11, 1983.

Letter from Kevin Tvedt to California Board of Education, January 21, 1983; reply February 11, 1983.

California Instructional Materials Law, Compiled by Curriculum Frameworks and Instructional Materials Unit, California State Department of Education, January 1983.

Letter from California State Board of Education to Laidlaw Brothers, April 1, 1983.

Letter from Carmelita Moore to California Board of Education, April 28, 1983.

Instructional Materials Compilation Form for Citations of Noncompliance, April 1983.

Response to Notice of Citation (Macmillan), May 15, June 21, 1983.

Letter from Ginn and Company to California Board of Education, May 16, 1983.

Letter from California State Board of Education to Macmillan, May 25, 1983.

Report of the Findings of the First Level Appeals Panel of the Legal Compliance Committee of the State Board of Education, July 1983.

Report of the Findings of the Second Level Appeals Panel of the Legal Compliance Committee of the State Board of Education, July 1983.

Curriculum Development and Supplemental Materials Commission: Social Science Subject Matter Committee Meeting Minutes, July 27, 1983.

Letter to Silver Burdett Publishing Company from California Board of Education, September 6, 1983.

Minutes, California State Board of Education, September 16, 1983.

Letter from Riverside Publishing Company to California Board of Education, September 28, 1983.

Letter from Leroy F. Greene to Superintendent Bill Honig, November 16, 1983.

Program Descriptions for History - Social Science Instructional Materials, 1983.

Report to the State Board of Education on the Evaluation of History–Social Science Instructional Materials Recommended for Adoption in 1983, n.d.

Instructional Materials Sunset Review Report, 1984.

Science Framework Addendum, 1984.

Survey of Textbook Evaluation and Adoption Processes in Adoption States and in Sample Districts in Nonadoption States, 1984.

Roger Lewin, "Evidence for Scientific Creationism?" *Science,* May 17, 1985.

Curriculum Development and Supplemental Materials Commission, Recommendation of Instructional Materials for Adoption for Science, Science Subject Matter Committee, July 25–26, 1985.

Letters from Creation-Science Research Center to California Board of Education, September 12, 1985.

Letter from Thomas H. Jukes to Superintendent Bill Honig, September 5, 1985.

Letter from the San Francisco Chapter of American Atheists to California Board of Education, September 12, 1985.

Statement of G. Brent Dalrymple to the California Board of Education on the Age of the Earth and Geologic Time, September 12, 1985.

Statement of Thomas Jukes to California Board of Education, September 12, 1985.

Statement of Carol Magee to California Board of Education, September 12, 1985.

Statement of Kevin Padian to the California Board of Education on the Adoption of Life Science Textbooks in Grades K–8, September 12, 1985.

Statement of Vincent Sarich to California Board of Education, September 12, 1985.

Statement of Michael Weber to California Board of Education, September 12, 1985.

Minutes, California State Board of Education, September 13, 1985.

Model Curriculum Standards, Grades Nine through Twelve: English/Language Arts, Foreign Language, History–Social Science, Mathematics, Science, Visual and Performing Arts, 1985.

Minutes, California State Board of Education Meeting, October 10, November 14, 1986.

Letter from California Department of Education to William E. Walstrom, December 19, 1986.

Standards for Evaluation of Instructional Materials with Respect to Social Content, 1986 ed.

Letter from Traditional Values Coalition to California Board of Education, April 22, 1987.

Letter from Gay/Lesbian Youth Advocacy Council to California Department of Education, June 6, 1987.

Letter from American Latvian Association to California Board of Education, June 10, 1987.

Letter from California Council for the Social Studies to California Board of Education, June 10, 1987.

Memorandum from Creation-Science Research Center to California Board of Education, June 10, 1987.

Presentation at Public Hearing on the Social Studies Curriculum Framework, Commission on Teacher Credentialing, June 10, 1987.

Statement of Duane E. Campbell to the California Board of Education, June 10, 1987.

Statement Detailing the Reasons for Our Disagreement with the Comments on the Holocaust, n.d. (internal evidence suggests the June 10, 1987, public hearing).

Statement by the Women's Lobby to the California Board of Education, June 10, 1987.

A Survivor's Testimony, Presented to the California Board of Education, June 10, 1987.

Testimony of the American-Arab Anti-Discrimination Committee, June 10, 1987.

Testimony on the History–Social Science Framework Before the California State Board of Education, June 10, 1987.

Presentation by the Traditional Values Coalition to the California Board of Education, Summer 1987.

Board Highlights, July 9–10, 1987.

Letter from Gay and Lesbian Educational Services Committee to California Board of Education, July 19, 1987.

Letter from John P. De Cecco to Superintendent Bill Honig, July 31, 1987.

Letter from Federation of Turkish American Societies to California Board of Education, August 4, 1987.

Letter from National Association of Christian Educators/Citizens for Excellence in Education to California Board of Education, August 10, 1987.

Comments to the Board of Education on the Proposed Curriculum by Community United Against Violence, Lesbian/Gay Speakers Bureau, August 11, 1987.

Letter from Amnesty International to California Board of Education, August 11, 1987.

Letter from the Islamic Center of Southern California to California Board of Education, August 11, 1987.

Model Curriculum for Human Rights and Genocide, Summary of Comments, August 11, 1987.

Notes for Testimony Before Policy and Planning Committee State Board of Education on Model Curriculum for Human Rights and Genocide, Los Angeles County Commission on Human Relations, August 11, 1987.

Remarks by ... the Polish Association of Former Political Prisoners of Nazi and Soviet Concentration Camps, August 11, 1987.

Statement by the Director of the Martyrs Memorial and Museum of the Holocaust in Los Angeles, August 11, 1987.

Statement of Chinese for Affirmative Action, August 11, 1987.

Statement of Montebello Unified School District to California Board of Education, August 11, 1987.

Statement of the Armenian National Committee to the California Board of Education, August 11, 1987.

Statement of the Baltic American Freedom League to California Board of Education, August 11, 1987.

Statement of the Catholic League of California to California Board of Education, August 11, 1987.

Statement of the Consulate of Estonia to California Board of Education, August 11, 1987.

Statement of the Turkish American Association to the California Board of Education, August 11, 1987.

Statement on the Model Curriculum for Human Rights and Genocide to the State Board of Education, California Teachers Association, August 11, 1987.

Statement Presented at the Public Comment Session of the California Board of Education, Polish American Congress, August 11, 1987.

Testimony before the State Board of Education Committee on the Model Curriculum on Human Rights and Genocide, Lois C. Leffert, August 11, 1987.

Letter from Attorney General's Commission on Racial, Ethnic, Religious, and Minority Violence, September 2, 1987.

Amendments Adopted by the State Board of Education on September 4, 1987, to the *Draft* Document, Model Curriculum for Human Rights and Genocide.

Minutes, California State Board of Education, October 2, 1987.

English/Language Arts Framework, 1987.

English/Language Arts Model Curriculum Guide, Kindergarten through Grade Eight, 1987.

Family Life/Sex Education Guidelines, 1987.

Handbook for Planning an Effective Literature Program, 1987.

Science Model Curriculum Guide, Kindergarten through Grade Eight, 1987.

Minutes, Curriculum Development and Supplemental Materials Commission, English–Language Arts Subject Matter Committee, March 2, 16, July 22, November 3, 1988.

Instructional Materials and Framework Adoption: Policies and Procedures, June 10, 1988.

Response to Notice of Citation, Harcourt Brace Jovanovich, June 17, 1988.

Response to Notice of Citation, The Wright Group, June 24, 1988.

Minutes, Curriculum Development and Supplemental Materials Commission, July 21–22, 1988.

Recommendations of the Curriculum Development and Supplemental Materials Commission, 1988 Adoption California Basic Instructional Materials in English–Language Arts, July 20- 22, 1988.

Report of the Findings of the First Level Appeals Panel of the Legal Compliance Committee of the State Board of Education, July 1988.

Letter from California Board of Education to McGraw-Hill Book Company, August 16, 1988.

Letter from The Wright Group to California Board of Education, September 7, 1988.

Elaine Woo, "State Reading Experts Hit 'Dumbing Down' of Books," *Los Angeles Times,* September 8, 1988.

Minutes, Curriculum Development and Supplemental Materials Commission, November 2, 4, 1988.

Highlights of the Presentation by Bill Honig to the Curriculum Commission on November 3, 1988.

Highlights of the Special Presentation by Diane Ravitch to the Curriculum Commission on November 3, 1988.

Special Presentation by Zoe Acosta, Rod Atkinson, and Diane Brooks on the Model Curriculum, Guide for History/Social Science (K–8), November 3, 1988.

Model Curriculum for Human Rights and Genocide, 1988.

History/Social Science Framework, 1988.

Secondary Textbook Review: English, Grades Nine through Twelve, 1988.

A Handbook for Curriculum Review and Instructional Materials Selection, Kindergarten through Grade 12, January 1989.

State Board of Education Policy Statement on the Teaching of Natural Sciences, January 13, 1989.

Minutes, Curriculum Development and Supplemental Materials Commission, January 19, March 2, July 20, 1989.

California State Senate Bill No. 594 to amend the Education Code, February 22, 1989.

California State Assembly Bill No. 2225 to amend the Education Code, March 10, 1989.

Professional Code of Conduct, May 18, 1989.

American Library Association, *Newsletter on Intellectual Freedom,* January 1990.

Minutes, Curriculum Development and Supplemental Materials Commission, January 25–26, March 22, 1990.

Correlation of Prentice-Hall Earth Science to California Science Curriculum Framework, n.d.

Instructional Materials Review Forms for Use by the General Public, n.d.

Chapter Nine: Market Force

Miscellaneous textbook proclamations, Board of Education minutes, and letters from the public, 1928–1960. Texas's current adoption process, including systematic public input and publishers' replies, began in 1961.

State Textbook Committee Hearing, September 14, 1961.

Minutes of the State Board of Education, November 13, 1961.

State Textbook Committee Hearing, September 14, 1962.

Minutes of the State Board of Education, November 12, 1962.

Protests and Statements on Certain Textbooks Being Considered for Adoption in 1962.

Minutes of the State Board of Education, November 11, 1963.

State Textbook Committee Hearing, October 14, 1964.

Letter from Creation Research Society to Mel and Norma Gabler, October 26, 1964.

Letter from Creation Research Society to Board of Education member, November 4, 1964.

Minutes of the State Board of Education, November 9, 1964.

State Textbook Committee Hearing, October 12, 1965.

Minutes of the State Board of Education, November 8, 1965.

Protests on Certain Textbooks Being Considered for Adoption in 1965 and Publishers' Answers.

Publishers' Replies to Protests of Certain Textbooks Being Considered for Adoption in 1969.

State Textbook Committee Hearing, September 16, 1969.

Minutes of the State Board of Education, November 10, 1969.

Protests and Statements on Certain Books Being Considered for Adoption in 1969.

Protests of Certain Textbooks Being Considered for Adoption in 1969.

State Textbook Committee Hearing, September 15, 1970.

Changes Requested of Publishers, 1970.

Protests of Certain Textbooks Being Considered for Adoption in 1970.

Publishers' Replies to Protests of Certain Books Being Considered for Adoption in 1970.

State Textbook Committee Hearing, September 14, 1971.

State Textbook Committee Hearing, September 21–22, 1972.

Minutes of the State Board of Education, November 10, 1972.

Changes Requested of Publishers, 1972.

Textbook Adoptions Process Policy Statement, May 12, 1973.

Transcript of Proceedings, Textbook Hearings Before the State Board of Education, November 9, 1973.

Bills of Particulars Filed in Protest of Certain Textbooks Being Considered for Adoption in 1973 and Publishers' Answers to the Bills of Particulars.

Changes Requested of Publishers, 1973.

Transcript of Proceedings, Textbook Hearings Before the Commissioner of Education, September 11–12, 1974.

Minutes of the State Board of Education, November 8, 1974.

Transcript of the Proceedings Before the State Board of Education, November 8, 1974.

Bills of Particulars Filed in Protest of Certain Textbooks and Systems Being Considered for Adoption in 1974 and Publishers' Answers to the Bills of Particulars.

Changes Requested of Publishers, 1974.

Changes Requested of Publishers, 1976.

James C. Hefley, *Textbooks on Trial* (Wheaton, Ill.: Victor Books, 1976).

Transcript of Proceedings Before the Commissioner of Education and the State Textbook Committee, August 17–19, 1977.

Bills of Particulars Filed in Protest of Certain Textbooks and Systems Being Considered for Adoption in 1977 and Publishers' Answers to the Bills of Particulars.

Changes and Corrections Requested of Publishers, 1977.

Hearing Before the Commissioner of Education and the State Textbook Committee, August 16–18, 21–22, 1978.

Bills of Particulars and Publishers' Answers, 1978.

Changes and Corrections Requested of Publishers, 1978.

Bills of Particulars and Publishers' Answers, 1980.

Minutes of the State Board of Education, November 8, 1980.

1980 Textbook Adoption Changes and Corrections Requested of Publishers.

Minutes of the State Board of Education, November 12, 1981.

Bills of Particulars and Publishers' Answers, 1981.

Changes and Corrections Requested of Publishers, 1981.

Transcript of Proceedings, Textbook Hearings Before the Commissioner of Education and the State Textbook Committee, August 9–13, 1982.

Minutes of the State Board of Education, November 11, 1982.

Report of the Commissioner of Education on Textbooks, November 12–13, 1982.

1982 Textbook Adoption Changes and Corrections Requested of Publishers.

Texas Textbook Law, 1982.

Transcript of Proceedings, Textbook Hearings Before the Commissioner of Education and the State Textbook Committee, August 1–3, 1983.

Minutes of the State Board of Education, November 10, 1983.

Bills of Particulars, 1983.

Rebuttals by Petitioners and Publishers to Bills of Particulars on Textbooks, 1983.

1983 Textbook Adoption Changes and Corrections Requested of Publishers.

Transcript of Proceedings, Textbook Hearings Before the Commissioner of Education and the State Textbook Committee, July 9–11, 1984.

Bills of Particulars, 1984.

Report of the Commissioner of Education Concerning Recommended Changes and Corrections in Textbooks, 1984.

Minutes of the State Board of Education, November 9, 1985.

Report of the Commissioner of Education Concerning Recommended Changes and Corrections in Textbooks, 1985.

Minutes of the State Board of Education, October 30, November 6- 8, 1986.

Report of the Commissioner of Education on Alleged Irregularities in the Textbook Adoption Process, November 8, 1986.

Report of the Commissioner of Education Concerning Recommended Changes and Corrections in Textbooks, 1986.

Texas Administrative Code and Statutory Citations, Title 19, Part II, Instructional Resources, Chapter 81, Subchapter D, amended 1986.

State Board of Education Rules for Curriculum, July 1987.

Report of the Commissioner of Education Concerning Recommended Changes and Corrections in Textbooks, 1987.

Responses to Written and Oral Testimony at the Hearings Before the Commissioner of Education and the State Textbook Committee, 1987.

Written Comments 1987 Adoption.

John Williams, "Backlash Unlikely on Evolution Vote," *Houston Chronicle*, March 13, 1988.

Recommendations of the Commissioner's Ad Hoc Committee on the Operation of the Texas Textbook System, July 8, 1988.

Minutes of the State Board of Education, November 12, 1988.

1988 Responses to Written and/or Oral Testimony.

Report of the Commissioner of Education Concerning Recommended Changes and Corrections in Textbooks, 1988.

Written Comments, 1988 Textbook Adoption.

Report of the Commissioner of Education Concerning Recommended Changes and Corrections in Textbooks, 1989.

Responses to Written and Oral Testimony, 1989 Textbook Adoption.

Transcript of Proceedings Before the Commissioner of Education and the 1989 State Textbook Committee.

Written Comments, 1989 Textbook Adoption.

Transcript of Proceedings Before the Commissioner of Education and the 1990 State Textbook Secondary Science Committee, July 10–11, 1990.

"Texas Gives Tentative OK of Texts Covering Evolution," *Northern Virginia Daily*, November 9, 1990.

Robert V. Camuto and Joe Cutbirth, "Battling Over Man's Beginning: Evolution Hits Books, but May Skip Tarrant," *Fort Worth Star Telegram*, November 10, 1990.

"Creationists Lose in Texas Texts: State Tentatively Approves New Biology Books with Evolution Details," *Arkansas Gazette*, November 10, 1990.

Terrence Stutz, "Evolution Goes on the Books: Education Board Vote Quiets Debate on Texts," *Dallas Morning News*, November 11, 1990.

Memorandum from Michael Hudson to PAW headquarters, November 14, 1990.

"Out of the Dark Ages," *St. Louis Post-Dispatch,* November 21, 1990.

Report of the Commissioner of Education Concerning Recommended Changes and Corrections in Textbooks, 1990.

Citizens for Excellence in Education, "News from Around America," n.d. (internal evidence suggests late 1990 or early 1991).

American Library Association, *Newsletter on Intellectual Freedom,* January 1991.

Committees of the State Board of Education Minutes, February 2, 14, 15, March 7, 8, 1991.

Minutes of the State Board of Education, February 2, 16, March 8, 1991.

English Language Arts Framework, Kindergarten–Grade 12, n.d.

Science Framework, Kindergarten–Grade 12, n.d.

Social Studies Framework, Kindergarten–Grade 12, n.d.

Chapter Ten: Into the 1990s

Eagle Forum, *Education Reporter,* January, March, April 1989; February 1991.

Citizens for Excellence in Education, *Education Newsline,* October/November 1989; January/February 1990.

Concerned Women for America, *Concerned Women,* January 1990.

Citizens for Excellence in Education, President's Report, June 1990.

Eagle Forum, *Phyllis Schlafly Report,* February, July 1990; August 1991.

American Library Association, *Newsletter on Intellectual Freedom,* September 1990; January, March, May, July, September, November 1991.

People for the American Way, *Attacks on the Freedom to Learn: 1990-1991 Report.*

Brown v. Woodland Joint Unified School District, First Amended Complaint, February 14, 1991.

American School Board Journal, February 1991.

People for the American Way mailing, n.d. (internal evidence suggests February 1991).

Brown, Woodland Parents' Answer in Intervention to First Amended Complaint, April 5, 1991.

People for the American Way, *Press Clips,* Spring/Summer 1991.

J. Gordon Melton, Jerome Clark, Aidan A. Kelly, *New Age Almanac* (Detroit: Visible Ink Press, 1991).

Brown, Second Amended Complaint, n.d.

Index

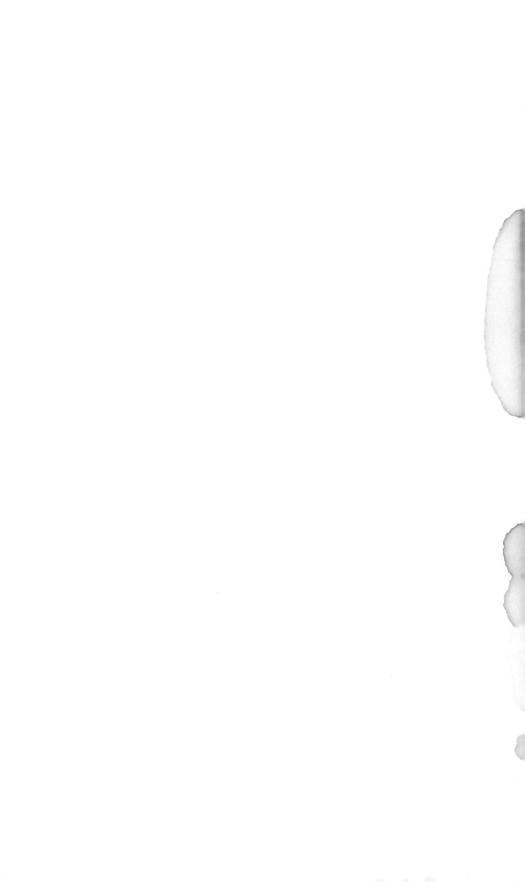